Spiraling Downward

Thinking About and Planning for Economic Collapse

by

Peter Damaris

PrepperPress

Your Survival Library

www.PrepperPress.com

Spiraling Downward

Thinking About and Planning for Economic Collapse

ISBN 978-0615782409

Printed in the United States of America.

Prepper Press Trade Paperback Edition: March 2013

About the Author

Peter Damaris has spent more than 30 years working in a variety of financial institutions and consulting firms both in the US and overseas. He has specialized in risk management, financial analysis, equity portfolio management, and distressed debt resolution. He holds bachelors and masters degrees in International Affairs with concentrations in Economics and East Asia. He and his wife currently reside in North Carolina.

Table of Contents

Introduction

Hollywood loves making movies about Armageddon. They always find an audience. One website, www.doomsdaymovies.com, lists "over 400 movies about doomsday, Armageddon, apocalypse, nuclear war, plague, disaster, and other end-of-the-world scenarios," including the film *Armageddon* (1998). Almost all of these show mankind triumphing or at least surviving. A search of the internet reveals more than one hundred doomsday prophecies over the course of human history. As far as we know, none of them have come true. Yet we remain fascinated by predictions of an end to the world as we know it.

Those who predict economic collapse also grab our attention. On September 12, 2012, the commentator Rush Limbaugh stated, "The country's economy is going to collapse if Obama is re-elected." On June 2, 2010 the famed economist Arthur Laffer, known as the theorist behind supply-side economics, predicted economic collapse in 2011 due to the Obama Administration's tax policies. A group of MIT researchers predicts global economic collapse and precipitous population decline by 2030 if we continue to consume the world's resources at our current pace. Ray Dalio, the head of the world's largest hedge fund, predicts economic collapse by 2013 due to inflation and government printing of money. And it goes on and on.

Spiraling Downward is <u>not</u> another one of these prophecies. It forecasts neither dates nor timelines. Nor does it deal in probability; one will find no odds-making here. And there is no list of conditional events which, if they occur, lead with certainty to economic breakdown.

This book starts from a different premise. It accepts economic collapse as a possibility without looking at probability. It accepts that we have just experienced a severe economic crisis stemming from the collapse of the real estate market so that we are weaker today than we were prior to 2007. It then looks at the world as it exists today and seeks to identify factors which have the capacity to cause another market crash and credit crunch with severity similar to that experienced during 2007-2009. The reason for doing so is that a market crash and a credit crunch during a period of ongoing economic weakness have the greatest potential to produce an economic collapse. This again is only logic, not probability. Market crashes administer a shock to the economy. If the economy is already weak, the effects of the shock will be more powerful than otherwise.

Assuming a market collapse and credit crunch have occurred, the book then looks at a path the US might follow towards collapse. Description of this path is driven by an analysis of imbalances which exist in the US today and which may become unsustainable in the wake of a crash. The path is a downward spiral, with each stage becoming progressively worse in its economic, political, and social effects.

In all the talk of "collapse" above or elsewhere in the media, there are no specifics as to what the word might actually mean. Just like Hollywood, the word is used for its shock value. Does it mean a new depression? A bad recession? An extended period of economic stagnation? The word is used very loosely. We also use the word very broadly here, but as shorthand for a drastic change in the American life as we know it. We are agnostic as to whether the collapse should be classified a depression, a recession, or stagnation. Rather than apply an economic label to what each chapter describes, we ask the reader to think about the downward spiral as a worst-case scenario, for what is described in Chapters 3-6 is probably worse than what most can imagine today.

The purpose of this book is thus to think about the unthinkable, even if you do not think it will really happen. Like the title of the book, each chapter spirals downward with conditions progressively worsening. The chapteral division of the book has been adopted so that we can see, from an analytical standpoint, how a spiral might descend. The chapters are thus an intellectual construct and so may bear no resemblance to the sequence of how events might actually play out. Some stages may occur before others, others may occur simultaneously, and some may never even take place. Indeed, there is no reason of necessity that the spiral descend to the depths of Chapter 6, i.e., for a variety of reasons, it could be stopped or moderated. We do not consider such reasons here except briefly in the Afterword: our focus is solely on the spiral and how bad things might become.

Going hand-in-hand with each chapter are thoughts on how to plan for it. Some might ask: why should I waste time and effort planning for an event I think is unlikely to happen? *Spiraling Downward* may take no position on probability but I think the odds are low. This comment has merit but we would respond as follows.

Probably, maybe tucked away in cubbyholes in a corner of its basement, the Pentagon has plans on how to invade every country in the world. Plans for the world's hot spots have undoubtedly moved upstairs to individual desks and working groups for real-time analysis and updating. Left behind among the yellowing paper is perhaps a plan for taking Quebec, maybe modeled on Benedict Arnold's disastrous expedition of 1775. Or a plan for taking Veracruz modeled on Pershing's success of 1914. The Pentagon is a vast bureaucracy. Maybe every ten, twenty, or fifty years, some low-level officer is charged with pulling out all of these old plans, dusting them off, reviewing the history, updating them for current capabilities and needed resources, and filing them away again. Not having a plan is unforgivable in a military context. Just because a war or invasion is improbable or unlikely does not mean you should not think about it or, in some way, plan for it. Focusing only on the conflicts of the moment means neglecting those of the future which may be equally if not more dangerous.

God came to Noah and forecast a deluge. The Bible does not give us Noah's response. He may have been skeptical, like the Noah portrayed by Bill Cosby, for he presumably had no experience of catastrophic events during his lifetime. God gave Noah detailed instructions on how to build an ark and how to employ it. If Noah considered a flood improbable, planning for it would have seemed a complete waste of time — but he did what he was told.

We may likewise think that the probability of a collapse is low but, even if it is low, it would be unwise to ignore it entirely. Why would we not consider the possibility that conditions could be far worse than they are today? Does it make sense to ignore the possibility entirely? If the reader feels that the probability of collapse is non-trivial, then it would make sense to plan for it in some way. Even if one feels the probability is miniscule, thinking through the issue will still help one lay out a better plan for the future. By thinking through all possibilities and ruling out those that do not make sense, one's overall personal planning process becomes more rigorous and disciplined.

Each chapter begins with its own introduction which describes the next downward step in the spiral. It then looks at early warning signs which signal that further deterioration is becoming more likely. The book then considers how to prepare for it. In some cases this will mean developing a plan. In others it may mean thinking about the issues in more detail. The early chapters identify red flags to be monitored subsequent to the appearance of early warning signs. Once these appear, the next downward step will be even more probable. Appearance of red flags would normally call for activation of other parts of the plan. Chapters 1-2 are more concrete because there are many facets of the issues and action steps to be considered. Chapters 3-6 are a bit more speculative so the structure of early warning signs, preparation, and red flags used in the earlier chapters have been modified in favor of thinking more deeply about how events will affect one's way of life. The downward spiral ends at the conclusion of Chapter 6. Chapter 7 addresses a possible path to recovery after things have hit bottom.

In the end, the reader may not agree with the downward spiral as presented. Its fact pattern may seem too tenuous and shaky to justify its conclusions. Information may seem to have been skewed or misused solely to present worst-case scenarios. One may conclude that the downward progression of the spiral does not ring true with one's own analysis of current issues and view of the world. One may decide it is a very strange and depressing vision of America's future, a vision one chooses not to contemplate.

The key to the spiral is America's current position of weakness. In the aftermath of an economic shock, weakness will mean that a shock has the potential to impact our economy and way of life in ways never seen before. That they have never been seen before in America does not mean they can never happen. Our major failing as Americans, and as human beings, is that we are either unwilling or unable to consider alternative visions of reality. We are locked into the ways we have always thought. The teachings of our parents, schools, and churches govern the way we see America and the rest of the world. We believe strongly what we have been taught. We have trouble accepting data or narratives which do not conform to it.

Spiraling Downward highlights some of the blind spots in American life. For all that we find good in America, there is history we cannot be proud of. For all of the progress we have made since the founding of the republic, there are still fundamental issues which remain unaddressed. These issues are already with us today—they do not suddenly emerge during a downward spiral. Rather, the downward spiral both makes them more visible at the same time it makes them harder to solve. We are in a position of weakness today in part because these issues have not been addressed. They are holding us back from the future we want to achieve. If, in spite of any faults found in this book, the reader gains a sense of the issues that face us and begins considering different ways to analyze and address them, then this book will have achieved its goal.

Chapter 1

Market Crash

Definitions and Characteristics

A *market crash* is a dramatic decline in the values of assets across a financial market that takes place over a relatively short period of time. It is usually associated with the stock market; however, a market crash may originate in any market, financial or non-financial. A *financial market* is a venue, either physical or network/web-based, where buyers and sellers trade financial assets. *Financial assets* include stocks, bonds, foreign currencies, derivatives, and commodities and can be thought of as "paper assets." Even though buyers of some commodity futures contracts, such as gold, can choose to accept physical delivery (instead of cash) at maturity, the futures contract is a "paper asset" prior to maturity and thus is classified among financial assets.

One side of every transaction in every market settles in cash: a buyer pays cash to purchase 100 shares of General Motors, or a seller receives cash proceeds from selling a US Treasury Note. Even though a crash may originate in one market, its effects will be transmitted to all markets because of their common mechanism of cash settlement. For example, assume an investor has bought a home for which closing is scheduled in 5 business days and that his required payment at closing will be $100,000. Let's also assume the investor had planned to borrow 50% (the maximum margin loan vs. stock permitted by regulation) against the value of his $200,000 stock portfolio in order to make the $100,000 payment. If the value of his stock portfolio has crashed 20% prior to date of closing, the investor no longer has sufficient margin loan resources to close on the purchase, i.e., total margin loan resources are: $80,000 (50% of the $160,000 stock portfolio after a 20% decline), but he owes $100,000. He then has two choices: (1) default on the agreement to buy the home; or (b) sell a portion of his stock portfolio outright to raise enough funds to make the payment at closing. If he fails to buy the house, the drop in the stock market has been directly transmitted to the real estate market. If he has to sell stock, obligations overhanging the investor from the real estate market have forced more selling into a stock market that is already under severe pressure. Similar actions taken by other market participants directly transmit the effects of a stock market crash to other markets and add additional pressure on the stock market itself. In other words, markets — especially financial markets — are deeply intertwined. The reason is that cash sits on one side of every trade.

Central to the concept of a market crash is price *discontinuity*. We normally think of prices moving in relatively smooth, even gradations, a few cents here and there up, a few down; a few dollars up, a few down. Discontinuity looks like this:

Chart 1.1

Stock Price & Discontinuity

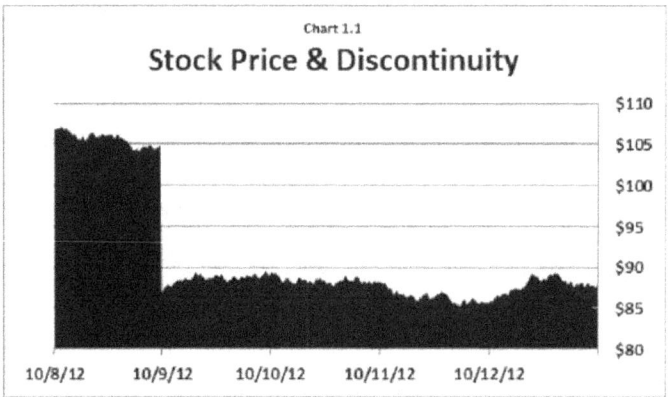

10/8/12	10/9/12	10/10/12	10/11/12	10/12/12

At the end of the day on October 8, the stock in Chart 1.1 was trading around $105 per share. It dropped to $87 at the opening of October 9 and then hovered in the $85 - $90 range the next few days. There was no gradual movement down to $87. There was a gap, a *discontinuity*, between prices on those two days. We do not know the reason for the drop in price. Presumably, the company announced something negative. What can we say about investors holding its stock? Well, they panicked. They did not like what they saw, they wanted out immediately, and they wanted out at virtually any price. The volume of shares offered for sale overwhelmed firms who made a market in the company's stock, who had no choice other than to slash bid prices in order to match buyers and sellers, i.e., the market maker must find a buyer for nearly every share bought from sellers, because no market maker has sufficient capital to hold a significant market position for very long. Here we have a single stock. A crash occurs when actions similar to what we see in this example happens across an entire market. In other words, investors seeking to flee their positions

6

try to dump financial assets across the market at the same time, and thereby create a crash.

Markets do not collapse just because of dark clouds on the horizon. If everyone can see them, the clouds get *embedded* in market prices.[1] Yes, investors can get it wrong, they may underestimate the magnitude of the risk, but they do know the risk is there. Today we see a European recession, US deficits, stalemates in Congress, high unemployment rates, and a weak housing market, all of which present risks. Investors' decisions to invest in financial assets in the face of such risks reflect their conclusions, their expectations about how political and economic events will play out. The prices they are willing to pay for any financial asset reflect those expectations.

Markets do not collapse just because a recession may be on the horizon. Economic cyclicality is recognized as an ongoing market risk by most investors. Certainly today's market prices must take account of the risk of recession, but they also, unconsciously, take account of the fact that economic cycles eventually hit bottom and turn back upward. Thus we can say that the eventual upturn is also embedded in market prices.

Shocks

What causes a market crash is a *shock*. A shock creates lack of confidence, mistrust, and, most importantly, fear. Investors' fear in reaction to a shock generates the crash. Why does the shock have such a devastating effect? The key point: the risk of the event that generated the shock was not embedded in market prices or, if it was, markets sorely misjudged it.

Shocks can be classified by the type of event or phenomenon that generated them: either the event or phenomenon was *unexpected* or it was *misperceived*. *Unexpected* shocks are generated by events very few saw coming. They were not captured in market pricing in virtually any way. Examples of such events might be a war that comes out of nowhere, a foreign exchange (FX) rate devaluation, or a rapid central bank-driven increase in interest rates.

Misperceived shocks are usually associated with market bubbles. A *market bubble* is defined as a rise in asset prices far in excess of the intrinsic value of the asset. By its nature, "intrinsic value" is difficult to define, being to some degree in the eye of the beholder. What unites bubbles is the failure to recognize that assets, financial or otherwise, can only be bought and sold in cash. When investors look out across all asset classes, they apply metrics, either consciously or unconsciously, to compare one against another in terms of cash, because cash is normally viewed as a limited resource and so is the universal standard for valuation. Bubbles almost always occur when cash is readily available. Investors during a bubble assume, implicitly, that cash will <u>always</u> be available: easy to earn, easy to borrow, and relatively cheap. The flip side is that if cash is cheap to borrow, bond and fixed income investors receive what are perceived to be below-average or insufficient yields. This creates a natural tendency to move into equity-type investments where price appreciation offers the prospect of acceptable or superior returns. With easy money, normal methodologies for valuation get abandoned in the face of heavy speculation because the opportunity cost of being wrong is believed to be low; however, once the easy money disappears, investors must decide how to reallocate/sell assets in light of diminished availability of cash (exactly the same as the homebuyer in the example). They begin evaluating each class of assets they own against each other. The class with prices most of line with other asset classes, i.e., the bubble asset class, is the most likely to be sold. This generates the shock.

Two Market Bubbles

Recent examples of bubbles are the dot.com boom of the late 1990s and the real estate boom of the mid-2000s. The excesses of the dot.com boom began around 1997. The boom focused on investing in internet and related telecom and technology stocks under the belief that these sectors offered a new paradigm to the global economy. There was no shortage of ideas when the dot.com boom began. Let's lay thousands and thousands of miles of fiber-optic cable and wire up the entire United States because internet traffic will grow tenfold every year and the world is changing—no one calculated how much cable was really needed. Let's start up an internet store because bricks-and-mortar retailers are dinosaurs and the world is changing—nobody asked why an internet retailer should carry a valuation radically above that of bricks-and-mortar. Few of the newly formed companies had prospects for generating meaningful profits or cash flow in the near-term, but what united investors during the dot.com boom, a characteristic of every bubble, is the belief that 'this time it's different.' The NASDAQ, heavy with technology and internet stock listings, started 1997 at 1,280.97. By March 10, 2000 it had reached its high of 5,048.62. The bubble burst on the heels of Fed interest rate increases and a *Barron's* article questioning high internet stock valuations.[2] By March 31, the NASDAQ had declined by over 9% from the high. By the end of 2000 it had declined 51% from the high.

The real estate bubble lasted over a longer period. The recession which began as a result of the bursting of the dot.com bubble ended, by National Bureau of Economic Research criteria, in November 2001. The S&P/Case-Shiller Home Price Index,[3] the most widely cited measure of home price movements, stood at 116.38 in the 4th quarter of 2001. The index reached a high of 191.01 in the first quarter of 2006, meaning 12.4% compounded annual growth. Housing prices accelerated during 2004 and 2005, with the Index growing by 14.6% in each year. We have cited national data. Housing price inflation in California, Arizona, Nevada, and Florida exceeded US national housing price inflation by wide margins.

The reasons for the bubble are many, including accommodative Fed monetary policy reflected in low mortgage rates, accommodative government regulatory policy reflected in loosened Fannie Mae and Freddie Mac[4] guidelines for banks, lower lending standards on the part of banks and other mortgage originators, and egregious behavior on the part of some market participants. Nevertheless, these explanations overlook the demand side. Americans had an intense desire for home ownership. The reasons varied household to household but included the long-held dream of home ownership in the hearts of most Americans and the related belief that homes represent an excellent financial investment for the long-term. Demand grew over the period as Americans tried to get in on the action. In the hottest markets, demand met tight supply. This generated a swathe of new home building across the country, which was supported in some regions by wild speculative fever. Florida in particular saw investors (including Europeans) take positions, through placement of deposits on homes and condos yet to be built, not with the idea of living in them but with the goal of selling their positions at a profit.

As with its causes, the reasons for the bust are many. The market only began to realize there was a problem when many sub-prime[5] borrowers began to default on their loans in 2006-2007 and that the structuring of these loans at origination had been negligent.[6] Then it began to understand that Wall Street stood at the center of the problem through structuring these mortgages into mortgage-backed securities for sale to investors. It was eventually learned that the problem was not limited to sub-prime: loans to so-called prime borrowers had most of the same defects. The aftermath of the sub-prime crisis revealed a variety of structural imbalances throughout the economy, including a weak, poorly regulated financial sector. Most analysts concluded that at the heart of the crisis was one glaring reality: Americans, including American businesses, were carrying far too much debt—debt of all types—relative to their capacity to repay. This imbalance was unsustainable over the long-term.

It is interesting that people only understood the imbalances once the crisis had burst into the open; but was it so hard to see? We noted that housing prices were accelerating at a growth rate of 12% per year, yet contemporaneous economic data for the same period showed relatively flat personal income. How can an individual (or an economy) handle higher and higher housing costs if he or she does not have the higher cash flow to pay them? The answer should have been obvious, but one of the key characteristics of the *misperceived* shock is that people do not understand what is going on when they are in the midst of it. On a personal note, I had heard many anecdotes about lending abuses well before the real estate crisis erupted front-stage even though I was not involved in mortgage lending. I knew that many loans being originated were high-risk, but I had no inkling of the magnitude of those originations (especially among West Coast thrifts) or of the gross negligence of regulators who could have shut down the worst of those practices. In other words, I knew all this was happening but I was wrong on the dimensions.

It is also a characteristic of a *misperceived* shock that, when naysayers express doubts, they are routinely ignored or shouted down. Former Fed Chairman Alan Greenspan warned of "irrational exuberance" in 1996, before the dot.com boom reached its height, but no one paid much attention even though most remember his words. In 2005, he commented on "froth" in the real estate markets but was largely ignored (but unlike the rest of us he had the power to take action and chose not to do so). Those who shout down naysayers routinely accuse them of being stupid, delusionary, anti-business, or even quasi-anti-American, of seemingly wanting markets to collapse. The fever of speculation tends to bring on deafness in most other market participants. They do not even hear the naysayers.

The Case-Shiller Index fell from its 1Q06 high of 191.01 to a low of 126.37 in 4Q11 (compounded annual rate of decline of -8.3%). The year 2008 (-18.3%) showed the greatest annual decline. The centers of greatest real estate activity—California, Arizona, Nevada, and Florida—had price declines greater than what is shown in the national data. The US stock market, as measured by the Dow Jones Industrial

Average, reached its all-time high of 14,280 on 10/9/07 somewhat oblivious of the ugly heads of the real estate crisis which were already beginning to emerge from the muck. A year later on 10/9/08, in the midst of an election campaign, it stood at 8,579, down 39.9%. Thus the bursting of the real estate bubble was the event which generated a shock to other markets. This shock caused stock market investors to doubt and then fear the solvency of large financial institutions which stood at the center of the real estate debacle, critically important to the financial sector representing more than 20% of total market value. This fear caused the crash of the stock market. Moreover, the problem was not just American: the bursting bubble sent tremors throughout Europe and revealed imbalances in its own property sector and, more importantly, its governmental structures. Those imbalances are at the heart of today's European debt crisis.

Overview of Market Crashes

Table 1.1 sets out stock market crashes during the 20th and 21st centuries. Note that, with the exception of the Japanese asset bubble, this select list focuses on US crashes. This does not mean that international financial crises have nothing to teach us. We will introduce one of them below and others in Chapter 2. The market panics of the 19th century were caused by financial panics accompanied by bank runs, for which financial excesses of various types were the cause. The last pure financial panic occurred in 1907. One might conclude that establishment of the Fed in 1913 put an end to pure bank run-driven market crashes. After 1913 and through 1974, market crashes appear to have been rooted more in structural imbalances.[7] Yet we can perceive a change beginning in 1989 with crashes rooted in market bubbles. While financial issues were not the prime movers in inflating those bubbles, banks' loose and sometimes slipshod lending practices played a major supporting role. Some may have thought that the absence of market crashes caused by bank runs proved the success of the Fed in providing stability to the financial sector. Those thoughts have obviously been put to rest.

Table 1.1
Selected Stock Market Crashes

Period	Market High	Market Low	Hi-to-Lo Loss	Worst Month	Type of Shock	Reason for Shock	Detail
1907	70.06 Jan-07 DJIA	38.83 Nov-07 DJIA	-44.6%	-14.8% Oct-07 DJIA	U	Financial	Failed attempt to "corner" (acquire a dominant position in) the stock of United Copper Co caused Knickerbocker Trust Co to fail, causing runs on other banks. Intervention of J.P. Morgan stopped the crisis. Government reaction to the panic led to creation of the Fed.
1919 - 1921	119.62 Nov-19 DJIA	63.90 Aug-21 DJIA	-46.6%	-12.9% Nov-19 DJIA	U	Structural	A period of rapid adjustment to the end of World War I caused what is known as the Depression of 1920-1921. The economy was already weak because of a recession dated from Aug-18 thru Mar-19.
1929	386.10 Sep-29 DJIA	195.35 Nov-29 DJIA	-49.4%	-20.4% Oct-29 DJIA	M	Structural	Start of the 1929-1933 Great Depression. DJIA reasched a low of 40.56 in Jun-32. The boom of the 1920's created global imbalances which were exacerbated by heightened speculation aided by easy money. Profits on Wall Sreet masked distress in other sectors, such as agriculture.
1973-1974	1,067.20 Jan-73 DJIA	570.01 Dec-74 DJIA	-46.6%	-14.0% Nov-73 DJIA	U	Structural	Market reacted to (a) the "oil shock", a reaction to an increase in oil prices generated largely by OPEC's reaction to the Yom Kippur War, and (b) devaluation of the US$, which put an end to the Bretton Woods system of fixed FX rates.

Year	Peak	Trough	Decline				Description
1987	2,746.65 Aug-87 DJIA	1,616.21 Oct-87 DJIA	-41.2%	-23.2% Oct-87 DJIA	U	Structural	Market up ~45% from Aug-06. A normal market correction may have been turned into a crash by program trading/portfolio insurance. Long-term impact ultimately less important than other crashes cited here: no immediate recession or severe economic adjustment.
1989-1990	38,915.97 Dec-89 Nikkei	19,782.00 Oct-90 Nikkei	-49.2%	-19.2% Sep-90 Nikkei	M	Bubble	A Japanese asset bubble, centered in real estate and aided by easy money, existed for most of the 1980's. BOJ successfully burst the bubble (which it had helped create) by raising its benchmark interest rate in steps from 2.5% (Apr-89) to 6.0% (Sep-90). The Lost Decade followed.
2000	5,048.62 Mar-00 NASDAQ	2,312.51 Dec-00 NASDAQ	-54.2%	-22.9% Nov-00 NASDAQ	M	Bubble	See discussion in Chapter 1. Unlike the other crashes, this one was centered more in technology and Silicon Valley. The ensuing recession was hence more regional than national. The other crashes cited here were followed by nationwide downturns.
2007-2009	14,280.00 Oct-07 DJIA	6,440.08 Mar-09 DJIA	-54.9%	-14.0% Oct-08 DJIA	M	Bubble	See discussion in Chapter1.

DJIA = Dow Jones Industrial Average. Nikkei = Nikkei 225 Index. NASDAQ = NASDAQ Composite Index U = Unexpected M = Misperceived.

We have looked at the characteristics of unexpected and misperceived shocks. We have also taken a look at past crashes. One factor which was not present in crashes prior to 1990 was the capacity of large capital flows to cause or exacerbate a shock. Hedge funds and other large pools of capital have changed the playing field. Hedge funds alone are estimated to have ~$1.74 trillion in investor equity assets under management (AUM).[8] Combining AUM with leverage[9] means hedge funds can hold staggering positions. The growing strength of hedge funds can be traced directly to the low interest rates of the past decade which are due to accommodative monetary policy; without low rates, the cost of carrying large leveraged positions would have been higher, and hedge funds would have been more selective. More importantly, the availability of cash to invest in hedge funds would have been less under tighter monetary policy. Another factor which has contributed to hedge fund growth has been globalization and the lowering of regulations and investment barriers. Globalization has made it easier for any investor, including a hedge fund, to take advantage of attractive opportunities anywhere in the world.

A key point: hedge funds and other large capital pools are traders, not long-term investors. If they are shocked by any event, be it unexpected or misperceived, their *modus operandi* is to react, and react with speed. The size of the capital they can inject or withdraw has the capacity to cause or exacerbate a shock. In a sense, hedge fund actions in a distressed environment can have the same effect as depositors standing in a teller line during a bank run. Indeed, one might argue that bank runs have disappeared with large capital pools replacing them as potential drivers of financial panic.

The poster child for the importance of large capital pools in financial crises was the Asian debt crisis of 1997, nicknamed the "Asian flu." The crisis began in Thailand in May 1997. Thailand had pegged its Baht at 25 to the US Dollar. Its government had an aggressive national economic development plan and so kept interest rates high to attract foreign capital. Thailand, considered a relatively stable country, attracted huge inflows of capital in search of interest rates that were more attractive than elsewhere. Many of these investments were short-term, deposits with maturities as short as six months. Key to these investment decisions was investment manager confidence that they could invest at B25 and withdraw at B25. The incoming flows of foreign capital swamped the actual need for productive capital and ended up funding real estate speculation. At some point, investors realized that the Thai economy was becoming overheated and wanted out. Their need to convert Baht back to Dollars put huge pressures on the Thai central bank: there were no new Dollar inflows which could be used to fund those wanting to leave, so the central bank was forced instead to use its foreign exchange reserves. When those were exhausted, it was forced to float the Baht, which fell to $B56$ by January 1998.

The shock of the float caused a Thai stock market crash and financial crisis that sent its economy into a tailspin. Let's look at why. Prior to the devaluation, a Thai bank (banks and other financial institutions were, once again, at the center of this crisis) would take in, say, a one-year deposit of, say, $B25$ million owned by an international investor which had converted $1 million into Baht. The bank would then lend this $B25$ million into the local economy, presumably to borrowers who could repay. The bank usually assumed that the investor would roll over the deposit but, if the investor wanted out, it assumed it would be easy to pay him off and take in a deposit from somebody else. This model broke down once investors became uneasy. They all started to want out and few new depositors replaced them. Even though the FX rate was still fixed at $1:B25$, our theoretical bank had insufficient liquidity to meet withdrawal requests of this size. In order to raise Baht to repay deposits at maturity, it began calling in loans, but many of these loans had been used for speculation and borrowers could not repay. Thus the bank was thrown into crisis. For a Thai bank which had borrowed Dollars directly and then converted them to Baht, the crisis was even worse. Once the Baht fell to, say, $1:B56$ the bank had to deliver $B56$ million, instead of $B26$ million, for every $1 million borrowed. Accessing such huge amounts within the Thai economy was clearly a Herculean task. Few banks had the capacity to do so without government support. The effects were devastating. Focusing on a single bank is an oversimplification of what happened overall, but it does illustrate how the decisions of foreign investors can directly influence a local economy. Some will point out that the devaluation would help Thai exports and that it is true, but that comment misses the key point about shocks of this sort: devaluations have an "instantaneous" effect, whereas projected earnings from higher exports take place only over a period of years. And the comment ignores the fact that importers must now pay more than double the price of what they were previously buying, and that is "instantaneous" as well.

The experience of hedge funds and other large investors in Thailand caused them to look more critically at all their Asian investments. They started withdrawing capital, much of which had also been extended as short-term loans or deposits. These withdrawals caused credit crunches throughout Asia (to be discussed in further detail in Chapter 2). Indonesia, South Korea, the Philippines, Malaysia, Singapore, and even China were all thrown into financial crises of varying degrees.

These large capital pools then turned their eyes to their investments in Latin America. The same story played out there. Admittedly, there were areas of economic concern in each Asian and Latin American country, but any possibility of executing reasonable, measured plans for dealing with them was foreclosed, trashed by investors with a short-term view and limited understanding of where they were investing yet, at the same time, enormous market power. When they decided to exit emerging markets, it was like everyone trying to exit a burning theater through a single emergency door. What was impressive about this crisis is the sheer speed with which this crisis, which began in Thailand, spread to the rest of the world: less than one year.

These countries all recovered eventually, but the cost in terms of economic damage and human suffering was high. Most analysts believe the after-effects of this crisis played a crucial role in the Russian debt default of 1998.

The US did not suffer a market crash or a financial panic because of the Asian flu, although the stock market did experience significant pullbacks. The US economy was undoubtedly affected as import demand from emerging markets slumped. The more important impact from the Asian flu was that hedge funds and large capital pools now were no longer making the same level of liquidity available to global markets—they had become more conservative. This lack of liquidity created imbalances and these imbalances undoubtedly created the crisis that led to the collapse of Long-Term Capital Management in 1998.[10] One cannot help but think that reduced liquidity fed into the collapse of the dot.com boom. Given the size of hedge funds, their lack of regulation, and the opaqueness of their operations, one cannot also help thinking that a future market crash has the potential to be worse than any seen in the past century. This is not a prediction. It merely identifies a heightened risk, a risk that is evident from the so-called "flash crash" of May 6, 2010 in which the market dropped ~600 points within five minutes. An investigation of the flash crash pointed at large directional bets and high-frequency trading as among its causes.[11]

So, you might ask, market collapses are dangerous but didn't we just see one a few years ago? Once a bubble bursts, how much more likely is another to form quickly? After all, market crashes do not happen that often. Maybe it does not make sense to overkill this issue. This argument has merit, but the counter-argument is that we do not really know where the next shock will come from. If we did, we could take actions to prevent it. With misperceived events, it is difficult to understand what is happening even when we are in the midst of them. One of our fundamental shortcomings as human beings is our belief in the power of reason, that we can understand what is happening and that, once we understand it, we can manage it — and then the market slaps us in the face. Since at least the time of the philosopher Descartes, man has believed he can apply reason to the world around him and make sense of it. Market collapses are a way, perhaps God's way, of demonstrating that we do not know that much. The response is thus: how do we really know that the probability of a collapse is low?

Some might respond that they are long-term investors and do not want to overreact to short-term problems. Yet even if we accept the proposition that the probability of a market collapse is low, how do we know that we are not in the midst of our own Lost Decade, similar to that experienced by the Japanese during the 1990s and outlined in Table 1.1 and discussed in more detail in Chapter 2? That period of stagnant growth has been in many ways more devastating to Japan than its 1990 stock market collapse. One 2008 study of 15 countries that have suffered severe financial crises shows that the downturn after the crisis averaged 6 years for real housing prices, 3.4 years for real equity prices, 4.8 years for unemployment, and 1.9 years for decline in GDP.[12] Note that these are averages and that, in some countries, recovery took longer. One of the key changes in mental outlook that supports market bubbles is the belief that 'this time it's different.' Reversing the logic with respect to the time it takes to recover from a market collapse, how do we really know a recovery is <u>not</u> going to take many years?

In the end, even if collapses are truly "low-probability" outcomes, it still makes sense to think about the conditions which produce them given the horrific impact that shocks can have on the economy and our way of life. Thinking through the issues, even given the shortcomings of human understanding, places us in a better position to act more effectively than ignoring them altogether.

Early Warning Signs

Although, by definition, it is difficult to predict where the next shock will come from, we can point to early warning signs which, if they appear, will mean that the market is more vulnerable to a shock.

Unexpected Shock: Sudden Increase in Interest Rates

As noted earlier, market bubbles are periods of easy money with interest rates lower than experienced in the past. Low interest rates contribute to the bubble by making it easier to purchase assets. The level of interest rates is fundamental to the valuation of all assets. Let's take the simple example of a 100-unit apartment complex, which is shown in Table 1.2. This example shows that the cash flow generated before debt service (called net operating income (NOI) in commercial real estate parlance) is about $669,000. A shorthand way of valuing the apartments is to divide NOI by the *cap rate*, short for capitalization rate. How is the appropriate cap rate determined? Real estate investors look at recent sales of similar properties in the marketplace and collect data on their respective NOIs and sales prices. They look at the cap rate on each sale, which is determined by dividing NOI by sales price. They then estimate a cap rate for the market as a whole by averaging, calculating the median, or some other method. The next step is to do the reverse of how the cap rate was derived: divide our apartment complex's NOI by the market cap rate, here assumed to be 6%, to determine its current market value: about $11,200,000.

The market has determined the market cap rate by looking at comparable sales transactions, but where does the cap rate actually come from? The cap rate, at least on a theoretical basis, reflects an investor's weighted average cost of capital (WACC):[13]

Cap Rate = WACC = $(i \times k) + (r \times (1 - k))$ where

i = interest rate on bank debt
k = % of bank debt used in making the purchase
r = the rate of return on equity that investors demand

Table 1.2		
Effect of a 2% Increase in Interest Rates on Valuation		
Amounts in $000		
Income		**Comments**
Rent	900,000	100 apartment units fully occupied @$750/month
Laundry Income	6,750	
Potential Gross Income (PGI)	**906,750**	
Less: Vacancy	(45,000)	Expected average vacancy of 5%
Less: Credit Losses	(4,275)	Expected losses of .5% due to tenant non-payment
Effective Gross Income (EGI)	**857,475**	
Expenses		
Real Estate Taxes	(53,000)	
Rental Office Expenses	(12,000)	
Insurance	(8,000)	
Repairs & Maintenance	(31,000)	
Advertising	(4,000)	
Management	(45,000)	
Utilities	(27,000)	Utilities not paid directly by tenants
Other	(8,000)	
Total Expenses	**(188,000)**	
Net Operating Income (NOI)	**669,475**	EGI minus total expenses
Cap Rate	**6%**	Capitalization rate
Value of Apartment Complex	**11,157,917**	NOI divided by cap rate
Bank Debt	7,252,646	Bank debt available @65% of value
Debt Service	(521,536)	25-year monthly fixed rate amortization @5.25%
Net Cash Flow	147,939	NOI minus debt service
Debt Service Coverage	1.28x	NOI divided by debt service
Owner's Equity	**3,905,271**	Value minus bank debt
Net Operating Income (NOI)	**669,475**	EGI minus total expenses
Cap Rate	**8%**	Capitalization rate
Value of Apartment Complex	**8,368,438**	NOI divided by cap rate
Bank Debt	7,252,646	Same as above
Owner's Equity	**1,115,792**	Value minus bank debt

In our example, the calculation is: $6.00\% = (5.25\% \times .65) + (7.39\% \times .35)$. Note that we have found, from the hypothetical data given, the return on equity that investors expect. Under the mathematics of this example, the investor would have had to put up about $3.9 million in personal funds, equity, to buy the property. Now let's say the Federal Reserve Bank decides to push interest rates up quickly by 2% in order to curb inflation and/or reverse its

19

accommodative monetary policies. Let's also say this action pushes cap rates to 8% from 6%. If our investor actually purchased the apartments with $3.9 million in equity, our shorthand methodology would now say his equity is worth just $1.1 million. Note that the value of the property has fallen by 25% but that the investor's equity in the property has fallen by 71%: he or she feels immediately poorer. The reason for this is that the mortgage must still be paid even though the value of the property has fallen. This illustrates the ever-present downside risk accompanying use of leverage in financial transactions.

When a central bank raises interest rates abruptly in an unexpected manner — the emphasis here is on *unexpected* — financial market participants revise their valuations of the assets they hold — all assets — using a thought process similar to the preceding example. The thought process may also take into account the impact of higher rates on US federal budget deficits. We would suggest that either an increase in the Fed Funds Rate by 1.00% - 1.50% over a relatively short period of time, or speculation beginning in the financial media that the Fed may be contemplating a change to its monetary policy, be used by as early warning signs that changes in market conditions have the capacity to produce a crash. That a rapid increase in rates can produce a crash is borne out by the Bank of Japan's actions during 1990 as outlined in Table 1.1. This is not the first time in history that this has happened.

Unexpected Shock: Europe and the Euro

With the notable exception of China, the foreign exchange (FX) rates of major countries float freely based on demand and supply for currencies in FX markets. It is easy to forget that this system of freely floating exchange rates is relatively new in human history, having emerged only since the 1973 break-up of the Bretton Woods system which had been in place since the end of World War II. A world of fixed FX rates is a world that frequently produces shocks that can produce market crashes. The reason for this is that, while FX rates are fixed, trade and capital flows are not. When these flows get out of balance, the FX rate cannot be adjusted to match demand and supply for the currency. A so-called "attack" on the currency ensues which the central bank tries to combat by using its FX reserves or borrowing from other central banks. When FX reserves run out and borrowings are no longer available, the central bank has no choice other than to devalue its currency. The Thai example discussed mirrors the pattern all devaluations tend to follow. The effects of a devaluation on the domestic economy depend on the extent to which it imports and exports goods and services and/or borrows foreign currencies. For a country with high exposure to international markets, the impact of devaluation on the local economy usually produces a shock capable of generating a market crash.

There were hundreds of devaluations around the world in the two centuries prior to 1973 but we have probably forgotten how they work for lack of recent experience. The European debt crisis contains elements that have the potential to reintroduce them. The Euro came into existence in 1999 as European governments agreed to swap their local currencies (German Deutschmarks, French Francs, Italian Lira, Spanish Pesetas, Greek Drachmas, etc.) for a brand-new currency that could be used throughout Europe. The ratios at which governments were able to swap their local currencies for Euros were established in 1999; the agreement to establish the Euro included limitations on budget deficits and other macroeconomic metrics designed to ensure that the relationship between the swap ratios of 1999 and fiscal performance within each country remained within reason. Although the European Central Bank was established (with weak powers) to manage monetary policy for the Eurozone, countries could go their own way on national budgets, and they did. While the 1999 agreement prescribed various penalties and other controls on national economic performance, they were never enforced so that imbalances between countries grew, culminating in the recent Greek and Spanish debt crises.

To date, the Eurozone has been able to muddle through. The region is in recession and policymakers have begun taking steps, albeit slowly, to reform the current system and address imbalances. The period of adjustment will take years. This crisis has been playing out in front of us on TV and in the media. We think we understand it. Nevertheless, the market has probably not thought about what would happen if a large country (not Greece) left the Euro and new national or regional currencies came into being. If the Euro were to break apart, there is no way to calculate, from today's perspective, the rates at which new currencies should trade against each other, the old Euro (for those countries that still used it), or the US Dollar. The market's inability to calculate proper exchange rates means there is a high probability of an *unexpected* shock if the Euro breaks apart. This shock would have high potential to cause a market crash. We suggest that observation of any information or reports in the media that suggest any major European country is experiencing distress greater than what we see today be established as an early warning sign of a market crash.

Unexpected Shock: Chinese Turmoil and the Chinese Yuan

The Yuan was fixed at 8.27 per US Dollar from 1997 – 2005. In 2005, in part due to international pressure, the Chinese Government allowed the Yuan to float but has since managed movements within a tight range. Over the next seven years through October 2012, the Yuan had gradually appreciated to ~6.27, a gain of ~32% (about 4 - 5% per year). In spite of the managed float, many foreign politicians and market participants continue to press China to allow the Yuan to appreciate at a greater rate. At this writing, there is no sign of Chinese willingness to depart from the managed float.

Its managed float allows the Chinese Government to create certainty for the significant number of Chinese businesses that depend on imports and exports; however, by maintaining the float, it has created a major problem for itself. As of 9/30/12, its FX reserves had risen to $3.29 trillion (a portion of this is held in Euros and other currencies but dollars represent the bulk of it). American politicians and the media keep raising the same old chimera: what happens if China dumps its dollars? This question demonstrates very little understanding. China cannot convert dollars to other currencies without hurting itself. First, the volume of other currencies is not large enough to accommodate such a conversion. And second, "dumping" dollars would crush current foreign exchange rates and create losses for the Chinese. They understand this well. The only step they can take is to convert a portion of their US$ to Yuan and use the proceeds to expand their money supply. Given the growth of its economy, demand for credit has been insatiable. The downside to conversion to Yuan is that expanding the money supply can increase inflation. China has been walking the fine line of matching money supply growth to economic need without exacerbating inflation or rampant speculation. It has had some success. From 1994 through 2012, Chinese inflation has averaged 4.3%. Consumer price inflation (CPI) was 6.1% in September 2011 but had fallen to 1.9% by September 2012. This was due to lower GDP growth and to tighter monetary and lending policies.[14] In sum, inflation, rather than dumping dollars, represents the greater risk for China when setting policies on how to manage its large FX reserves.

If China chose not to convert its FX reserves to Yuan, then its second concern is making sure it gets paid for holding US Dollars or, for that matter, any foreign currency. Due to economic problems in the Eurozone, a slowly improving US economy, and a flight to quality, the US Dollar still appears to be the currency of choice for investors around the world. This and accommodative Fed policy have kept interest rates extremely low. If US economic growth improves and brings higher inflation, all fixed income investors (not just China) will look for higher interest to compensate them for the increased risk. The first early warning sign speaks to this risk. In sum, interest rate increases on the large amounts of US debt outstanding are far more important than any concern about dumping dollars, both to China and the rest of the world.

Nevertheless, China has abandoned one tool for dealing with imbalances within its economy by sticking to the managed float. We discussed the risk of a Euro break-up. Devaluation in any country has the "benefit" of allowing "immediate" adjustment to economic imbalances, however painful that may be. As long as the Euro remains intact, the adjustment process is long and grinding, exactly what we see in Greece and Spain. Some argue that an immediate devaluation would serve Europeans better. At the same time, they understand that Europeans have strapped themselves to the Euro politically, so a break-up is hard for most to imagine.

With the managed float, the Chinese Government faces a dilemma similar to the Europeans with respect to its own imbalances. It does not discuss these imbalances openly. They include, but are not limited to: (a) rampant real estate speculation accompanied by a booming construction industry (although the Government has met recent success in dampening the frenzy in this market); (b) a wide gap in standard of living between the Chinese middle class, estimated at 300 million people, and the remaining 900 million, many of whom live in the countryside; (c) a moribund state-controlled banking industry with troubled banks standing alongside solvent private ones which must also operate under government directives; (d) various moribund state corporations standing alongside dynamic quasi-private corporations; (e) what appears to be growing labor unrest; (f) an aging population with an inadequate healthcare system; and (f) a non-democratic Communist government sitting atop a quasi-private enterprise system which, though China is the 2nd largest economy in the world, believes it can still "command" in accordance with Marxist-Leninist principles. It is hard to forecast how, and over what period, such imbalances can be reconciled.

Until 2012, Chinese GDP growth had been dynamic, exceeding 8% in each of the prior five years. The global recession has reduced demand for its exports. GDP growth for 2012 year-to-date has fallen below 8%. As long as global growth remains slow, there appear to be no near-term factors which will stimulate higher Chinese growth; further slowing is indeed possible, although growth rates should still exceed those of the US, Japan, and Europe by a wide margin. The Chinese Government has geared its economy for rapid growth. Any economy (or company) that is structured to achieve rapid growth feels more pain than a developed economy that experiences a slowdown. It is analogous to two cars traveling the same road, one at 60 mph and the other at 40 mph which are forced to reduce speeds to 30 mph over a short distance; the first car obviously experiences the greater stress. Similarly, for the high-growth economy, the slowdown quickly brings new imbalances and chafes at those that already exist. Market observers wonder if, for the first time, the Chinese labor force will be exposed to lay-offs of meaningful size.

No one can predict with accuracy the impact that a longer period of slower growth might have on the Chinese economy and Chinese society. Nevertheless, it is possible that a period of slower growth will create turmoil. Uncertainty about the future is reflected in the Shanghai Composite stock index, which has shown virtually no growth during the course of 2012 through October and is down ~39% from its 2009 high. How the Chinese Government addresses this possible turmoil and how it manages the float of the Yuan in response have the capacity to produce shocks that are not registering on today's economic seismograph. In particular, should the Government, at some point, decide to allow the Yuan to float freely as a means of dealing with imbalances, then an unexpected shock would almost certainly be generated which would have the strength to produce a market crash, not just in China but around the world.

Japan invaded Manchuria in 1931 and waged a massive war in the eastern regions of China until 1945. This war had little impact on US or European markets. Today, however, China is a major player given the size of its economy. Due to increased globalization and integration of markets, any major event in China has the potential to produce an unexpected shock elsewhere. As hinted at, we believe growth, or lack thereof, is the primary factor that could create new imbalances and make it more difficult to cope with existing imbalances. A slowing of GDP growth to ~7.0% should be established as an early warning sign of an unexpected shock.

Unexpected Shock: War

Heightened tensions in the Middle East or between North and South Korea; between China and other countries over territorial claims to islands in South China Sea; between China and Taiwan; or between India and Pakistan should be regarded as an early-warning sign of a possible shock. A breakdown of the Pakistani state and participation of radical Islamists in its government should also be regarded as an early warning sign because of its stockpile of nuclear arms. Of all these, a potential attack on Iran appears the most likely to occur. A recent opinion piece in *Foreign Affairs* said the US should not turn way from a war within Iran because it can somehow control/manage/deal with the results.[15] A review of history over the last three centuries and of the American experience in Iraq and Afghanistan would seem to belie this contention. War by its nature is unpredictable. A war that starts with an air strike on Iran could lead to closing of the Straits of Hormuz, sinking of oil tankers, a counter-strike on Israel and other Middle Eastern countries, or an all-out regional war. Who can predict the outcome of any of these?

As an early warning sign, we believe investors should focus on any change in US Government pronouncements that would suggest less discomfort with the option of an Iranian airstrike. We suggest close monitoring of the news to see how the nuclear proliferation crisis with Iran develops; any indication of materially heightened tensions should also be used as an early warning sign.

Misperceived Shocks

By definition, market bubbles are not understood by the vast majority of market participants when they are in the midst of them. During a bubble, the popular media and financial press will be full of articles commenting on the success of the bubble sector: growth in sales, earnings, and employment; stellar stock market performance; and new paradigms which urge us to look at investing in a new way. It is hard for any of us not to be influenced by the hype. Yet in the midst of the hype there will be naysayers. Look for articles that express contrarian views and try to evaluate them. In the end, looking for sources of misperceived shocks requires you to ask one question: what if the hype is wrong? Every one of the market crashes in Table 1.1 saw high-to-low losses in excess of 40%. The costs of being wrong potentially outweigh the gains from being right. Sometimes it is best to use gut feeling: if it sounds too good to be true, maybe it is.

Preparation

We have discussed events capable of producing shocks which lead to a market collapse. The next step is to ask: what steps can I reasonably take to respond to or be positioned for a collapse? The time to prepare is ideally before the early warning signs appear. Planning for the future, whether you forecast good times or bad, should be part of any disciplined approach to managing your finances. Disciplined planning forced you to think through the alternatives and position yourself in a way that is appropriate for your views of the market, your lifestyle, and your appetite for risk.

Once you have completed the plan, you must go one step further and ask: what if I am wrong? Do not assume you are correct, allow for the possibility that your analysis is off-base. Your plan needs to reflect the costs and benefits of the choices you have made in a way that is objective as possible. Furthermore, it is wise to get a second opinion to see if what you have decided makes sense. Some may prepare a plan with the help of a certified financial planner. Others may ask a trusted relative or friend with expertise in financial areas to look it over. Either may serve as a sufficient double-check.

Once you have completed a plan, it is never set in stone. Review it on a periodic basis to ensure it remains appropriate. Moreover, early warning signs and red flags must be regularly monitored. The appearance of any of them should cause you to revisit your plan. Furthermore, other early warnings signs and red flags may emerge that have not been envisioned here and so must be evaluated in accordance with your plan. Following we will discuss financial assets, non-financial assets, and personal lifestyle & budgeting in turn. The discussion of fixed income below is more at a bird's-eye view level and more focused on interest rate risk. More detailed discussion of fixed income, with a focus on credit risk, will come in Chapter 2.

Financial Assets

The starting point is what your portfolio looks like today. What it looks like today limits some of the steps you can take: you cannot perform a wholesale transformation of your portfolio overnight to address newly perceived risks. Furthermore, your portfolio presumably reflects some of your risk preferences, which must be taken into account in any planning process.

Do you understand what you own? Do you monitor your portfolio on a regular basis and make adjustments when necessary? Repeated surveys have shown that many Americans do not have a high financial IQ: they do not have a good feel for how markets work or how to analyze investments. Moreover, repeated surveys have shown that Americans remain wary of investing directly in the stock market, presumably due to the recent market crash. The Investment Company Institute (ICI) shows that households have pulled money out of direct stock market investments each year for the past ten years with net disinvestment of over $1 trillion in 2007 alone. At the same time those households have moved more into mutual funds. Much of direct stock market disinvestment has moved into mutual funds. ICI data shows mutual funds representing 23% of household financial assets at the end of 2011, which is an all-time high.[16]

The move out of the stock market into mutual funds also probably reflects Americans' feeling that they do not have enough expertise to manage direct stock market investments on their own. Nevertheless, one wonders on what basis they have selected the funds they currently own. A material percentage of Americans' holdings of mutual funds are within 401K plans but many of these plans have limited menus of choices so many participants probably just "check the box" instead of making an informed investment decision. Outside 401Ks, one suspects that too many investors have selected funds based on historical performance without enough attention paid to whether they are appropriate for their portfolios. Furthermore, one suspects that only a minority returns to their mutual fund holdings and gives them a hard look once they have made the initial purchase.

Now is the time to take another look at your portfolio, even if you have been monitoring it closely all along. The first step is to inventory your assets and liabilities and project your income and expenses. You may have done this once on your own or with the help of a financial advisor, but now is the time to bring it up to date. The Personal Financial Statement in Appendix I provides a template for how to do this and shows the kind of information you need to gather. Once you have gathered this information, you can start further analysis.

Appendix II sets out a very basic Financial Plan Worksheet to help you sketch out where you are today, where you want to go, and the steps you will take to meet your targets. There is no one-size-fits-all when it comes to creating a financial plan. Your plan must reflect, among other things, your age, the degree to which you need to rely on your financial assets for income, and your risk appetite; nevertheless, any plan you develop will need to consider the following:

The initial focus should be on the division of financial assets between fixed income and equity. Financial assets are those items listed in Schedules A – E in Appendix I. Fixed income assets are those listed in Schedules A & B; equity assets are those listed in Schedules C & D. Also, split your retirement assets between fixed income and equity based on the composition of your 401Ks and IRAs shown in Schedule E. A good benchmark to start from in thinking about your plan is 40% fixed income, 60% equity (40:60) but as noted, no one size fits all. If you have retired or plan on retiring in the next 5-7 years, you should probably think about having a higher proportion in fixed income. The key determinant: the sooner you will need to begin relying on your financial assets for income, the more your portfolio should tilt towards fixed income. On the other hand, if you are younger and further away from retirement, your need to rely on your assets for income should be minimal, in which case a ratio lower than 40:60 may be appropriate. Regardless of your age, two factors are all-important. First, your investments should never cause you to lose sleep at night (of course that it is hard to say in the midst of a market crash) so the mix of your assets between fixed income and equity must make you feel comfortable. Second, a corollary to the first: do not invest in anything you do not understand. Your friends and associates may all be touting the latest hot investment idea, but if you cannot get your arms around it, walk away. This general maxim of investing is too often forgotten. If early warnings signs suggest that a market crash is more probable than before, then tilting your portfolio more towards fixed income would be appropriate.

Though fixed income is usually less risky than investing in common stocks, your plan must incorporate the increased risk inherent in the current level of interest rates. Interest rates are at an all-time low and, with the Fed Funds rate close to 0%, cannot fall further. Investors have earned significant gains from investing in fixed income as interest rates have fallen, but one wonders if they have become complacent and are only looking backward at historical performance. Fixed income assets, as with the example of the apartments in Table 1.2, are subject to the inexorable law of bond and fixed income mathematics: interest rates down, prices up; interest rates up, prices down.

To take an example, the market price of a newly issued 10-year bond with an interest coupon of 1.75% would fall by over 16% if market interest rates on 10-year bonds jumped to 3.75%. Fixed income assets with longer maturities experience greater price swings than shorter-dated ones. The market price of a newly issued 30-year bond with an interest coupon of 3.00% would fall by over 30% if market interest rates on 30-year bonds jumped to 5.00%. Given where we are today, this argues for a bias towards shorter-term fixed income. The dilemma is: shorter-term assets pay very little in terms of interest and so you may lose cash flow which you need to support your household budget if you make this switch. Given the current level of rates, you should view any shift into shorter-dated assets as movement into a short-term holding pattern that gives you time to assess what is coming. If interest rates do rise, you can move back into longer-dated assets and take advantage of higher rates or, alternatively, buy stocks at a discount from today's prices.

Though fixed income is generally less risky, high-yield bonds are not. Investors have ploughed into high-yield searching for interest rates higher than can be achieved on Treasuries and investment-grade corporate bonds. High-yield bonds will see greater price declines in the wake of a market crash due to the increased likelihood of higher corporate defaults. Consequently, they should generally not be part of a plan focused on preparing for a market crash. We view high-yield as an aggressive strategy. Except for experienced investors and traders, we would recommend that aggressive strategies, in total, not comprise more than 5% of your financial assets.

Be wary of how the current level of low interest rates has distorted normal investing patterns. Dividend yields on many common stocks exceed those on Treasuries and investment grade corporate bonds. This is an abnormal situation not sustainable over the long-term. As with high-yield bonds, investors in search of income have piled into utility, telecom, MLP,[17] REIT,[18] and other stocks with high dividends. Stock dividends also tend to grow over time so investors presumably also regard investing in these sectors as a partial hedge against inflation. Due to the current low level of rates, some investors appear to have even expanded their definition of fixed income to include these types of stocks: you sometimes hear the new term "bond substitute." The result is that investors have seen large gains from investing in these sectors and sector performance has been better than the market as a whole (see Table 1.4 under Red Flags in this chapter). Today, however, analysts are increasingly questioning valuations and some see these sectors as overbought. Investors have not reacted much (though they are concerned about current political discussions over raising tax rates on dividend income), perhaps enamored with historical performance. As with the apartments in Table 2.2 and bonds, stocks with valuations heavily linked to dividend yield will go down when interest rates rise. Thus, when the overall market pulls back in the wake of an interest rate increase, they will experience losses due to overall market movements <u>and</u> the rate hike. Conclusion: stocks in these sectors have the potential to underperform during a market crash driven by an interest rate shock. As part of your plan, it may make sense to take some of your gains in these sectors and move the proceeds into shorter-dated fixed income assets, mirroring our suggestions in the bond area.

Should you decide to remain invested in these sectors, focus on stocks with good prospects for earnings growth. These sectors generally have more moderate earnings growth than the broader stock market but investors' buying patterns have made them look like quasi-growth stocks. The reason why so many analysts question current valuations in these sectors is that current prices imply earnings growth higher than what is achievable. One measure often used to screen for stocks that are more at risk of a pullback is the Price/Earnings to Growth (PEG) ratio. This ratio is defined as the P/E ratio (price divided by earnings-per-share, in this case <u>projected</u> EPS) divided by the <u>projected</u> EPS growth rate. A PEG ratio significantly higher than 1.00 may mean that the stock price is incorporating an implicit earnings growth rate that is out of whack with the growth rate a company can actually produce.

Diversification is the key to a sound financial plan. Diversification reduces risk because the impact of a decline in the price of any specific investment or asset class on the overall portfolio is less. The division into fixed income and equity discussed is the first step towards achieving diversification. Chapter 2 will talk about diversification within fixed income, focusing on credit issues. Within the equity sector, whether you invest directly in the market yourself or use mutual funds, you should make sure your investments are spread across the investment spectrum. Nevertheless, diversification for diversification's sake makes little sense. Whether in good times or bad, try to position your portfolio in those sectors which should perform the best given your economic forecast. To arrive at an economic forecast, review financial advice or publications and select the forecast that makes the most sense to you. This can be achieved by comparing the projections you finally select to those projected by others.

Appendix III shows a way to classify businesses by sector and industry. Since our goal is to position our portfolio to outperform other sectors after a market crash, we have forecast how each of these sectors is likely to perform during a downturn. The industries with a '+' sign after them are those that should have the best chance of outperforming the market. This forecast reflects the subjective, idiosyncratic view of the author. What drives this view is focus on industries whose products and services consumers and businesses must continue to buy, even after a horrific crash. This means concentrating on basic needs people cannot go without: food, clothing, housing, water, sanitation, energy, transportation, and education. This view assumes that "nice-to-haves" will perform more poorly than those companies which provide basic needs. As such, it tends to focus on traditional "defensive" stocks and those in other sectors which the author believes have defensive characteristics. In designating a portfolio that you believe will make sense in view of a possible downturn, we recommend that you review Appendix II carefully and determine if that the author's selection conforms to your view of the economy and the world. Forecasting how markets will perform is inherently challenging and so requires we give it the best scrutiny that we can.

Another key factor in investing after a market crash is the concept of *entry point*. It is not enough just to pick the right industry. It is not enough just to pick the right stock. We must buy it at the right price. Since we are in the aftermath of a severe market collapse and possibly an oncoming credit crunch, we need to buy cheaply to compensate us for the increased risk. The *entry point* is the price at which we would buy the stock, perhaps from cash and other short-term assets into which we have moved in anticipation of a market crash. We need to look at the fundamental "intrinsic value" of the stock in order to calculate the entry point. In the aftermath of a market crash, fundamental value should exceed the entry point by a material amount so that an investor is protected even if the market descends further. Knowing the methodologies of how to value stocks is critical to determining fundamental value. *Malkiel* provides a good high-level overview of this subject but you will need to go more in-depth to feel more comfortable.[19]

If you invest in individual stocks, we recommend establishing a plan for reallocating your current portfolio over time in order to reach your "plan" portfolio. Unless you feel you have neglected your current portfolio and are very uncomfortable with it today, there is no need to sell stocks immediately in order to create the "plan" portfolio. One approach might be to create a series of "review dates" at which you will reconsider whether to move forward towards the "plan" portfolio. Another approach might be to create a series of "action steps" to be taken on certain target dates. A third approach might set out a series of actions to be taken once an early warning sign appears accompanied by additional actions to be taken once a red flag occurs. Whatever you decide to do, your plan must reflect your considered judgment of how to protect you and your family in the face of a market crash. You may have other plans for an upside scenario and those are fine, but what we are focusing on here is the downside.

For those who use only mutual funds to invest in stocks, you need to evaluate sectors and industries just as the direct stock market investor does. Your task is not quite as easy but it is not hard either. Forget all the data on historical performance and focus on two pieces of information that are always available on every mutual fund company's website: (1) breakdown of the mutual fund's portfolio by sector and industry and (2) disclosure of the fund's top 10-15 stock holdings. With respect to (1), you should focus on mutual funds which are invested in the target sectors you feel will perform best after a market crash. If your target sectors do not represent a significant proportion of the assets held by the mutual fund you are investigating (or that you currently own), then it is probably not a good fit for your downside financial plan. With respect to (2), take a look at the fund's actual holdings, even if they are 3 months old:[20] are the 10 or 15 holdings that the fund discloses stocks you would have picked if investing directly? Mutual fund holdings reflect the investment manager's philosophy. Your plan must have good congruence with the investment manager's philosophy.

One example: I was looking at a mutual fund about two months after the collapse of Lehman Brothers. I saw Lehman Brothers in its top holdings and immediately excluded the fund because I could not trust the investment manager's judgment. A second example: I was looking at a Large Cap Value fund as an investment a few years ago. When I looked at its top 10 holdings, lo and behold, 5 of them were banks. At that time, I had determined I did not want to own any bank stocks and so excluded it from further consideration. Someone else, on the other hand, might have looked just at historical performance and type of fund. You need to look further and the information is there for you to evaluate. Even if, unfortunately, the information is dated, it still bears examination.

   Be realistic. Even though you are trying to position your portfolio to perform well through a market collapse, you cannot escape the fact that your portfolio will suffer interim losses. What you hope to do is tread water until conditions begin to stabilize and move upward. Also, keep in mind that the upturn may take a while because of the damage that a massive collapse may create across the economy (the subjects of Chapters 2 through 7). Some might reply: can't I escape all of this if I move all of my financial assets to cash? The answer is: theoretically yes, but the better question to ask is if I move all of my assets to cash and there is no crash, what happens? We have all heard of people making sweeping changes to their portfolios either to take advantage of or avoid certain situations. The costs can be huge. Such decisions ignore one vital question: what if the event you are forecasting never comes? You have tailored your entire portfolio to meet one objective. You need to ask yourself two more questions: (1) what makes me so sure of myself and what do I know that others do not? We spoke to man's predilection for thinking he can reason his way through this world. We suggest a dose of humility. And (2) may I not have abandoned significant upside in search of maximum protection? We suggest a careful assessment of risk vs. reward in every decision you make, and sometimes the risk is limiting your upside, i.e., the reinvestment decision is just as important as the decision to withdraw funds from one sector of the market. We return to our emphasis on diversification discussed. It is not only diversification by sector or stock that is important: your strategy must also be adaptable, flexible, and balanced. It should not be unidirectional. Your overall strategy should address both upside and downside forecasts appropriately, weighing one appropriately against the other. In sum, we believe it is better to use a trimmer than a roto-tiller when weeds start to pop up.

   In addition to positioning a portfolio more defensively, is this not a good time to bet on the downside to produce greater returns? One way you could bet on a coming market crash would be to engage in short selling or purchase put options, whether on individual stocks or on Exchange Traded Funds (ETFs) based on stock market indexes.[21] These strategies have three major defects for someone in your position, someone who is planning for the possibility of a market crash. First, with respect to puts, you must deal with the possibility that you cannot match the expiry dates of the options you like to the timeline of your projected market crash. You could buy puts today, pay the option prices (known as premiums) and if nothing happens, watch them expire worthless. And if you still want to maintain your position at expiration, you must buy another set of options, pay another set of prices, and then possibly watch them expire worthless. You will find it very expensive to continue this strategy of buying puts over and over again if you never get to exercise them. This is just one aspect of the cost/benefit trade-off discussion. Second, shorting stocks and buying puts are strategies more appropriate for experienced investors who already understand how these products work and their attendant risks. And third, buying puts (unless you already own the stock) and selling short are aggressive, high-risk strategies. As noted, we recommend that high risk strategies in total represent no more than 5% of your financial assets.

Don't gold and precious metals make sense as a way to protect myself from a market crash? Let's think about gold for a moment. It is a yellow metal in limited supply. It has a few commercial uses (e.g., jewelry) but mostly it is perceived as a store of value. Trading in gold is dominated by commodity funds, hedge funds, and other large pools of capital.[22] For some of these funds, investing in gold may be outright speculation, for others it may be a way to diversify portfolios because the price of gold is uncorrelated with stock and bond market movements. Since gold does not produce cash flow, the price of gold is whatever someone wants to pay for it. Some claim that gold retains purchasing power so it is a good hedge against inflation, but the same argument could be made for wampum: if investors think it has value because it is scarce (and, found only in museums, it is very scarce today), then it has value.

To put gold in perspective, look at the iShares Gold Trust (IAU), an exchange-traded fund (ETF) listed on the New York Stock Exchange that invests only in gold bullion. Here is the performance of IAU, based on net asset value, since its inception in 2006 through July 2012:

2006	2007	2008	2009	2010	2011	2012
22.35%	30.91%	5.92%	23.45%	27.94%	8.64%	5.79%

The average annual return over this period is 18.91%, but IAU's 5-year standard deviation is roughly 22%. In crude statistical terms, this means that 68% of the time IAU's return should lie between -4% and

41%. The remaining 32% of the time, the crude statistics would say that we should see returns that are either above or below those boundaries. Even if you are not familiar with statistics, the upshot is: gold is a very volatile commodity, much more volatile than the average common stock. We have seen the price only go only in one direction the past ~6.5 years, yet what statistics should remind us is that it could just as easily have gone down. Remember, gold produces no cash flow and has little relationship to most human activities: its value is what people say it is. An investment in gold is thus a very aggressive strategy. As such, it cannot be at the core of a plan that seeks to address a possible market crash. Rather it should only be held as one way of diversifying your portfolio and capped at the 5% recommended in total for aggressive strategies (except for traders).

Non-Financial Assets

Your plan for your non-financial assets, including current debt, should consider the following:

Primary residence. Does the size and style of your current home make sense if looked at in the light of a possible market crash? What is the current market price of the home vs. your current mortgage? What is your outlook for the overall direction of market prices in your immediate area over the next five years in the absence of a market crash? If you have a significant amount of equity in the house, does it make sense to sell the house and downsize? The equity proceeds not used to purchase the smaller house could be invested in financial assets in accordance with your overall plan or used to pay down non-mortgage debt. Or would it make more sense to sell your current house and rent instead? If you have negative equity in the house, you might seek agreement from your bank to consider a short sale as a way to get yourself out from under the debt load you are carrying, but the topic of short sales, as well as their impact on your credit standing, is too complicated to consider in detail here.

Second Homes. Do they still make sense in light of a coming market crash? Are they key to your lifestyle or just nice to have? As with your primary residence, you need to consider market pricing and mortgage debt in order to develop a plan.

Vehicles. How many vehicles does your family own? How many are actually needed to get to work and school? How many are just "nice to have"? Are the vehicles utilitarian or luxury in nature?

How much debt is owed on each? Thinking all this through will help determine if you need to make a decision.

Boats and RVs. As with second homes, do these still make sense in light of a coming market crash?

Investment Real Estate. This is real estate that you control and manage directly (even if it is owned in an S Corp or LLC in which you do not have 100% ownership). The focus of this review must be on current NOI, projected NOI, current debt, market interest rates, and overall market conditions—in other words, on everything you originally evaluated at the time you bought it. After this assessment, you must estimate how a market crash is likely to affect market demand and real estate prices and then formulate a plan for how you might best respond. The focus must be on how you might monetize your investment in light of a possible market crash. Unlike financial assets, it takes time to reposition an investment real estate portfolio, so your plan should aim at taking near-term action rather than defer decisions until early warning signs appear.

Business Assets. As with investment real estate, these are businesses that you control and manage directly and the focus should also be on cash flow (EBITDA), debt, and how the business will perform in a downturn. Perhaps you already have an exit strategy, a way to monetize your investment. In light of a possible market crash, it may make sense to execute that strategy. At the same time you must also evaluate your dependence on the business for household cash flow. If you sell the business, what will you do then? Will you rely on cash flow derived from reinvestment in financial assets? Or will you get a new job or buy a new business that is likely to perform better in a down-cycle? As noted, you need to evaluate the risk and benefits of every piece of your financial plan, and the reinvestment decision is just as the important as the decision to sell.

Personal Lifestyle & Budgeting

The focus here must be on your household budget with an eye towards dividing essentials from "nice to have." Review all memberships: country club, swim club, dining, etc. How often do you really use them? Review satellite/cable TV, internet service providers, cellphone, smartphone, and tablet costs. How many of these do you really need and how many are just "nice to have"? How many devices does your family own and are they used that often? Consider also how often you dine out and the costs of your most recent vacation. Are there ways you could trim these without a major difference in your quality of life? Private school and college tuition represents a significant portion of some families' budgets. Even though some might consider these essential, you still need to look at them as objectively as possible and determine if there might be alternatives. Last but not least, review your health insurance plans. If you pay the regular monthly premium but are not using many of the services, switching to a high-deductible plan may fit your needs and thereby lower your family's expenses.

Only you can determine the right path in each of the areas discussed. The goal in this review is to determine the "baseline budget" for your family. The baseline budget is what you cannot avoid spending. This budget is what you must cover even if you or your spouse loses a job after a market crash. Knowing your baseline then allows you to evaluate to what degree your financial assets can cover any cash flow shortfall. A baseline budget is thus integral to the rest of your plan.

Red Flags

We discussed possible early warning signs of a market collapse. In this segment, we discuss red flags which, if they emerged, would indicate the probability of a collapse is materially closer than when you first began planning for it. We suggest that the following be identified as red flags but you may establish others based on your own analysis of the markets.

Further Increases in Interest Rates

We suggested that a rapid movement in rates by 1.00 – 1.50% should be designated an early warning sign. Data or information that suggests a movement closer to 2.00% should be designated a red flag.

Brinksmanship

The summer of 2011 saw a debt limit crisis that threatened US default on its debt obligations if not resolved. A "band-aid" was placed over these issues until after the recent reelection of President Obama in November 2012, which created the so-called "fiscal cliff." We suspect that the two political parties will find a solution to resolve the debt's challenges but, just as in the summer of 2011, the solution may be to kick the can down the road once again. Kicking the can down the road resolves the immediate crisis but sets up a new limit, trigger, or date that can be used, once again, for those who prefer crisis to managing through the issues. We suspect that the US can straddle up to the brink only so many times before going over, not because anyone desires to go over, but because someone miscalculates and accidentally loses footing.

The US economy is slightly stronger now than in 2011, but it is still struggling. The Eurozone economy is in recession, weaker than a year ago. Chinese growth is slowing. In spite of it all, the rest of the world looks to the US and China to drive the engine of global economic growth. While federal deficits are a long-term US structural issue that must be addressed, they cannot be successfully addressed until US economic growth strengthens. To suggest draconian budget cuts in the midst of this economic backdrop is, quite frankly, delusional. There is no immediate hint of inflation because economic recovery is so slow, but deficit hawks would have Americans believe that deficits threaten our very survival today. The Eurozone prescription for Greece and Spain has been, essentially, to kill the patient in order to save it. The human costs are incalculable at this time. The vague prescriptions being bandied about in the US are little better and almost as reckless. One can impose reckless solutions on Greece and Spain; sad to say, they do not really matter because they are not economic powers. Increased recklessness in the US, however, risks producing the shock that produces a market collapse, not only in the US but for the world as a whole. This would be an *unexpected* shock because market participants would not have predicted that US Government leaders would go so far. We suggest monitoring news reports carefully to see how US budgetary issues play out.

Mutual Fund Withdrawals

Net cash flow invested/disinvested in mutual funds provides a source of data which is usually viewed as a good indicator of investor sentiment. Table 1.3 shows net cash flows into mutual funds since 1997. We can see that the stock market crash of 2008 caused withdrawals of $225 billion from longer-dated mutual funds. Of this amount, $228 billion were withdrawals from equity mutual funds, $26 billion were withdrawals from hybrid debt/equity funds, and $30 billion were new

Table 1.3

Net New Cash Flow to Mutual Funds

Billions of dollars, 1997–2012

	Money market funds	Equity, bond, and hybrid funds	Total
1997	103	272	375
1998	235	242	477
1999	194	170	363
2000	159	229	388
2001	375	129	504
2002	(46)	121	75
2003	(263)	216	(48)
2004	(157)	210	53
2005	62	192	254
2006	245	227	472
2007	654	224	879
2008	637	(225)	412
2009	(539)	390	(149)
2010	(525)	228	(297)
2011	(124)	24	(100)
2012-YTD	(138)	201	

Source: Investment Co Institute. Money market flows are thru 8/12, others thru 9/12.

investments in bond mutual funds. A significant portion of the withdrawals from equity mutual funds was presumably reinvested in money market funds. After 2008, we note progressive disinvestment in money market funds, presumably due to lower interest rates and investors' search for more attractive yields. This observation is buttressed by continuous reinvestment in bond funds. For the period from 2009 through 2012 year-to-date, net investment in bond funds has been $982 billion, while net disinvestment in equity funds was $230 billion. These statistics add support to our discussion of the impact of low interest rates under the "Preparation" section discussed.

In searching for red flags, we want to identify indicators of fear. As has already been noted, fear is associated with any event that causes a shock. We would suggest that withdrawals from <u>equity</u> mutual funds (as opposed to bond) are a good red flag because they provide palpable information on investor sentiment toward the stock market.

The pattern of monthly withdrawals by type of fund is graphed in Chart 1.2.Withdrawals by themselves provide little information of value. Since 2006, withdrawals from equity funds have averaged $5.6 billion per month. There have been net withdrawals from equity funds every month (save one) for the 17 months ending September 2012. The mathematics of these monthly flows are thus all negative but we are not suggesting that they are indicators of distress that suggest a coming shock; indeed, movement out of equity funds looks like the "new normal" when we look back over the past five years. Of course, those swept up in a market bubble fervently believe that the bubble is the "new normal." Here, however, progressive disinvestment from equity funds, whether viewed as normal or abnormal, actually evidences risk aversion and so cannot support a bubble or shock.

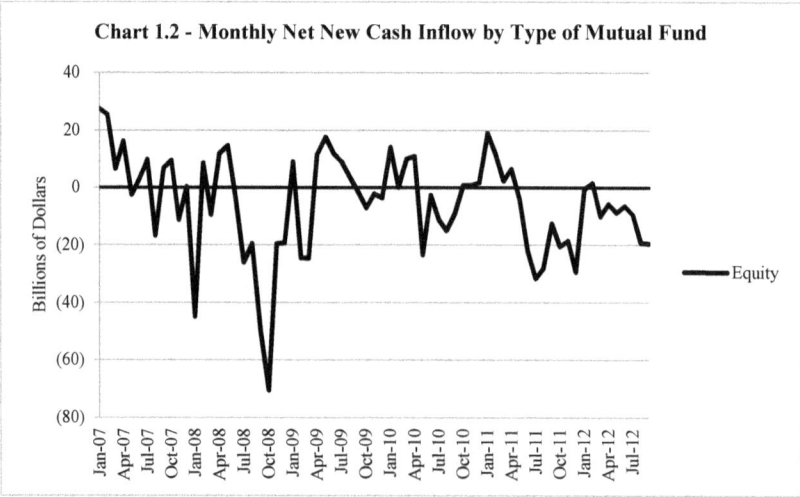

Chart 1.2 - Monthly Net New Cash Inflow by Type of Mutual Fund

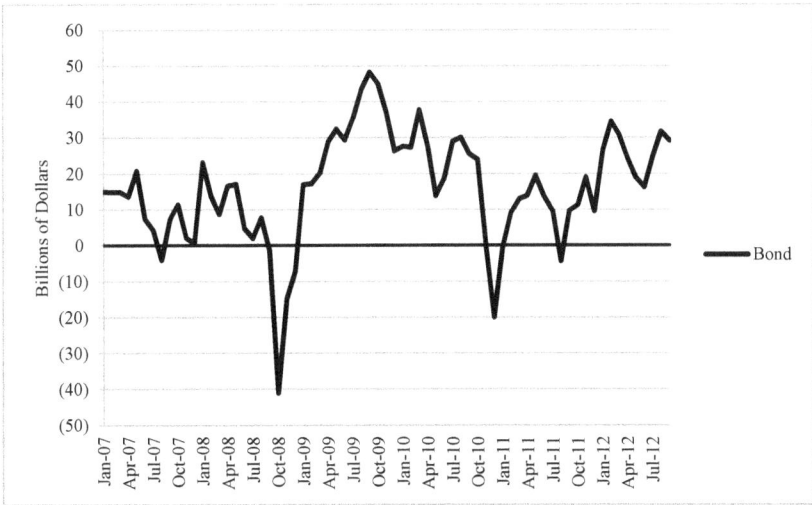

Bond

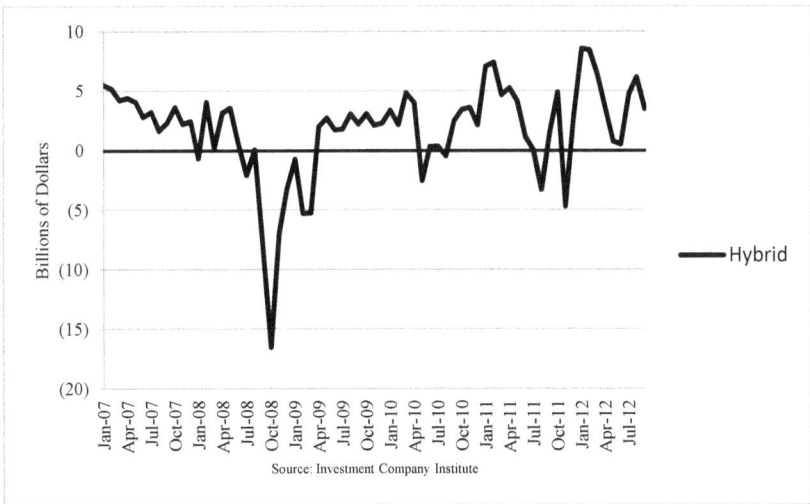

Hybrid

Source: Investment Company Institute

What we want to focus on instead is a pattern of outsized withdrawals that might mean heightened investor fear and uncertainty. We suggest that monthly equity withdrawals that reach $23 billion during any single month should be the initial red flag that justifies intense scrutiny. Movements upward from there toward $30 – 40 billion within the following two months should confirm the red flag. By way of reference, the highest monthly equity fund withdrawal for 2012 through September occurred in September ($19.5 billion). The red flag we are establishing has an analogue to the 12.1% drop in the Dow Jones Industrial Average during the third quarter of 2011; during July and August of that quarter, equity mutual fund withdrawals were $31.7 billion and $28.1 billion, respectively. Note that we are not suggesting that those levels were indicators of a market crash—there was no crash during 2011. There was, however, a crash in 2007 – 2009, with equity fund withdrawals spiking to $70.5 billion in October 2008. The $23 billion red flag is designed to alert you well in advance of a crash so that you can take action. What we are suggesting is that higher-than-normal withdrawals should cause you to consider the possibility that negative investor sentiment is now making a crash more probable.

Hedge Fund Performance

As discussed, movements of large pools of capital have the capacity to shock or exacerbate a shock to financial markets. Hedge funds as a group have produced mediocre performance since 2009. The HFRX Global Hedge Fund Index was up 13.40% during 2009, but thereafter performance was +5.19% in 2010, (8.87%) in 2011, and +2.69% for September 2012 year-to-date.[23] Of course, this is an index of all hedge funds: some have done much better, some worse, but the industry data suggests that they are not the "masters of the universe" that some would make them out to be. They are human and can make mistakes just like other investors. Our concern in searching for red flags is that one of these mistakes should be seen as so *unexpected* that it generates hedge fund actions which would cause a market crash. It is impossible to get "real-time" information on hedge fund cash flow movements and so it is difficult to establish a "hard" red flag, but we suggest monitoring the financial press looking for signs of large hedge fund losses. Large hedge fund losses, coupled with financial commentary expressing concern, should be designated a red flag.

Exit from Dividend-Sensitive Sectors

Dividend-sensitive sectors like utilities, telecom, and real estate investment trusts (REITs) have outperformed the overall market as seen in Table 1.4:

Table 1.4 DIVIDEND-SENSITIVE SECTORS VS S&P 500			
	Annualized Returns		
	1 Year	**3 Year**	**5 Year**
S&P 500 Index	21.12%	11.61%	1.30%
S&P 500 Utilties Index	13.53%	11.96%	2.92%
S&P 500 Telecommunciations Services Index	28.74%	19.37%	2.48%
S&P US REIT Index	27.56%	21.82%	2.20%

Last updated: 10/19/12, 4:35 pm EDT
All calculations are based on total return.
Source: S&P Dow Jones Indices

Only the 1-year annualized return for utilities trails that of the broad S&P 500. The popularity of these sectors for investors seeking yield has already been discussed. If market performance in these three sectors begins falling and/or all three sectors begin to underperform the S&P 500, this may be an indication that investors, who have heretofore used them as havens of relative safety, are changing their minds. Whether it is fear of a rate hike or fear of overall market conditions or fear of a tax increase, fear matters most to us. Thus we would set underperformance in these sectors as a red flag.

Further Preparation

Now that red flags have appeared, it is time to go back and revisit your original plan. Go over the action steps you have previously established and, if it is appropriate, take action. If you decide not to take action, this means that you have decided that (a) your original plan has shortcomings even in the face of the red flags you have established and/or (b) the red flags you originally established are not good indicators of a possible market crash. You need to bring your plan up-to-date and amend it to reflect your latest, best thinking.

At this point, a key consideration is that the market crash may be accompanied by a credit crunch, which is discussed in Chapter 2. The prospect of a credit crunch brings a period of heightened risk for your fixed income portfolio. Planning for a credit crunch can proceed in one of two ways. First, you could have already incorporated it within your initial plan, or as an adjunct to the plan. In other words, your initial plan could have called for specific action steps to be taken upon the occurrence of the red flags outlined. Alternatively, your original plan could merely have required, upon emergence of red flags, a review of all your fixed income positions with an eye to analyzing their vulnerability to a credit crunch. Whatever approach you adopt is acceptable: it depends on your overall view of the risk of market collapse and how you feel it is best to respond to it. Chapter 2 presents the dimensions of a credit crunch and then discusses how to plan for it.

---

[1] One of the foundations of financial theory is that a company's current stock price reflects buyers' and sellers' collective evaluation of all known information about it. This foundation rests on the assumption that markets are efficient, i.e., if a new piece of information appears, one buyer may immediately try to take advantage of it, but other buyers and sellers immediately wade in and place their own value on the new information, the stock reacts accordingly, and momentary balance between buyers and sellers is restored. Obviously, this is theory and theory does not always reflect what we see on a day-to-day basis. For example, it assumes that everyone has access to the same information, but we know this is not true in real life. Nevertheless, it is hard to deny that investors look at events, make conclusions, and act (or not act) on them. Thus, to some degree market prices do embed investors' view of the risks that exist. For more discussion of this topic, the popular classic is: Burton J. Malkiel, *A Random Walk Down Wall Street: The Time-Tested Strategy for Successful Investing* (New York: W.W. Norton & Company, 2007).

[2] Jack Willoughby, "Burning Up," *Barron's*, March 20, 2000.

[3] The S&P Case-Shiller Home Price Indices track changes in the value of residential real estate nationally by tracking home prices in 20 metropolitan regions. The Index we have cited is its US National Index, seasonally adjusted. For more information see: http://www.standardandpoors.com/indices/sp-case-shiller-home-price-indices/en/us/?indexId=spusa-cashpidff--p-us----

[4] Fannie Mae is the nickname for the Federal National Mortgage Association (FNMA). Freddie Mac is the nickname for the Federal Home Loan Mortgage Corporation (FHLMC). These are so-called government-sponsored enterprises (GSE's) and were publicly traded prior to the real estate crisis. Although privately owned, the market always regarded them as quasi-governmental organizations, meaning the government would back them up if they ever had trouble. Their mission was to support the financing of residential real estate. The primary means by which they did so was through guaranteeing residential mortgages and purchasing mortgages from banks and other financial institutions. In the wake of the collapse of the residential real estate market, both entities are now 100%-owned by the US Government.

[5] Sub-prime is defined in many ways, depending on the financial institution, but the most common definition is a loan to an individual with a credit score (FICO) of 640 or less.

[6] The negligence included but was not limited to: (a) Alt-A and other types of "low-doc" loans under which borrowers were not required to provide full financial disclosure; (b) interest-only, pick-a-pay (under which the borrower had the option of skipping payments in various ways), and adjustable rate mortgages (ARM's) with low introductory teaser rates; (c) mortgages representing 95–100% of appraised value; and (d) debt service coverage ratios with calculations based solely on interest-only payments. All of these had the practical effect of allowing

borrowers to qualify for loans for which they would ordinarily not qualify. The fundamental principle of sound lending is demonstrating that the borrower has capacity to repay, but the majority of mortgage originators no longer cared about capacity to repay because they had no intention of holding the loans. Their sole goal was selling the loans to Wall Street so it was only Wall Street's purchase criteria that mattered. Wall Street's purchase criteria were not a constraint because, like the originators, they also had no intention of holding the loans. They cared only about packaging the loans and selling them to investors, who for a variety of reasons did not understand clearly what they were buying. Investors were the ones in this process who <u>should have</u> cared most about borrower capacity to repay; however, capacity to repay was often masked by unwarranted Aaa/AAA ratings from Moody's and Standard & Poors and by credit enhancements from mortgage insurers and corporations like AIG which lacked sufficient capital to back up their commitments. Investors themselves bear some responsibility for not understanding fully what they were buying. Keep in mind that the vast majority of investors were large pools of capital (mutual funds, pension plans, etc.) managed by well-trained, experienced individuals. We have to conclude that the individuals who managed these pools did not do their homework.

7 Admittedly there were bank runs in 1929 and thereafter during the Great Depression. These bank runs, however, were not a cause of the market collapse but a reaction to it. They took place until the bank holiday imposed by Franklin D. Roosevelt after his inauguration in 1933. Note that the market collapse had occurred well before then.

8 Eurekahedge Research Data, "Asset Flows Update for the Month of August 2012," September 2012, http://www.eurekahedge.com/news/Eurekahedge_Sep_2012_Asset_Flow.asp (accessed October 14, 2012).

9 In financial terms, leverage means using debt as well as equity in order to make an investment. A borrower that is said to employ high leverage is one that uses a higher proportion of debt to equity than other market participants.

10 Long-Term Capital Management (LTCM) was a large hedge fund established by well-regarded, experienced Wall Streeter professionals, with two Nobel Prize winners on its board of directors. Its focus was on computer-driven trading aimed at capturing mispricing, even in tiny amounts, between related markets or financial assets. The financial models which drove its trading were based on pure "rocket science." Since the models were designed to capture the tiniest amount of mispricing, LTCM could only produce large returns for its investors by employing large amounts of leverage. Think of it this way: if it could only scrape a little bit off each investment position, each investment had to be huge if it wanted to make a lot of money. In fact, debt exceeded LTCM equity by astronomical amounts, ironically appropriate for practitioners of rocket science. While LTCM management recognized that leverage potentially brings higher risk, they believed in the superiority of their models. They believed that their investments, a long position typically being offset by an appropriate short, were effectively hedged. This belief rested on the implicit assumption that the long and short positions could be closed

at any time, i.e., management's entire business model rested on the assumption of market liquidity. Imbalances, to which the crisis which started with the Asian flu undoubtedly contributed, meant that liquidity had shrunk in many of the markets and financial assets in which LTCM was trading. This meant that LTCM could not liquidate many positions it held, so that many of them became *de facto* unhedged. The size of LTCM's positions threatened the stability of world markets as its losses began to mount. In the end, the Fed was forced to intervene in order to prevent a financial panic and, with the cooperation of money center and large investment banks, was able to prevent a crisis, but LTCM went bankrupt in the process. For additional information, a popular study is: Roger Lowenstein, *When Genius Failed: The Rise and Fall of Long-Term Capital Management* (New York: Random House, 2001).

[11] U.S. Securities and Exchange Commission and the Commodity Futures Trading Commission, "Findings Regarding the Market Events of May 6, 2010," September 30, 2010.

[12] Carmen M. Reinhart and Kenneth S. Rogoff, "The Aftermath of Financial Crises," (Draft dated December 19, 2008 presented to the American Economic Association on January 3, 2009).

[13] We disregard the effect of taxes in this presentation.

[14] Given the size of the Chinese economy and recent rampant real estate speculation, one questions if the Chinese Government's inflation statistics really capture on-the-street inflation as experienced by its average citizen. Nevertheless, this data is all we have.

[15] Matthew Kroenig, "Time to Attack Iran: Why a Strike is the Least Bad Option," *Foreign Affairs*, January/February 2012. The author is a former Special Adviser in the Office of the Secretary of Defense who served earlier during the Obama Administration.

[16] Investment Company Institute, *2012 Investment Company Fact Book*, p. 9, http://www.ici.org/pdf/2012_factbook.pdf (accessed October 16, 2012). ICI defines net investment/disinvestment in financial assets as net new cash inflow/outflow plus reinvested interest and dividends.

[17] Master Limited Partnership. MLP's are publicly traded limited partnerships. These are found most often in the energy sector. They typically hold oil and gas gathering, pipeline and storage assets which produce relatively predictable cash flows.

[18] Real Estate Investment Trust.

[19] See footnote #1. "Intrinsic value is usually calculated via (a) discounted cash flow analysis using (in the environment after a market crash) very conservative cash flow projections and/or (b) comparable public company analysis. Discounted cash flow analysis is more important during a severe market downturn. This book is not a book on stock analysis or fundamental analysis but you need to know about it if you intend to invest in stocks and/or stock mutual funds. There are is an innumerable number of books available on this subject. Look for one which spends at least part of its time on discounted cash flow analysis.

[20] As an aside, disclosure of mutual fund holdings leaves much be desired. Some funds publish monthly, some quarterly, and some as infrequently as semi-annually. Mutual funds are custodians of individual assets and individuals have every right to know what investment managers are doing on a frequent basis; monthly disclosure should be a minimum by regulation but weekly would be desirable. Mutual funds have this information electronically at their fingertips. For what reason can they justify failing to disclose it when all they have to do is hit a button to put it on their website? Some might reply that more frequent posting is costly and risks disclosure of competitive information. This reasoning is without merit. The cost of updating a table on a website is minimal. Furthermore, posting of stock holdings a month or a week late discloses only history. Fund managers may have changed major portions of their portfolios after date of disclosure and so the argument of confidentiality does not hold up. In addition, purchases and sales by mutual funds or hedge funds are not invisible to other market participants. Many large participants already have a good idea of where these funds are investing even in the absence of publication of updated results. But, sad to say, average investors do not.

[21] To short a stock means to sell shares without owning it. A short seller generally borrows the stock from another investor who owns it (a broker or other financial institution usually acts as the intermediary between borrower and lender) and sells the stock in hopes that its price will fall. Once the price has fallen, the short seller will buy back the stock, pocket his profit, return the stock, and thereby close out the transaction. When one buys a stock (going "long"), the maximum one can lose is one's initial investment. A short seller's loss, however, is theoretically unlimited: if the stock price skyrockets (for example, due to a takeover) instead of falling, losses could be huge. A put option gives the investor the right, for a specific period of time, to deliver to the party that sold the put, shares of stock at a defined price (the "strike price"). Once the strike price falls below the current stock price, the put buyer will consider exercising his option, or will consider selling his option. Purchase of a long put option thus protects the investor against downside movements in stock prices. If, however, the stock price never falls below the strike price, the put option will expire worthless at maturity.

[22] On a side note, one of the issues in today's commodity markets is the extent to which commodity funds dominate trading in all types of commodities, not just gold. With no commercial interests, these funds focus solely on capital gains from speculating on price movements. Today, many participants in agricultural commodity markets who use them for hedging of harvest deliveries have been frustrated with the high volume of trading and the anomalies these funds have created. Soybeans could be gold: they are both trading vehicles, both the same from a commodity fund's perspective. The sheer volume of trading generated by commodity funds, their sheer size and power, reflects the volume of easy money sloshing about in today's markets seeking higher returns.

[23] Hedge Fund Research, Inc., https://www.hedgefundresearch.com (accessed on October 19, 2012).

Chapter 2

Credit Crunch

Introduction

Definitions

Investopedia defines *credit* as "a contractual agreement in which a borrower receives something of value now and agrees to repay the lender at some date in the future, generally with interest. The term also refers to the borrowing capacity of an individual or company." Production of goods and services is the heart, brain, and lungs of every economy, but credit is its lifeblood. An economy cannot exist without the motive force, power, and dynamism of production. Credit, however, sustains the economy by enabling delivery of the fruits of production in an as efficient as possible manner. Without credit, there is no way to bridge the difference in needs and capacity between buyer and seller. Credit rests on one foundation we have already discussed: trust. A clothing manufacturer which ships apparel to a department store trusts that it will be paid 30 days after shipment. A bank which makes a loan to a car buyer trusts that the buyer has the capacity and willingness to pay it off over 60 months. Credit collapses without confidence and trust.

Profile of Financial Institutions

We are all familiar with the normal types of personal credit: residential mortgages, car loans, student loans, home equity lines, credit cards and the like. Think of how you would manage your life if none of these were available or if they were in very limited supply. Yet, however important they may be, they do not run your life, they do not dog your every waking hour. That is not the case with Wall Street. As Table 2.1 shows, equity represents just ~10-11% of assets at large financial institutions. If we were to somehow include the credit equivalent amount of off-balance sheet derivative and other positions, then the calculated equity/asset ratio would be even lower. Of course, the equity/asset ratio says nothing about the quality of the assets on the institution's balance sheet or the management of its trading and derivatives positions. We could only make a conclusion in that regard if we had full access to the institution's books and spent a good deal of time examining them. That is, needless to say, impossible.

What we can say, however, is that financial institutions are highly leveraged relative to every other sector of the economy. For those who cringe in alarm, that is the reality and always has been. Financial institutions cannot make money without leverage: if we demanded that liabilities not exceed equity (as is the case with most large industrial companies), then they could not earn enough to satisfy their shareholders.[24]

Reliance on Short-term Liabilities

More important than pure leverage is a financial institution's reliance on volatile short-term liabilities to finance its needs. Table 2.1 shows that the average large financial institution finances about one-quarter of its assets from volatile sources.

What are these volatile sources? Other large financial institutions represent a substantial portion: financial institutions borrow from each other. Large certificates of deposit and corporate short-term commercial paper, which are purchased by mutual funds and investment vehicles, are also very important. For the purposes of this chapter, we will term the aggregate of these sources the short-term credit markets, or just the *credit markets*. When a bank needs an overnight loan to fund its portfolio, it may borrow from another bank which has excess funds available and needs to put them to work; that other bank is part of the credit market. When a broker-dealer or investment bank has increased its securities portfolio as a result of trading during the day, it may borrow from other firms to finance the need, pledging a portion of that portfolio to secure the loan; that other firm acts as part of the credit market. It is not just banks and broker-dealers that depend on credit markets. Hedge funds and other large pools of capital are also heavy short-term borrowers.[25]

Table 2.1

Balance Sheet Composition

Large Financial Institutions

	Large Banks	Large Brokers
Liquid Assets	22.9%	38.5%
Securities & Investments	20.6%	40.6%
Loans	46.7%	1.9%
Other Assets	9.8%	19.0%
Total Assets	100.0%	100.0%
Deposits	71.1%	7.6%
Short-Term Debt & Trading-Related Liabilities	8.0%	25.8%
Long-Term Debt	6.4%	15.8%
Other Liabilities	3.4%	40.2%
Memo: Volatile Liabilities	26.7%	25.8%
Equity	11.1%	10.6%
Total Liabilities & Equity	100.0%	100.0%

Large banks = Composite of US banks with assets of $100B or more per FDIC data at 6/30/12. Brokers is median of 8 large broker-dealers per most recent 10Q. Grouping of assets is per the author. Volatile liabilities is as per FDIC reporting. For brokers, author has assumed short-term debt & trading-related liabilities are volatile.

The seeds of a *credit crunch* are sown when market liquidity, the availability of cash, declines dramatically. Sometimes it occurs after a market crash. Sometimes, in pursuit of the goal of combating inflation or excessive speculation, it results from direct Fed or central bank action to raise rates accompanied by reduction in the money supply. In the example in the early part of Chapter 1, our prospective homebuyer was suddenly caught short of cash due to the market crash and began scrambling for ways to cope. After a crash, any individual investor who has margin loans outstanding scrambles to meet margin calls, whether by drawing down bank deposits or selling other assets. The impact of the withdrawal of liquidity on the lives of individual investors can certainly not be overlooked — we all remember the sad stories of people jumping from buildings after the crash of 1929 — but, in dollar terms, the stress imposed on financial institutions is far greater. Why is that?

The Impact of Reduced Liquidity on Financial Institutions

Let's begin with how life looks to a large financial institution that relies heavily on short-term financing. Every day it wakes up and looks at a significant portion of its assets — loans, securities, or whatever — that must be refinanced. Any increase in assets requires incremental financing beyond that. It spends every minute of every day in the credit markets arranging financing to help fund itself. Sometimes this is accomplished by rolling over existing loans. Sometimes it is accomplished by pledging additional collateral so existing financing can remain in place. Sometimes it involves establishing new credit arrangements with new counterparties. By the end of each business day, each firm has financed its portfolio in a way it finds appropriate. Its staff then gets to rest overnight, but when they come in the next morning, they have to do it all over again. But does the firm really get to rest overnight? No, because trading is now global. In almost every time zone you will find someone trading. If someone is trading, those trades must be financed. So workers in New York or London can go home thinking they have done their jobs, but workers in Tokyo are now at it, plugging away to ensure financing remains in place. Thus, for the firm as a whole, keeping existing short-term financing in place and arranging new short-term financing is a 24/7 function.

Now if you asked a bank or brokerage house today whether the picture drawn in the prior paragraph is true, they would say it is overdrawn. They would say it looks too much like a titanic struggle between borrowers and lenders. They would respond that borrowing from day to day is not really that hard. In Chapter 1, we said that implicit belief in the availability of cash — easy to earn, easy to borrow, and relatively cheap — underlies every market bubble. Financial institutions, even in the absence of a bubble, believe even more strongly in the availability of cash. That belief underlies how they would respond to your question. For if they did not believe, which of them would be in the market every day arranging billions of dollars of short-term financing? Stress tests, liquidity plans, collateralization, and risk policies — which are all very helpful — are designed to bring mathematical rigor to balance sheet management. They are all designed to prove to the firm's senior management that the firm can withstand a crisis. Yet they also serve to mask the fact that the hypothesis of future cash availability cannot be substantiated with certainty. Is there not great complacency here? In fact, history has shown the falsehood of this hypothesis time and again: when credit crunches occur, they strain the capacity of even the strongest institutions. Just because markets have not experienced a credit crunch in a long time does not mean one cannot occur.

Complacency is directly connected to our belief that we can reason our way through the world. In everyday activities, we all look at trendlines and implicitly assume the trend will continue; that is how our minds work. We humans love forecasting the future using trendlines (and this book lays out a trendline, though it is only an intellectual construct to think about the issues). Sportswriters love trendlines. If a team has been winning, they assume it keeps on winning and prattle on endlessly about its strengths. If it loses a game, the team now has all sorts of insoluble weaknesses which will cause it to keep on losing. For an example of this, compare the stories about the Miami Heat and LeBron James during the regular season and after they lost Game 1 of the 2012 NBA Finals with the stories after they went on to sweep the last four. In the world of stock trading, use of trendlines represents the heart of technical analysis. Technical analysis uses charts based on past trends to try to predict future performance; one doubts that it does any better than reading tea leaves.[26] In the world of business, if times are bad, we tend to assume they will get worse; if markets are booming, we tend to assume they will get even better. Prediction from a trendline seems to be built into our DNA—yet we obey these instincts at our peril. Would J.P. Morgan's notorious "London Whale" fiasco have occurred if a less complacent mindset towards risk management existed within large banks?[27] We are not saying that financial institutions should stop borrowing short-term or that they should stop trading. What we are saying is that they need to recognize that all the stress tests, liquidity plans, collateralization, and risk management procedures in the world may not be enough to help a firm manage through a financial panic. If firms choose to rely on short-term credit, caution must be a byword.

There are generally three ways in which financial institutions experience the liquidity crisis directly:

1. The value of a firm's securities portfolio declines after a market crash, which lowers its equity position. As a result, the firm may be at risk of breaching required regulatory capital ratios; breaching capital ratios threatens regulatory intervention/takeover and, in the most severe cases, insolvency. In a down-market, capital is king for every financial institution: every firm focuses on maintaining capital because it is capital that enables it to survive a financial panic. Every firm going through a financial crisis thus becomes inner-directed. There are essentially three options to ensure capital remains adequate:

a. A firm can sell assets and thereby reduce the capital need, but selling assets into a down-market is usually unpalatable: it will likely produce additional losses which will lower capital still further. Selling only makes sense if the firm can sell at prices close to the values reflected in its financial statements, which probably means selling its best assets—but selling your winners and keeping your losers is a recipe for failure in all walks of life.

b. A firm can use liquidity on its balance sheet to pay down debt. Reducing debt makes the firm less volatile and thus less at risk of breaching capital requirements.

c. It can try to raise capital, but raising capital during a crisis is difficult and, more important, unappealing: the firm can be expected to pay dearly for it.

So only option (b) is really feasible near-term. When much of the firm's liquidity is directed towards reducing its own debt, that liquidity is no longer available to other firms, the credit markets as a whole. The liquidity crisis becomes more severe to the extent that this inward focus on paying down debt is replicated across the credit markets.

2. The second way firms experience the decline in liquidity is through what are known as "haircuts." Haircuts are directly related to the discussion in the preceding paragraph. Much of the financing on Wall Street is extended on a secured basis. When a firm agrees to make a secured loan, it "haircuts," i.e. discounts, the market value of the collateral in order to calculate the maximum loan it is willing to make. Haircuts are used by the lending firm to protect itself from the risk of a market decline—they are not set by regulation. Every firm sets its own

haircuts based on its view of the liquidity/saleability of each individual piece of collateral and the volatility of its market price (illiquidity and volatility usually correlate to some degree). Haircuts can range from as low as .5 – 3% for US Government securities to 15 – 25% for US, European, and Japanese common stocks. Every firm engaged in this type of financing provides a detailed schedule listing every type of asset it will accept as collateral and spelling out the related haircuts. The crucial point is this: the lending firm recalculates the haircut every single day (and sometimes, depending on the asset, intra-day) and tells the borrower whether collateral is excess or deficient. If it is deficient, then the borrower must either pay down the loan or put up additional collateral—"immediately" or by close of business. Paying down the loan, if that option is chosen, becomes part of the firm's overall plan for reducing the debt discussed in the prior paragraph. If the borrowing firm cannot put up additional collateral, then the lending firm can sell the existing collateral in order to protect itself. Letting the lending firm sell the collateral is usually unsatisfactory because it risks even more losses in a falling market, but if the borrowing firm's liquidity is spent, there are no other choices.

Providing additional collateral may be the easiest short-term solution, but only if the lending firm will accept it. Presumably most of the best collateral was already pledged prior to the crash. New collateral will be of lesser quality and so the haircuts may be significant and punishing relative to the borrowing firm's overall needs. At some point, the borrowing firm's pool of unpledged, satisfactory collateral may become so small that it cannot meet the many conflicting demands on its liquidity, which threatens insolvency. Whether the borrowing firm pays down the loan or puts up additional collateral, the net effect is that liquidity disappears which might otherwise have been available to lend in the credit markets.

3. The third way in which firms experience the decline in liquidity is changes in haircuts. Sometimes lending firms decide that certain types of collateral are no longer acceptable. For example, before the sub-prime crisis, mortgage-backed securities (MBS) composed of sub-prime loans were probably acceptable collateral at most firms. After the crisis came into the open, they were either no longer acceptable or, alternatively, were "haircut" to such a large degree that they no longer provided much in collateral value to borrowing firms. Sometimes lending firms raise haircuts even on normally acceptable collateral. They do this to protect themselves from the risk of higher market volatility after a crash. Increasing haircuts usually comes as a

shock to borrowing firms because they had not planned for it. Whatever the motivation for increasing haircuts, its effect on the liquidity crisis is pro-cyclical, i.e., it makes already bad market conditions worse. Increasing haircuts drains further liquidity from the marketplace.

Significant declines in liquidity have great potential to develop into a *credit crunch*. Declines in liquidity, by themselves, bring great uncertainty. A credit crunch adds fear to that uncertainty. This is what we saw after the market crashed in 2008. At some point, it is no longer just a question of availability of funding. At some point, a threshold is crossed. Unlike an industrial company, one cannot really understand how well a financial firm has been managed until it faces adversity: during good times, even shaky borrowers make their loan payments and the stock market lifts even leaky ships. The results of poor financial management can only be seen when things turn ugly. Given the breadth of financial markets, there are many different areas in which ugliness can appear.

A Digression on Derivatives

What is special today is the variety of products traded in financial markets. Many of these products did not exist ten years ago and, even if they did, trading volume was modest when compared to today. Derivatives have been the area of greatest financial product growth. Those seeking to reform the US financial sector have bandied about *derivative* like a four-letter word, as if it can be held responsible for many of our problems. In truth, the problem is not derivatives, but how humans have used (or misused) them. *Derivatives* are hard to understand for most people because so many financial products are encompassed within this category, but the basics are relatively simple.

A *derivative* is merely a contract between two parties. Cash to be paid between the parties is measured by the performance (most often a change in price) of an underlying asset (usually called the *reference asset*). The word derivative has developed in daily use because cash payments are <u>derived from</u> the performance of the underlying asset. The most common types of derivatives are options, swaps, futures, and forwards. Most are used for hedging, but investors without a commercial need for hedging trade in derivatives markets as well.

An example of an *option* is a call option on a stock. In return for payment of the option price (the premium), a call option buyer receives, for a specified period of time, the option to buy the stock at some price (the strike price) which is higher than the current market price; the value of the option at any point in time is <u>derived from</u> measuring the difference between the strike price and the market price and estimating how likely it is that the market price will move to the strike price. A call option buyer uses the option to speculate on a rise in the price of the stock without having to own it; a call option seller sells the option to earn income because he believes the stock price will not rise above the strike price by the option's expiry date.

An example of a *swap* is an interest rate swap. Under an interest rate swap, one party (the fixed-rate payer) agrees to pay the other (the floating-rate payer) a fixed rate, let's say 6% per annum every three months, on a *notional amount* of $1,000,000. In return, the floating payer agrees to pay a floating rate, let's say the London Interbank Offered Rate (LIBOR), every three months on the same amount.[28] Actual cash owed by one party to the other at the end of three months will be <u>derived from</u> the net difference between the payments due from the fixed-rate payer and the floating-rate payer, respectively. The amount of this difference is <u>derived from</u> changes in LIBOR. The motivation for the swap: the fixed-rate payer currently has floating-rate debt but wants fixed rate instead; the floating-rate payer currently has fixed rate debt but wants to pay floating.

A *futures contract* is an exchange-traded contract to buy or sell a commodity at a specific price at some point in the future. Its underlying asset is a specific commodity, such as wheat or heating oil, with the actual value of the futures contract at any point in time <u>derived from</u> the difference between the current spot price of the commodity and that specified in the futures contract and estimating how likely it is that the spot price will move to the futures price. A farmer will sell a futures contract to fix the price of the bushels of wheat he expects to have available at harvest time.

A *forward contract* looks very much like a futures contract but it is between two counterparties and is not traded on an exchange. For example, a forward FX contract is one in which one bank is willing to pay $1,000,000 three months from now in return for receipt of €750,000 from another bank. The value of the forward contract at any point during its 3-month life is <u>derived from</u> the difference between the spot $:€ exchange rate and the $1.00: €.75 exchange rate specified in the hypothetical forward contract laid out. Parties to an FX swap use it to fix the exchange rate on expected future cash flows; for example, the bank willing to pay $1,000,000 in 3 months knows that it will need €750,000 at that time and so wants to be sure, today, of what that will cost. Derivatives exist on virtually any underlying reference asset you can think of (and some you have never dreamt of); the wonders of financial engineering have produced this wave of new products for us. Who knew we even needed them?

The issue with derivatives markets is that they are relatively opaque compared to firms' normal lending and investing activities. Some products are so complicated that only experts and day-to-day practitioners really understand how they work and their attendant risks. The size of the overall derivatives market is monstrous in notional terms, perhaps $1,200 trillion ($1.2 quadrillion) by one estimation.[29] One doubts that senior management at most banks really understands what is happening on their derivatives trading desks.

It is not just the variety of financial products that makes today different from ten years ago. It is not just the size of derivatives markets that matters. Another issue is that trading in most derivatives is dominated by financial models. Models estimate fair value and it is on the basis of this fair value that trades are generated. Prior to closing out trades, models are usually used, in the absence of transparent market prices, to price current positions and determine <u>unrealized</u> profits and losses.

There is nothing inherently wrong with financial models, so long as one understands their limitations and acts accordingly. Models usually help firms better understand the way markets work. They take the old maxims and shibboleths about trading and investing, test them, and see if they really work in practice. The risk with using models is the human propensity to trust them completely, to believe they are scientific. The risks in models are fourfold. First, they are based on historical data, but there is no reason that the future should look like the past. Second, models are often based on the assumption that traders can buy or sell a position at the drop of a hat. In other words, they assume that liquidity is always available, a delusion we have been skewering throughout this book. This assumption is even more questionable for certain derivatives where trading is dominated by a relatively small number of firms; liquidity or other issues at any of the market makers could directly affect the volume of trading in the market for a single derivative, raise immediate questions about the fairness and accuracy of pricing, and thereby raise doubts about a firm's ability to hedge positions effectively. Third, models assume that prices move in fairly smooth, small gradations, unlike the stock price in Chart 1.1 which we have already discussed. And fourth, models seek to find statistical correlation between assets or different asset classes. The theory that underlies the construction of the model is critical. One worries that humans, when either constructing or using models, make the leap from correlation to causation and thereby embed fatal flaws in their investment methodology. It's the old joke (but not so funny here): do we eat ice cream in the summer because it's hot, or is it hot in the summer because we eat ice cream?

Most experienced market observers and participants realize these risks exist to some degree in all models, but many assume they can deal with them by, for example, evaluating model performance under stress test scenarios. Yet one doubts if the stress test parameters will bear close resemblance to how events will actually unfold during a market crash and a credit crunch. Others take comfort in the fact that financial institutions have experienced, talented risk managers overseeing trading activities. This comfort resides in the belief that these individuals can somehow intervene and override the model's conclusions when a market crash or credit crunch looms. One has to ask: are risk managers, being human, fast enough and smart enough to do what is needed? Is it possible to manage these risks effectively, or will humans always be too late? In 1995, one trader in Singapore, through losses on unauthorized derivatives trading, bankrupted the venerable Barings Bank which had been in continuous existence since 1762. We have seen multiple trading fiascos over the past 20 years, the latest being the noted London Whale. Every one of these can be linked to a failure in risk management.[30]

Moving Into a Credit Crunch

Now we return from our digression into derivatives and models to see what actually starts a credit crunch. What moves a shortage of liquidity into a credit crunch is when financial institutions start becoming suspicious of each other. They know better than the rest of us how hard it is to understand the quality of the assets on another firm's balance sheet. Yes, ABC Brokerage reports its results quarterly, but suspicion arises from a number of basic questions. In what is ABC actually investing? What strategies is it following? How is it managing the risk? Financial statements provide little detail to help answer these questions. And just as important, does the value of the investments reported in ABC's published financial statements reflect actual market value today? These suspicions arise from the miasma of gloom following a market crash. The thought process, which is often arrogant, works like this: 'If my firm, XYZ Bank, is well-run and is still experiencing issues in hard times like these, how much more worse off is ABC Brokerage, which I have always thought of as a schlock shop? They have to be hiding losses.' This thought process becomes even more intense if XYZ knows ABC is an active trader in derivatives, because it is even more difficult to grasp what ABC's true derivative exposure might be. At some point, XYZ's <u>suspicions develop into fear</u> about ABC's solvency and it cuts off all credit.

The *credit crunch* arrives when fear causes dramatic reduction in or complete termination of funds availability/financing to multiple firms across credit markets. Since so many financial institutions rely heavily on short-term funding, a cut-off in credit threatens the very existence of many of them. Multiple insolvencies of major financial firms have the capacity to threaten the very foundations of the economy. It should be noted that a credit crunch will usually produce a feedback loop back into the market crash because the credit crunch usually leads to even more selling as financial institutions scramble to sell assets and raise cash in order to remain solvent. The worst credit crunch in recent memory is the financial crisis which began with the Lehman Brothers bankruptcy filing of September 15, 2008. In March 2008, the Fed forced the troubled Bear Stearns into the hands of J.P. Morgan Chase, but the Fed elected not to save Lehman in September when it went into crisis. At the heart of Lehman's problems were large holdings of sub-prime mortgages and huge losses incurred on these positions. With Lehman's bankruptcy, financial institutions came to believe that the US Government might not stand behind other institutions that were experiencing distress and that more bankruptcies were possible in light of the severity of the mortgage crisis and the stock market sell-off to date. Fear set in. Banks and brokers stopped lending to each other because they did not have a good feel for others' mortgage holdings or derivative positions. Credit markets seized up. The stock market plunged further. This was not just a US crisis. Interbank lending locked up around the world. Central bankers were faced with true panic which, if left to run its course, may have brought on a financial collapse rivaling that of the Great Depression. Advocates of so-called free market capitalism speak to the power of free markets to correct themselves and eliminate imbalances, but in October 2008, the credit markets had, for all intents and purposes, ceased to exist. Central banks around the world had to step in and provide the liquidity needed for markets to reopen.

In the US, these actions culminated in the $700 billion Troubled Asset Relief Program (TARP), which provided capital to banks. This capital gave them the liquidity needed to operate normally and thus the time needed to work through the problem assets on their balance sheets. With TARP, banks came to realize that the financial system was not in danger of imminent collapse and credit markets gradually reopened. Nevertheless, normal operation was probably not achieved until the 2nd quarter of 2009. TARP has been much maligned in the US as politicians and commentators have demagogued the issue and called it a bailout for the banks, without reminding citizens how severe conditions were in late 2008. It is true that TARP was a bailout, but the US Treasury and the Fed had little choice. To allow multiple large institutions to fail would have taken the US into an immediate financial crisis the results of which could not be forecast. The results of this crisis would have affected all Americans and all businesses, not just banks, and that is what government officials were determined to prevent. In the end, the Bush and Obama Administrations, together with the Federal Reserve, had few choices and all must be commended for taking prompt, successful action during a critical time. One may quibble about the details with 20-20 hindsight, but not the results.

The credit crunch in the financial sector reduced liquidity available to businesses and individuals. Most experienced the credit crunch as "tighter lending standards," a reduced willingness on the part of banks and others to make loans on the same basis as before. Some businesses experienced the credit crunch as outright denial of credit. Those which normally depended on unused credit lines to fund temporary operating needs were often unable to access those lines for a variety of reasons (most of them valid). Those businesses which depended on regular access to credit went into crisis. Over the next few years, the US saw a deep recession and high unemployment accompanied by a spike in business bankruptcies. Part of these can be traced directly to the credit crunch.

To be fair to the banks, the lack of interbank liquidity made it difficult to refinance their existing loans, let alone make new ones, so bankers had to react with tighter lending standards because, as noted, maintaining solvency during a downturn is priority #1. TARP helped to fill some of the need but it could not fill all of it. And, to be fair, the creditworthiness of individuals and companies across the country was weaker in the wake of the market crash, and it is only prudent to recognize this in one's lending practices. In the midst of the credit crisis, you heard government officials say, "Banks need to start making loans to good borrowers." Politicians seem to think good borrowers are gentlemen and ladies, just all-around nice "guys." In fact, good borrowers are those with capacity to repay (something bankers often forget). Capacity to repay is weaker, and usually harder to evaluate, after a market crash and in the midst of a credit crunch and so tighter lending standards should be expected. Nevertheless, we cannot forget that the root of banks' unwillingness to lend lay in their own aggressive lending and egregious practices during the build-up of the real estate bubble, which led to the credit crunch when it burst. It is amazing to watch how banks line up in lockstep in opposition to financial regulation today. We rarely hear a word from them about their behavior and mistakes during the last financial crisis. It is as if everything has returned to normal. It is like a patient who has gone through severe trauma and lost everything except short-term memory.

We have already discussed how the Asian flu starting in Thailand engendered financial crises throughout Asia and Latin America. In Table 2.1, we outline other notable financial crises prior to today's European debt crisis to give a sense of historical perspective. A review of these crises reveals a common thread: (1) a period of bank deregulation/liberalization followed by (2) an economic boom with inadequate regulatory oversight which fuels real estate speculation followed by (3) a collapse of the real estate bubble, leading to (4) a bank financial crisis because of bad loans made during the boom. This parallels uncannily the US experience over the past few years.

Each of these crises was accompanied by market crashes. Although the chapter order in this book implies that a market crash creates the credit crunch, it can go in the opposite direction and there are clearly feedback loops between the two. While we have divided the market crash from the credit crunch in order to treat the particular issues that surround them separately, the reader should understand that they will always be very closely linked. Sometimes they are so closely linked that it is difficult to tell which of the two, the stock market crash or the credit crunch, actually started the crisis.

Table 2.2
SELECTED BANKING/FINANCIAL CRISES

Spain	1977	52 out of 110 banks experienced solvency problems during the late 1970's and early 1980's. Attributed to undisciplined lending, lax supervision, and heavy losses in the midst of a severe recession where unemployment soared to 25%. Central bank had to intervene with temporary liquidity to prevent contagion to stronger banks. 29 institutions failed in 1977-1978. Accompanied by a severe stock market crash.
Norway	1987	2/3 of all banks became insolvent or required central bank intervention. The banking industry was deregulated in 1984-1985. Optimism due to North Sea oil led to real estate speculation, partially funded by foreign borrowings. The price of North Sea oil fell by 46% in 1986. Foreign depositors fled. The stock market collapsed. The currency was devalued. The real estate market collapsed. Banks could not shoulder the losses. Central bank intervention was required.
Finland	1991	Deregulation of the banking industry during the mid-1980's led to rampant speculation in real estate and stocks in the late 1980's. Skopbank was one of the heaviest involved in the speculation and experienced heavy losses. Liquidity for the bank dried up as other banks refuse to lend to it in the interbank barkets. Taken over by the Finnish central bank. Central bank injected loans into all banks to stabilize. Cost of crisis to Finland estimated at 8% of GNP.
Sweden	1991	A real estate bubble collapsed, creating a credit crunch. The banking system was on the brink of total insolvency. The government ended up guaranteeing the deposits and creditors of all banks. Two major banks were nationalized.

Colombia	1998	Banking deregulation led to a booming economy with rampant speculation. Trade imbalances put pressure on the FX rate. The central bank hiked interest rates dramatically. This caused a rapid economic decline and revealed poor underwriting in the banking sector. A credit crunch followed with central bank intervention. There were 110 financial institutions in 1998. By 2001, there were only 57.
Argentina	2001	The Argentina peso had been fixed vs. the US$ since 1991 which created multiple imbalances which the government was unable to address. The imbalances created a crisis which led to economic and political chaos. Bank runs started at the end of 2001. The government responded by freezing all bank accounts. The government defaulted on its foreign debt at the end of 2001. Devaluation followed in early 2002, followed by economic hardship.
Iceland	2007	Banks were deregulated in 2001 and expanded rapidly. Since Iceland is a small country, they funded their growth with foreign loans and deposits. This fueled an economic boom, speculation, increases in household debt, and high inflation. The central bank hiked inerest rates to curb inflation. The Icelandic currency plunged. Icelandic banks could not pay/roll over foreign loans and deposits and so experienced a credit crunch. The central bank was forced to nationalize the 3 largest banks.
Ireland	2007	Irish banks funded a real estate bubble which was partly funded by foreign loans and deposits. The collapse of the US real estate bubble spread to Europe and led to a collapse of the "Celtic Tiger." The Irish banks experienced a credit crunch as they were unable to repay/roll over foreign debt. The Irish government was forced to guarantee all liabilities for 6 banks. The collapse caused an economic recession and political turmoil which remain to this day.
UK	2007	The collapse of the US real estate bubble spread to Europe. Certain UK banks with heavy exposure to booming residential real estate market were exposed to a credit crunch. This forced the Bank of England to nationalize one bank and take actions to stabilize the financial sector.

Early Warning Signs

In the wake of a market crash, it may be difficult to distinguish early warning signs from red flags, particularly if they appear very close together in time. Make sure you do not waste time trying to tell one from the other. If you wait too long, you could lose a step. Always consider the cost/benefit of the trade-off between acting and not acting.

Another point to consider is that early warning signs will probably not appear simultaneously. You must sift through what data you have in order to make a reasonable determination of what will likely come next. Unlike Chapter 1, the following warning signs focus most closely on indicators that credit quality is deteriorating because, as outlined, it is fear about other firms' creditworthiness that turns a period of tighter funds availability into a credit crunch.

Market Crash

Based on what we have discussed so far, a market crash is often a precursor to a credit crunch. We noted, however, that a credit crunch could precede a market crash or that they could both happen, more or less, simultaneously. Thus do not wait for a market crash and neglect the other early warnings signs that follow.

Central Bank Actions

Monitor news reports for any sign that the Fed or other central banks are providing increased liquidity to the financial markets not in line with overall monetary objectives but instead to meet banking and securities firms' needs. This may indicate that some financial institutions are in distress. Also monitor Fed commentary to see if new concerns are being expressed.

Credit Default Swap (CDS) Spreads

A credit default swap (CDS) is a type of derivative.[31] The swap can take a variety of forms but its most common is the following. The CDS buyer, which we will call the "protection buyer" pays a fee, known popularly as the CDS spread, to the CDS seller, the "protection seller." The "reference asset" is a loan to or a bond issued by, say, XYZ Corporation (the "reference entity") and usually owned by the protection buyer. Upon the occurrence of a credit event (at minimum defined as default by XYZ), the protection seller will make the payments due on the reference asset to the protection buyer until its maturity (in many respects, a CDS feels very much like a guarantee). The CDS spread at inception of the swap (which is fixed for the life of the swap) is <u>derived from</u> the buyer's and seller's views at that time of the probability of default on the reference asset by XYZ.

CDS spreads react very quickly to changes in credit market perceptions of borrower creditworthiness, much more quickly than do credit ratings issued by Standard & Poors and Moody's. As such, they are viewed as the best early indicator of credit distress. CDS spreads are expressed in basis points. One basis point equals .01%, one hundred basis points equals 1.00%. If the CDS spread for a specific bank is 100 basis points, the cost of buying protection against default by that bank is 1.00%, or $10,000 for every $1,000,000 of principal that the buyer wants to protect. Rising CDS spreads indicate greater perceived probability of default, falling spreads the opposite.

Our focus is on a credit crunch and, per our discussion, the source of the credit crunch will be the financial sector. As an early warning sign, we suggest monitoring the S&P/ISDA CDS US Financials Select 10 Index, which is composed of the CDS spreads of 10 large US financial institutions with which we should be most concerned.[32] Large US financial institutions can be expected to be on the front lines of any credit crunch. Chart 2.1 shows the performance of this index from the period 10/25/11 – 10/25/12.

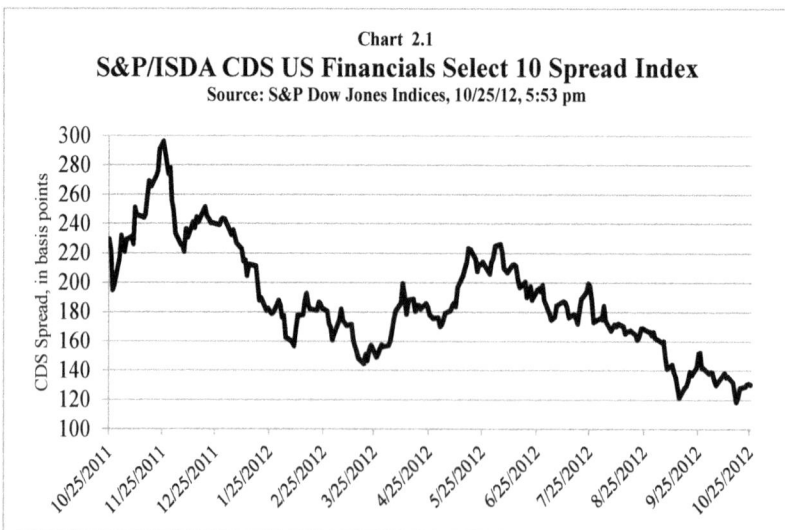

Chart 2.1
S&P/ISDA CDS US Financials Select 10 Spread Index
Source: S&P Dow Jones Indices, 10/25/12, 5:53 pm

The graph shows that this index's CDS spread fell from a high of 296 basis points on 11/25/11 to 130 basis points on 10/25/12. This shows strong improvement in the perceived probability of default of the ten financial institutions over this period: the cost of protection fell from $29,600 to $13,000 per $1,000,000.

We suggest that a 50 basis point upward movement in CDS spreads from current levels within a period of 3 months or less be set as an early warning sign, with increases above that level to be monitored carefully thereafter.

Difference in Treasury vs. Eurodollar Rates (TED spread)

A rise in the difference between Eurodollar and US Treasury rates is often used as an indicator that liquidity is being withdrawn from the credit markets and thus an indicator of a potential financial crisis. It is a broader measure of the market than the Index above and reflects the experience of borrowers and lenders globally.

The difference, nicknamed the TED spread, is calculated by subtracting the 3-month US Treasury Bill ("T-Bill") rate[33] from the 3-month rate for Eurodollars.[34] Chart 2.2 shows the history of the TED spread since 1970.

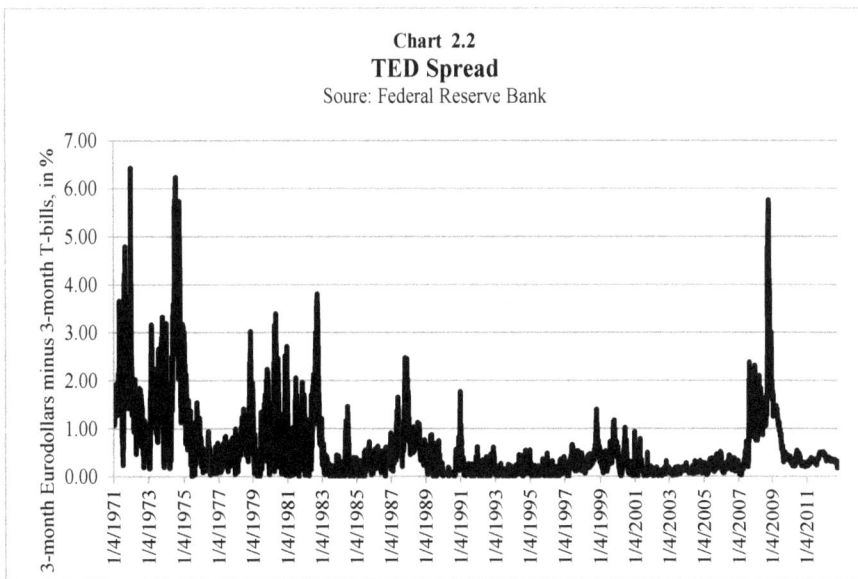

Chart 2.2
TED Spread
Soure: Federal Reserve Bank

The spikes in the TED spread correlate most closely with the selected stock market crashes shown in Table 1.1 of Chapter 1. Note of course the most recent spike in the TED spread. These large spikes reflect outright fear. They evidence reluctance of banks to lend to each other on any reasonable basis. While lending to a bank is more risky than lending to the US Government at any time, the spreads shown here at times of crisis are at panic levels. One should note that just because rates were quoted during these periods does not mean a bank could actually borrow; during a financial crisis or a credit crunch, many market participants have no access to borrowing, regardless of price. Furthermore, if one had to borrow at these rates, it is doubtful they could have invested the funds in loans or securities at a profit; however, during a credit crisis, no one focuses on the profitability of individual loans or trades. They focus on survival and they are willing to pay anything to achieve that. Lucky are those who have sufficient capital, and thus sufficient liquidity, on the balance sheet and so do not have to go into the credit markets at times like these.

One comment is in order about the spike in spreads from 1979 through 1983. This represents the period after the Second Oil Shock, which drove oil prices even higher than those resulting from OPEC's First Oil Shock a few years earlier. The Second Oil Shock brought on a period of high inflation and low growth (known at the time as "stagflation") which the Fed, under Chairman Paul Volcker, addressed with interest rate increases and a contraction of the money supply. This sent Eurodollar rates soaring to over 20% during periods of 1980-1981. Nevertheless, this period did not produce a financial panic or a banking crisis even though a recession followed. The reason for the high TED spreads during the period was probably that many market participants believed high rates would cause a crisis. They were wrong: the Fed somehow managed to avoid it. This demonstrates the point that reliance on the TED spread, or any single early warning sign as an indicator of a coming credit crunch must always be done with some degree of caution. One is reminded of the economist Paul Samuelson's 1966 comment that has been endlessly requoted:

> To prove that Wall Street is an early omen of movements still to come in GNP, commentators quote economic studies alleging that market downturns predicted four out of the last five recessions. That is an understatement. Wall Street indexes predicted nine out

of the last five recessions! And its mistakes were beauties.[35]

    The average TED spread for the period in Chart 2.2 is 62 basis points (.62%) with a standard deviation of 75 basis points. We suggest that an upward movement of the TED spread by 2 standard deviations, i.e. 150 basis points (1.50%) should be established as an early warning sign. From today's levels, that would mean an increase in the spread to roughly 1.50 – 1.75%. There is no easily accessible graph of the TED spread but information on Eurodollar and Treasury rates is available in major newspapers, financial magazines, and on-line which should allow the reader to perform a rough calculation.

    Note that it is possible to use other statistics as early warnings signs. Examples might be to compare A-rated corporate bonds against Treasuries of similar maturities to see how spread-over-Treasuries varies over time. An increase in spread usually indicates heightened risk. The shortcoming of this approach is that the data, as we analyze it, shows increases in spreads only once the credit crunch is underway, i.e., the historical data does "emit" the early warning sign we need. Nevertheless, there may be data sets we have not investigated that may provide better insight. In the end, CDS spreads probably provide the best insight and one could choose additional Standard & Poors CDS indices to get a broader perspective on risk than the narrowly-focused Financial Select 10 Index suggested.

Negative News Stories

    Monitor media sources for evidence of issues at financial institutions rising to the forefront. Also be sensitive to Wall Street commentary on the financial sector which is beginning to turn negative.

FDIC Quarterly

    FDIC Quarterly provides quality information on current trends in the banking industry.[36] Even though you may not be an expert in banking terminology, a quick review of this document will give you a good sense of where things are going. You will need to be sensitive to increases in problem loans and increasing loan loss provisions in order to decide whether the health of the banking system should be used as an early warning. At the current time, the banking industry continues to strengthen from the depths of 2007 -2009 and so we see no early warning.

It would be good to read *FDIC Quarterly* together with Wall Street analyses of major banks. See if both of them appear to be forecasting increases in loan loss provisions, which would indicate increasing problem loans, and thus a reversal of positive trendlines. Growth in problem loans, by itself, is never an early warning. Problem loans rise and fall during every economic cycle. What you need to look for are <u>rapid</u> increases in problem loans, and investigate further.

Preparation

Our focus in preparing for a market crash was on the totality of one's personal assets, both financial and non-financial. The focus in this chapter is more on safety. From the preceding discussion, it should be clear that the greater risk to an investor during a credit crunch is default and insolvency by major financial institutions or corporations. A credit crunch will cause a "flight to quality" as scared investors seek havens of safety for their money. This flight will cause a decline in interest yield on what are perceived to be the safest assets. US Treasuries are likely to receive the largest portion of cash inflows because the probability of default on these securities is perceived to be extremely low; thus Treasury yields can be expected to fall, sometimes by substantial amounts. Even though investors are being paid less, they do not care. For the moment, all they care about is seeing their money safe; interest yield thus is a minor concern when a credit crunch is at full roar. In a sense, investor actions imitate those of the traditional bank run.

It would be better to avoid the "flight to safety," better to avoid the chaos. Planning ahead is the key. Throughout the planning process, you will have thought through the issues and should have configured your financial assets in a way that you do not have to react in a panic. During your initial plan, you may have already tentatively created a target portfolio to address the risk of a market crash and credit crunch. Here we would like to supplement that planning with a greater focus on safety. As in Chapter 1, you may decide to lay out your plan with interim steps to be taken both on the appearance of early warnings signs and red flags. In planning for a credit crunch, you should consider the following:

Ensure that bank deposits are below the FDIC insurance limits. The deposit limit is $250,000 per depositor per bank for each account ownership category established by regulation. Be aware that the insurance limit encompasses only traditional deposit products; thus investment asset classes such as mutual funds (including money market mutual funds), annuities, life insurance products, stocks, and bonds offered by banks or their affiliates are not insured. Those with multiple accounts at one bank or a complicated financial picture may benefit from using FDIC's on-line Electronic Deposit Insurance Estimator (EDIE). Without making things too complicated, the easiest way to ensure that your deposits are below the limit is to make sure you have no more than $250,000 in any one bank; open new accounts at other banks if needed to keep below $250,000. For those who need more detailed guidance, refer to the FDIC website and/or use EDIE.[37] On a side note, keep in mind that the Securities Investor Protection Corporation (SIPC) only protects investors if cash or assets in their brokerage accounts go missing; it does not insure those accounts against risk of loss associated with trading and investing. Thus SIPC's place in the regulatory galaxy is entirely different from FDIC.

Be attentive to money market mutual fund holdings. Many investors believe that money market funds carry little risk of loss because their prices are "fixed" at $1.00 per share. They thus believe that these funds' Net Asset Values (NAV) are all $1.00.[38] This is not true. In fact, in September 19, 2008 at the height of the financial crisis, there was great concern that, for a variety of reasons, investment managers across the money market fund industry would lower prices below $1.00, i.e., they might have to "break the buck" because NAVs had fallen below $1.00. This fear was generated by Reserve Primary Fund, the largest US money market fund at the time with $64 billion in assets under management, which did in fact "break the buck." The reason it was forced to do so was that it owned a large amount of Lehman Brothers commercial paper (a little over 1% of the Reserve Primary Fund's total assets). As noted earlier, Lehman Brothers went bankrupt on September 15, 2008. When Reserve Primary Fund "broke the buck," investors panicked and, within a very short period, withdrew $300 billion from all money market funds; when those withdrawals took place, the effect was to reduce access to the commercial paper market for all but the best companies. The US Treasury, in order to quell the panic, provided a temporary program to existing owners of money market funds that guaranteed fund prices would remain at $1.00. This guarantee lasted until September 18, 2009 but there are no guarantees today.

Money market funds currently hold over $2.6 trillion. In view of the events of 2008, the US Securities and Exchange Commission (SEC) continues to examine proposals aimed at reducing the risk of panic emanating from these funds. One proposal calls for fund share prices to float freely and reflect actual NAV. The argument for this approach is that investors would get used to it and adapt accordingly; the argument against it is that no one can predict how such a proposal will impact investor behavior and willingness to invest in money market funds. Another proposal calls for reduced investor access to his or her holdings after a withdrawal; one idea is that, for the first 1-30 days after a withdrawal, an investor would have access to only 95-97% of his or her remaining assets instead of 100%. The argument for this proposal is that it would somehow reduce financial panic; the argument against it is that it is a very weak defense against a panic. The proposal most talked about is a requirement that mutual fund companies hold a small amount of capital (perhaps 1-3%) against money market fund assets under management which would help them maintain share prices at $1.00. The argument against this proposal is that it would increase the costs of money market fund management and that money market fund interest yields, already low, would have to fall further in order to absorb the costs.

We believe that, at this time, the third proposal remains the most likely to be promulgated but the question remains subject to fierce debate. Whatever the conclusion, we believe that investors must get used to the idea that losses, even if they be small, may be sustained on money market funds in a time of financial panic. One way to mitigate this risk is to look for money market funds with ratings from Standard & Poors or Moody's that reflect a forward view of a fund's ability to maintain share prices at $1.00. The best-rated money market funds carry S&P and Moody's ratings of AAAm and Aaa-mf, respectively; the drawback is that not every fund is rated because many mutual fund companies believe the additional expense of a rating provides negligible incremental value to investors.

We believe that, whatever the outcome, losses sustained by an investor during a financial panic should be relatively small when compared to other asset classes. Thus they should still be viewed as a relatively safe asset class. To reduce the risk that any one fund "breaks the buck," we recommend diversifying money market fund holdings among several mutual fund companies.

An investor must also remain sensitive to risk/reward trade-offs when investing in money market mutual funds. Given the breadth of short-term financial products in which investment managers can place fund assets, it is doubtful that one money market fund can produce yields that materially exceed those of another without pursuing a different strategy, i.e. a fund that has a lower yield than another may reflect the fact that it has a larger portion of its assets in 90-day US Treasury Bills than another which has a greater concentration in commercial paper. Given that money market fund yields are so low today, we believe there is little incremental value in picking money market funds on the basis of yield differentials. Thus we suggest a bias towards funds which hold a greater proportion of US Government and similar securities than comparable funds. Funds which hold such securities are less likely to "break the buck" because there will be greater demand for short-term Treasuries during a credit crunch. Conclusion: funds should be picked on the basis of safety rather than yield.

Government bonds and government bond funds will be havens of safety in a credit crunch. The trade-off is that yields will remain low. Your plan must take your need for current income into account and make an appropriate allocation of assets which reflects both this trade-off and interest rate risk as discussed in Chapter 1. On a side note, we would avoid Treasury Inflation-Protected Securities (TIPS) in preparing for a credit crunch; the likelihood of inflation after a market crash and credit crunch is very low, so TIPS can be expected to underperform other Treasury securities.

Intermediate term corporate investment-grade bonds or bond funds represent an asset class worth your attention. Although we must take Chapter 1's comments about interest rate risk into account, investment grade corporate bonds represent low-to-moderate risk from a safety perspective as shown in Chart 2.3.[39]

Investment grade for Standard & Poors and Moody's means bonds carrying ratings of at least BBB- and Baa3, respectively. Speculative grade means bonds with ratings lower than BBB-/Baa3.[40]

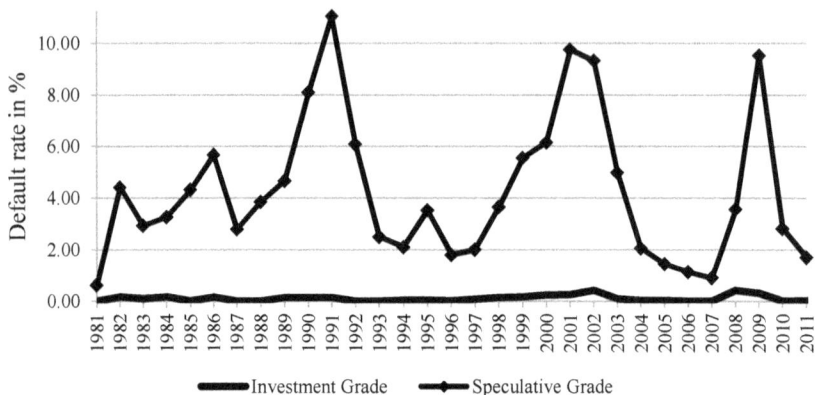

Chart 2.3
Global Corporate Default Rates over Time
Source: Standard & Poors

In Chapter 1, we noted that high-yield, i.e. speculative grade, bonds were not a good candidate for portfolios aimed at addressing a market crash because of prospective higher default rates which would lead to potential losses.[41] Chart 2.3 illustrates the point but it also shows that default rates on investment-grade bonds have been relatively low over time. Nevertheless, a sell-off in corporate bonds and bond funds during a credit crunch can be expected. This will reflect investors' fear that default rates will rise. What Chart 2.3 does not show is ratings migration over time. Investors will fear that certain bonds currently sitting in the investment-grade category may actually deserve a speculative-grade rating because of the changed environment after a market crash. They also take into account the fact that the rating agencies have often been criticized for being too slow to adjust ratings in line with deteriorating economic conditions from which one should expect more defaults.

Investors must understand that there is no way to avoid unrealized losses completely, at least for the short-term, when investing in corporate bonds. For the average investor, we believe mutual funds represent the appropriate vehicle for investing in bonds. In order to mitigate the risk of default, pick funds which have the bulk of their assets in bonds at the stronger end of the investment-grade spectrum. This means bonds with S&P/Moody's ratings of BBB+/Baa1 or better. The trade-off from this reduced risk is lower investment

74

yields, but the focus of planning for a credit crunch is on increased safety.

While a sell-off may bring some short-term losses, keep in mind that the sell-off reflects fear, perhaps irrational fear, which probably overstates the actual probability of default. Selling shares of your bond fund into the sell-off will make little sense if you have done your homework properly. We suggest it is more appropriate to try to hold your shares until the credit crunch moderates, at which point bond fund shares should be expected to recover part of their losses. If your plan has called for a meaningful portion of your financial assets to be moved into short-term funds upon an early warning, you might consider reinvesting a portion of those funds back into investment-grade corporate bond funds once their price has fallen to take advantage of prospects for capital gains. Needless to say, the timing of this decision is critical and so requires much thought. Please refer to the discussion in Chapter 1 around entry point.

Although we believe investment grade corporate bonds are a potentially attractive asset class, we must express one note of caution. Since financial institutions are large borrowers, we would generally exclude or limit corporate bonds issued by these institutions from your plan. The reason is that we are trying to avoid financial institution exposure in advance of a credit crunch because they are more directly exposed to its consequences. Except for the strongest of institutions, bonds issued by the financial sector are likely to fall farther than those by other sectors because of market fear about how the credit crunch, as it is happening, will affect bank capacity to repay. This also creates a dilemma when investing in corporate bond mutual funds. Since banks and others are such large borrowers, it is difficult for investment managers to construct bond mutual funds by avoiding them entirely. Nevertheless, such funds do exist. Seek them out or, alternatively, seek funds with relatively small exposure to bonds issued by financial institutions.

Municipal bonds may make sense for the right investor. The size of the municipal bond market is about $4 trillion. The variety of borrowers in the market is huge, ranging from the State of California to Hiawatha City, Kansas. Unlike corporations which have the SEC looking over their shoulders, municipal bonds are largely unregulated. The quality of financial disclosure by many municipalities leaves much to be desired. Credit ratings for municipalities have a greater likelihood of being inaccurate because rating agencies appear not to revisit ratings as often as they do for corporates. The credit quality of this sector has deteriorated during the last few years as falling tax revenues have hit the budgets of states, towns, and cities hard, perhaps harder than at any time since the Great Depression. Yet this is not reflected in higher default rates. In fact, there have been few municipal defaults over the past 25 years, in part because municipalities rarely default from a legal standpoint or go into bankruptcy; instead states often step in to help cities and towns navigate through difficult periods. Nevertheless, it is clear that this sector is weaker than at any time in the recent past.

Investors have bought municipal bonds and municipal bond funds based largely on the attractiveness of receiving tax-exempt interest. One doubts that most have focused on credit quality. In spite of the negative backdrop for this asset class, we believe that, for the right investor, munis may fit into one's plan for dealing with a credit crunch. First, munis are less affected by a credit crunch because most municipalities are not highly dependent on short-term credit. Second, as noted, default rates are low because troubled municipalities are usually able to muddle through.

Although munis deserve consideration, we suggest that only bond funds with the highest ratings be considered: we suggest that the vast majority of bonds be rated no less than S&P/Moody's A-/A1. This of course brings the trade-off of risk vs. reward. Second, from the standpoint of safety, we prefer national bond funds to state-specific because of the diversity they provide and because such bond funds probably hold more liquid issues from larger, more creditworthy borrowers. The trade-off from this approach is losing tax-exempt status for some of the interest earned. If one decides, for this reason, on a single-state bond fund, one needs to study the financial condition of the state and of individual holdings in the fund. As with corporate bonds in the face of a credit crunch, we prefer safety to yield in picking investments.

Review all holdings of stocks in financial institutions and of stock mutual funds with large holdings of these stocks. Financial institutions include commercial banks, investment banks, broker-dealers, insurance companies, and asset managers. As discussed, this sector is likely to be the most affected by a credit crunch. Consider selling the stock of all financial institutions with an S&P/Moody's rating of BBB/Baa2 or lower (or of stock mutual funds which have an overweighting in financial institutions).

Review all holdings of non-financial stocks and of any mutual fund with large holdings of stocks with weaker credit profiles. Consider selling individual stocks with a current S&P/Moody's rating of BBB-/Baa3 or lower. These companies are probably the most vulnerable to a credit crunch. For unrated companies, consider selling any company for which Funded Debt (outstanding debt) exceeds 35% of market capitalization.[42] These also are most likely to be affected by a credit crunch.

Red Flags

We suggest that the following be established as red flags for a credit crunch: (1) a 100 basis point increase in the CDS spread discussed (the Early Warning was a 50 basis point move); (2) a 225 basis point increase in the TED spread discussed (the Early Warning was a 150 basis point move); and (3) monitoring of Fed actions, news stories, and *FDIC Quarterly* reveals more distress in the financial sector than at the time of the early warning.

Further Preparation

On a philosophical note, in planning for a market crash and a credit crunch you will always be haunted by thoughts like: Have I done the right thing? Have I waited too long? Have I identified the right early warnings signs and red flags? Have I identified them correctly? To have doubts is human. It is a sign that you are thinking and trying to do the right thing, and it could be that you have done the wrong thing. Even so, you cannot look back and wring your hands over what might have been. Every day is a new day. Every day brings a new decision. Every day is a new portfolio day as well: disregard the unrealized capital losses you may have embedded in any position, for that is often just a tax issue. The question you must ask yourself is: What actions should I take (or not take) to reposition my portfolio for tomorrow? Try not to obsess on the past, which of course is easy to say but harder to do. Look forward, not back. This is one theme that unites the chapters in this book.

Upon occurrence of the red flags, you should activate plans already established. Also you should look more critically at what you own and, if appropriate, revise your plans. After a market crash and a credit crunch, some may be tempted to move a large portion of their holdings "under the mattress." We suggest that this temptation be resisted because, using a word from Chapter 1, this strategy is "unidirectional" and so the risk/reward trade-off is huge. Even if you have no notion of putting money under the mattress, you may still decide that moving more of your holdings into non-financial assets is appropriate based on your viewpoint and risk preferences. We recommend looking at the following points when considering such a decision:

Convertibility to cash, particularly after a credit crunch, is the test of any asset, financial or otherwise. Either an asset can be owned or employed to produce cash flow, or it can be sold at some point for cash because someone else sees value in it. When shifting into non-financial assets, test them for liquidity, for their ability to be sold for cash or generate cash within a reasonable period. Cash is king after a credit crunch. Assets that have little marketability or cannot be used to produce cash have much less value than prior to the market crash. The reason for this is that, given the lesser availability of cash within the economy, few can afford to purchase assets that do not produce cash. You should be looking for *value-in-use* and *value-in-cash-flow* assets. Buying a non-financial asset that produces nothing, speculating on a change in value over time, makes little sense within the context of a credit crunch.

We may not be able to sell *value-in-use* assets easily but we need them in order to live, even if someone else does not want to buy them at the moment. Examples of value-in-use assets are your home, your car, and appliances. Here, as in Chapter 1, we want to distinguish must-haves from toys. If you are thinking of moving your portfolio into non-financial assets, presumably you will not be buying new value-in-use assets. Your initial plan will have already reviewed value-in-use assets and so alteration of your plan upon emergence of red flags would generally not be appropriate; indeed, if you want to rethink value-in-use assets now, this would probably indicate that your initial plan was flawed.

If you want to move into *value-in-cash-flow* assets, you should be looking for assets that you can manage directly to produce cash flow that will support your household and your lifestyle during a market collapse or credit crunch. These are not financial assets and they are distinct from value-in-use assets. Examples of value-in-cash-flow assets are rental real estate, businesses that you currently own that you decide to expand, or new businesses that you can purchase/establish and operate yourself. When making any purchase decision of this type, the primary desideratum must be how much cash flow can be produced, both under current market conditions and under the stressed conditions subsequent to a market crash. If cash flow cannot be determined with accuracy or is weak, we would suggest that it does not make sense to purchase the asset. We would also suggest that if an asset does not have the capacity to produce annual free cash flow equal to 8% of your purchase price (after deducting debt) in the case of real estate, or 10% of your purchase price (after deducting debt) in the case of non-real estate, then it is not an appropriate candidate for purchase. Look for better candidates elsewhere.[43]

You will also to need to balance any major shifts in asset allocation with new demands for cash which may arise in the wake of a credit crunch. In particular, people may believe you have substantial financial assets. This may cause family and friends to ask for help. As part of your initial plan, it may make sense to think through how you will respond to such requests, and on what basis. Even if you decide that you will respond, it is best to think of such funds as "lost" from a conservative planning perspective. In other words, do not assume that repayment of personal loans will represent predictable cash flow which you can incorporate into your plan.

---

[24] Some crude but simple math will illustrate the point. Let us assume that investors are looking for a 20% return on equity. For an industrial firm levered at 50:50 liabilities/equity, this means it must earn a 10% return on assets. For a financial institution levered at 90:10 liabilities/equity, this means it must earn a return on assets of 2.00%. In fact, the typical bank has a return on assets of 1.00–1.50%. The reason for this is that lending is a "spread business" and the typical spread over cost of funds on a loan transaction is only 1.00–3.00%. If we were to turn financial institutions' business models on their head and require that they operate with dramatically lower leverage, the conclusion is that lending spreads would have to rise almost tenfold in order to ensure that investor returns are met, which would be unpalatable for the rest of the economy. If neither liabilities nor interest rate spreads can rise, the only prices that can respond, given the assumptions we have made, are stock prices. These must plunge so that investor return on bank shares is in line with potential returns from other stock market investments. This crude example also illustrates the delicate balance regulators and politicians must achieve in looking to reform the financial sector: demands for increased capital in order to protect depositors and creditors must be weighed against the need for financial institutions to achieve a satisfactory return.

[25] It should be added here than financing does not just encompass short-term borrowings to finance loan and security portfolios on the balance sheet. It also encompasses credit, known as "counterparty credit," which occurs when financial institutions engage in derivative, foreign exchange, and other types of trades. Counterparty credit consists of two components: (1) settlement risk and (b) pre-

settlement risk. The risk of loss on settlement occurs when counterparties cannot make payment to settle a trade at inception or maturity. Pre-settlement risk occurs when the value in your favor on a derivatives contract, so-called positive mark-to-market, cannot be realized because the counterparty has gone bankrupt; your loss depends on how you close out the trade under current market conditions.

[26] A good introductory discussion to technical analysis can be found in *Malkiel*. See footnote 1 in Chapter 1.

[27] One small trading group in London, headed by a very prominent trader now known as the London Whale, took very aggressive positions in a single market in order to "hedge" J.P. Morgan balance sheet positions. Although we do not know all the details of his trading strategies, the positions taken were so large that they dominated that market, such that JPM's positions became *de facto* unhedged. The fiasco was disclosed during the spring of 2012. All of this seems to have taken place without sufficient oversight from JPM's risk management executives. Announced losses to date are close to $6 billion. While JPM has survived and remained profitable, the fiasco has damaged not only the bank's reputation but the proposition that large financial institutions can be trusted to manage risk effectively.

[28] LIBOR is the most widely used inter-bank interest rate around the world. Almost all loans to large- and medium-sized businesses have an option for borrowing at a spread over LIBOR. A large number of other financial products, including some loans to individuals and many derivatives, are tied to LIBOR in some way. A scandal erupted in June 2012 when the US Commodity Futures Trading Commission announced that it had fined Barclays Bank for manipulating the setting of LIBOR. It is now believed that multiple banks may have been involved but the story is still playing out. Various measures designed to ensure the fairness of LIBOR rate-setting are in the process of development but final solutions have yet to be implemented.

[29] "Top Derivatives Expert Estimates Size of the Global Derivatives Market at $1,200 Trillion Dollars . . . 20 Times Larger than the Global Economy," *Washington's Blog* (May 18, 2012), http://www.washingtonsblog.com/2012/05/top-derivatives-expert-finally-gives-a-credible-estimate-of-the-size-of-the-global-derivatives-market.html (accessed October 25, 2012). Notional amounts refer general to the estimated market value of all reference assets, which overstates amounts actually at risk. What are at risk are the cash flows to be exchanged between counterparties. In the case of the interest rate swap mentioned, the amounts at risk would probably be in the range of 1.25% of $1,000,000 for each year of the swap. For a 5-year interest rate swap, its risk-equivalent might be 6.25%, i.e., $62,500. Even if we applied 6.25% across all derivative markets, the risk equivalent of $1,200 trillion would still be $75 trillion which is big enough to be important to most people.

[30] A best-selling book which focuses on our inability to predict random events is: Nassim Nicholas Taleb, *The Black Swan: Second Edition: The Impact of the Highly Improbable*, (New York: Random House, 2010).

[31] The credit default swap has been much maligned as a derivative which played a significant role in the sub-prime crisis. Again, it is not the product itself, but how humans failed to use it properly. The way the product was used was to provide

protection to buyers of mortgage-backed securities (MBS), many of which were composed of sub-prime mortgages. The first problem was that rating agencies vastly underestimated the probability of default (PD) on these MBS and gave many of them AAA/Aaa ratings (the very highest quality). Most market participants believed in the agencies' estimated PD's. In addition, the agencies rated these securities on the basis of credit protection provided through CDS. The second problem, related to CDS but in fact to any derivative, is *counterparty risk*. For a buyer of protection to lose money, two things have to happen: (1) a credit event, i.e., a default, must occur; and (2) the seller of credit protection must fail to make payment. The potential of the seller to fail to make payment is known as counterparty risk. A subsidiary of American International Group (AIG) was a major seller of credit protection. It too was rated AAA/Aaa (ratings agencies created their own feedback loop in rating AIG: the size of its obligations to perform as a seller of protection under CDS were deemed to be low, because the PD's on sub-prime MBS were felt to be low) so everyone thought counterparty risk was low. So investors thought both probability of default and counterparty risk were low on these MBS and snapped them up. We all know what happened. Sub-prime default rates skyrocketed. Then it turned out that AIG had negligible capital against all the credit protection it had sold and so did not have the resources to honor all of its obligations. It was the so-called "perfect storm." The US Government was forced to step in and provide capital and loan guarantees to AIG in order to prevent the global financial crisis from getting worse. There is nothing wrong with CDS. At their core, they are no different from insurance. If we have no problem with insurance, why do we have a problem with CDS? First of all, insurance products are heavily regulated by state insurance commissions whose first priority is protection of policyholders. On the contrary, CDS are unregulated products. While the International Swaps and Derivatives Association (ISDA) sets standards for the CDS market, it has no real enforcement powers. While bank regulators should have deep interest in ensuring this market functions properly, one sees little movement towards reform of market practices. In truth, one doubts that most regulators (and bankers) really understand CDS and CDS markets. Second, state insurance commissions perform their duties to policyholders by making sure insurance companies have sufficient capital to meet their potential obligations. On the contrary, from an accounting point of view, CDS are off-balance sheet and, as in the case of AIG, were often written in subsidiaries outside the purview of banking and insurance regulators. Capital held against AIG's CDS obligations was minimal. One expects that the new set of bank capital regulations known as Basel III will place greater focus on capital adequacy vs. off-balance sheet risk but it has yet to be fully implemented in the US. In the interim, all we can do is hope regulators understand better the potential threat from runaway derivatives trading operations and so curb reckless activities before they become too dangerous.

[32] This index can be accessed on-line at: http://us.spindices.com/indices/fixed-income/sp-isda-cds-us-finance-select-10.

[33]T-Bill rates are quoted on a discount basis for a 3-month period. Calculating the TED spread requires annualizing the T-Bill rate and also converting interest to an

effective-rate basis, as if the T-Bill were not traded at a discount but instead with interest paid at maturity, as with most other financial instruments. This is necessary to equate interest implied by the T-Bill discount rate to the Eurodollar rate.

[34] We have used the bid rate, the rate for Eurodollar deposits (so called LIBid), instead of the offered rate for loans, LIBOR.

[35] Paul Samuelson, "Science and Stocks," *Newsweek* (September 19, 1966, p. 92).

[36] *FDIC Quarterly* may be accessed on-line at: http://www.fdic.gov/bank/analytical/quarterly/index.html

[37] For more detail on FDIC deposit insurance and EDIE, go to: http://www.fdic.gov/deposit/deposits/

[38] The net asset value (NAV) of any mutual fund is determined at the closing of each trading day. It is calculated first by valuing each security owned at its closing market price. NAV is then calculated by dividing (a) the market value of all securities held minus fund liabilities (which should be few in the case of money market funds) by (b) total shares outstanding . It should be obvious from these calculations that there is no reason why a share price set at $1.00 should exactly equal NAV.

[39] S&P calculates default rates by looking at all bonds in each rating category one year prior to default and calculating the number that were in default one year later. Defaults also include those companies which no longer had a rating one year prior to default.

[40] For S&P ratings definitions, go to: http://www.understandingratings.com/. For Moody's rating definitions, go to: http://www.moodys.com/Pages/amr002002.aspx.

[41] Within the category of high-yield we would also include bank loan funds.

[42] Sectors, such as utilities and REIT's, should be excluded from these actions because leverage is consistent with the nature of their businesses. The focus should be on companies in sectors for which high leverage is not normal.

[43] The 8% and 10% benchmarks are established for a period after a credit crunch when cash will be king; prior to a credit crunch, one would hope that your business could exceed those benchmarks. Here we define free cash flow as: Earnings before Interest, Taxes, Depreciation & Amortization (EBITDA — but use net operating income, NOI, for real estate) minus (a) cash taxes related to your new investment minus (b) capital expenditures for which you will have to use cash instead of bank financing minus (c) increases in working capital required to support growth of the business.

Chapter 3

Breakdown of the US Economic Model & Job Market Collapse

Introduction

Imbalances

In Chapters 1 and 2, we discussed the market crash and the credit crunch, what to watch for and how to prepare for them. Those chapters were relatively concrete because history is full of crashes and panics. We have used this history to make measured forecasts of what the future might look like after a crash or a panic.

Beginning with this chapter, we depart from the concrete into areas a bit more speculative. After a crash and a panic, many will believe that recovery will come quickly, after 2-3 years like a normal recession. Others may predict that the recovery will take somewhat longer, perhaps as long as Japan's Lost Decade; yet even they forecast gradual recovery. Chapters 1 and 2 focused more on describing how a market crash and a credit crunch occur. What we did not emphasize in those chapters was how devastating they might be. That is what we start to discuss here. In particular, with the US economy still weak after the bursting of the real estate bubble, a new market crash and credit crunch would administer an electric *shock* that could scarcely fail to have a major impact on the America we know today. As described in the Introduction and in Chapters 1 and 2, *shocks* are central to major disruptions. Without a *shock*, little changes, even if all political, social, and economic indicators are net-negative. We believe that multiple *shocks* over a relatively short period of time, 10-15 years, cannot fail to change our way of life. We have already seen two, in 2000 and 2007-2009. Let us hope a third does not await us in the near-term.

In the prior chapters, we cautioned repeatedly against overreliance on trendlines and historical patterns. Yes, we must study the past to understand where we are now and how we got here. Yes, we must educate ourselves about the critical decisions and economic phenomena of the past so we will have a better sense of what will work in the future. Nevertheless, as we undertake such study, we must beware of the seductive power of human reason that believes it can always make sense of the world. We risk putting on blinders if we try to establish "hard" causal linkages between the past and the future. We risk ignoring outcomes that are not on anyone's radar screen today — but probably should be.

We have used the word *imbalance* repeatedly and some readers may feel uncomfortable because we never tried to define it. Just as with *derivative*, the word is somewhat general. Similar to *derivative*, it hides numerous concepts under one umbrella. The word carries with it the implicit belief that there is a point of *equilibrium* which, once reached, will cause the imbalance to disappear: if things are out of balance, that implies there is a balance to <u>return to</u>. Thinking of *imbalance* in this way risks drinking the Kool-Aid of *mean reversion* which has infected so many financial models, including those for derivatives. Our thought processes have been swayed in this direction since the time of Aristotle and his *golden mean*.

Per Investopedia, mean reversion is "a theory suggesting that prices and returns move back towards the mean or average." That is to say, if GHI Company's stock is currently trading at a P/E ratio of 16x versus its historical average of 13x, many on Wall Street would call it "overvalued" on the belief that 13x is the metric that should govern its long-term valuation. They believe that the price should fall so that GHI's P/E can revert to its mean. Some might seem to believe that the price <u>will</u> fall, almost as if the mean is a magnet pulling things back into place. Few are willing to concede that 16x might be the "new normal" until they have seen quarters of historical data confirming GHI's ability to achieve higher earnings growth. Mean reversion is just another example of overreliance on trendlines and historical patterns.

In this chapter, we want to strip from the word *imbalance* any idea that there is a necessary point of *equilibrium* to which we can <u>return</u>. There may indeed be one, but it may be just as likely that we never find our way back. The more severe the imbalance the harder it is to forecast the future. If we lean too hard on any scale, we risk tipping it over. In that case, there is no teeter-tottery return to equilibrium. If we find a critical imbalance, it is almost impossible to describe what the future point of equilibrium might be. It is beyond our capability to forecast with precision. All we know for sure is that there is a huge imbalance and that "something's gotta give."

One of the few good things about a market crash and a credit crunch is that it shows us the imbalances that created them. The market crash of 2007 – 2009 showed us that the mortgage origination machine was a Rube Goldberg contraption created by mad scientist-bankers who forgot to check its oil level — so it froze up. The credit crunch showed us radioactive "toxic assets" pulsing beneath the Emperor's New Clothes of the financial sector. Once we see imbalances, we can take action, but unfortunately we can do little about what has already passed. All our new decisions and reforms must be focused on the future.

That we are taking action provides great solace. We believe that everything will be set to right if we only take a few important steps. We recognize what went wrong and now we are doing something about it. In a debacle like our latest market crash and credit crunch, we can see what went wrong (sub-prime loans! big banks! derivatives!) and it is very satisfying when we take action to correct it. And if we correct it, we think can get back to the way things were, the *equilibrium*, the *mean*. But in focusing on the obvious, is it not possible that we will miss something both fundamental and critical? And if so, is it not also possible that we will never be able to click our heels and get back to Kansas?

Stagnation in Household Income

As shown in Charts 3.1 and 3.2, growth in real household income has been negligible over the past ten years. Chart 3.1 shows the annual rate of change in growth. Chart 3.2

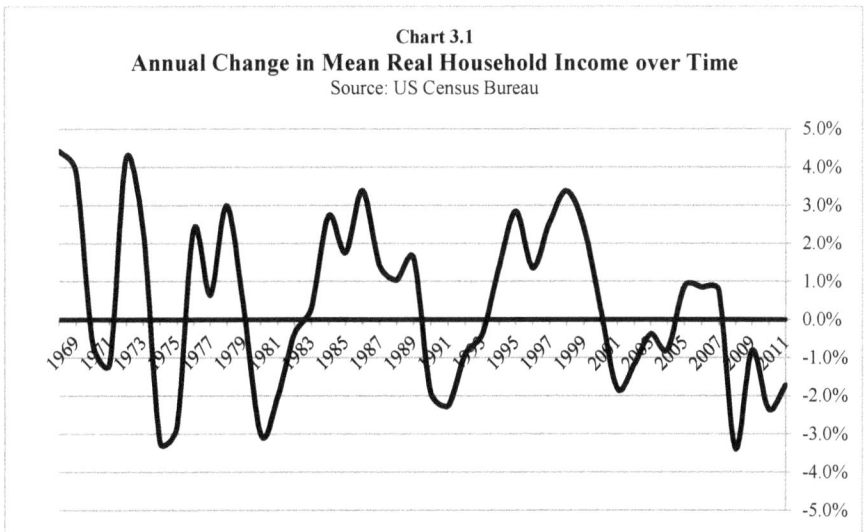

Chart 3.1
Annual Change in Mean Real Household Income over Time
Source: US Census Bureau

Chart 3.2
5-Year CAGR in Mean Real Household Income over Time
Source: US Censusu Bureau

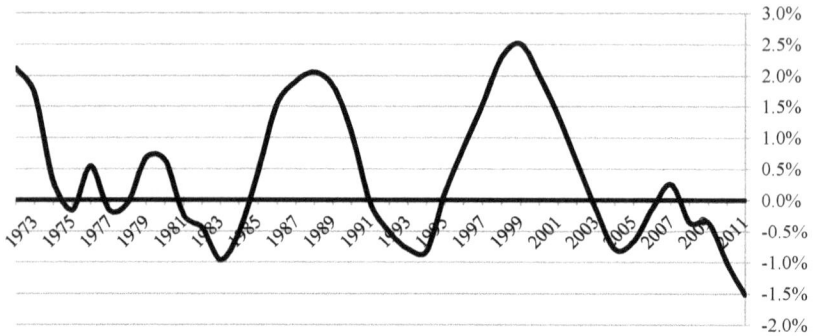

Each data point represents the compounded annual growth rate (CAGR) in real household income over the prior 5 years.

shows the compounded annual growth rate (CAGR) of real household income over the prior five years; it lays a "smoothing" effect over the volatile annual rates of change. The annual rates of change in Chart 3.1 have been under 1% since 1999. With the exception of 2007, right before the crash, 5-year CAGR has been negative in each year since 2003. 5-year CAGR has been under 1% for each year since 2001. The charts also show two periods of growth. Chart 3.1 shows annual growth of 1% or better during the periods 1984-1989 and 1994-1999; Chart 3.2 shows CAGR of 1% or better during the periods 1986-1990 and 1997-2001. With the exception of the recession which lasted officially from July 1990 to March 1991 (and is probably now a distant memory), we would guess that Americans in the 21st century look back with longing to the two decades of fairly good growth at the end of the last century during which they felt better off. We would also guess that they contrast those decades with their experience of the past ten years. Surveys and polls show that Americans' overall economic outlook remains net-negative.[44] Some might interpret the income data to show America's own particular "lost decade."

As shown in Charts 3.3 - 3.6, household income for the top quintile and top 5% of all households also declined over the past 10 years (the top 5% is a subset of the top quintile, which explains why the shapes of the curves are similar even though data points are different). Both sets of households performed better in the 20th century than the overall mean household. Even though upper-income households did experience significant down years, they performed much better during good times than the overall mean household. Better performance in good times plus the likelihood that they hold meaningful amounts of financial assets probably cushioned the recent crash and credit crunch for them. It should also be noted these households saw real income growth during 2011 whereas overall mean household income continued to fall. Although these households have performed better than lower-income ones, the charts should put to rest any populist implication that the well-off are somehow immune to bad times.

Chart 3.3
Top Quintile
Annual Change in Mean Real Household Income over Time
Source: US Census Bureau

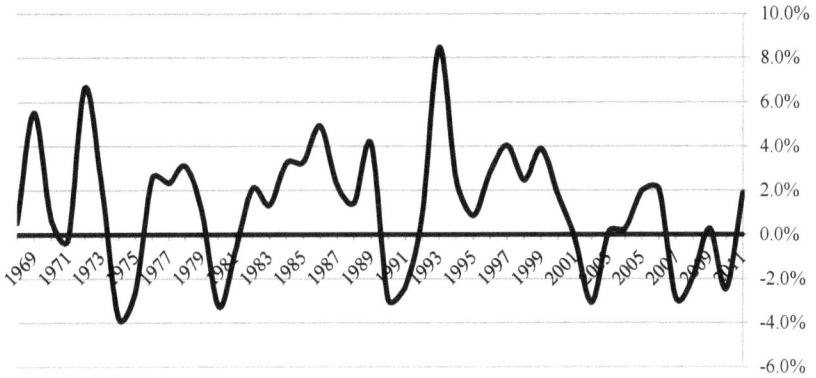

Chart 3.4
Top Quintile
5-Year CAGR in Mean Real Household Income over Time
Source: US Census Bureau

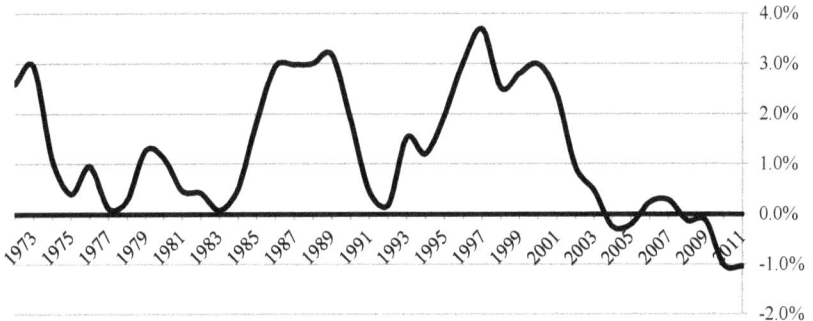

Each data point represents the compounded annual growth rate (CAGR) in real household income over the prior 5 years.

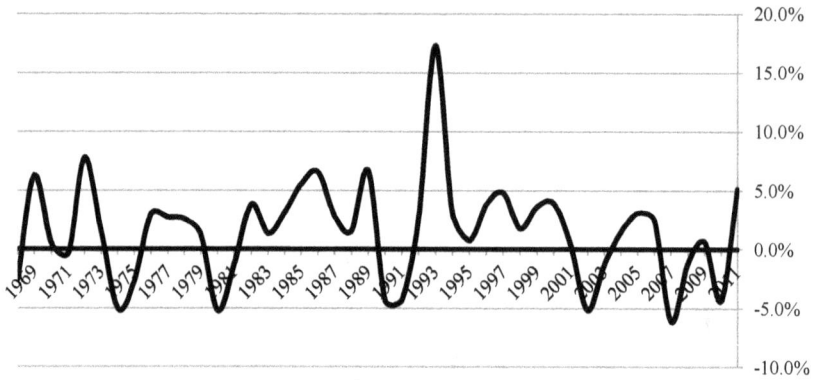

Chart 3.5
Top 5% of All Households
Annual Cahnge in Mean Real Household Income over Time
Source: US Census Bureau

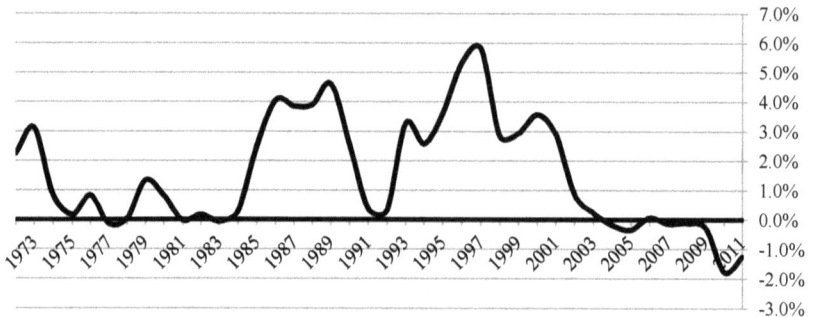

Chart 3.6
Top 5% of All Households
5-Year CAGR in Mean Real Household Income over Time
Source: US Census Bureau

Each data pont represents the compounded annual growth rate (CAGR) in real household income over the prior 5 years.

88

This decade of poor income growth started not with the collapse of the real estate bubble but with the collapse of the dot.com bubble. The economy continues to grow sluggishly, still unable to overcome the combined force of two crashes. Economists, politicians, academics, commentators and others have looked at these income numbers and offered multiple, sometimes dueling, explanations for why America seems stuck in a rut. In no particular order, these explanations include (but are not limited to):

Wage inequality due to race, ethnicity, and gender causes certain groups to be unable to obtain fair compensation.

Large corporations wield increasing power over the American economy and American government and countervailing forces are weak.

Labor union membership has fallen due to economic, corporate, and political pressure, meaning there are fewer Americans who can bargain with management on a relatively equal footing.

Geographic mobility, in part due to the rise of two-income households, has fallen, meaning Americans have less willingness to relocate in order to obtain higher wages that may be available in other parts of the country. Those who stay put may be locked into below-market wages because they have foreclosed the possibility of relocation.

Education and technology have been cited for much of the differences in wages, in that those with higher education and better technical skills earn more. The implication is that America is building a two-tier economy in which the lower tier has limited negotiating power.

Incentives provided to top earners represent meaningful portions of their compensation and boost income during good times, whereas lower earners have few incentives at any time.

Tax policies provide disincentives to get ahead and earn more.

Globalization and outsourcing hold incomes down because the American worker is now in competition with low-wage countries.

Corporate CEOs are grabbing a larger share of corporate free cash flow for themselves, leaving less available to both shareholders and employees.

Immigration, in particular illegal immigration, holds down US wage levels.

The American work ethic is weakening. Americans are no longer willing to work hard to get ahead.

The size of government and the social safety net creates disincentives for entrepreneurs to form businesses or for individuals to take on jobs that offer more reward but at the same time more risk.

Without speaking to the merits of any of these arguments, we would like to return to the subject of *imbalance* as an explanation. While these arguments point to a plethora of imbalances, few of them rise beyond the level of political rhetoric or have been substantiated with independent research. Yet there is a critical imbalance in the American economy that few want to address. The reason few want to address it is that it cannot be solved quickly. Many of the explanations are, implicitly, arguments for a "quick fix" which will supposedly solve everything or, alternatively, arguments to do nothing because "the fault…is …in ourselves."[45] Americans are impatient, they want answers. They have been led by politicians and commentators to believe there are "silver bullets" which will solve most anything. Americans' attention wanders when the reality is more complex.

Goods versus Services

Chart 3.7 shows Goods' and Services' shares of non-farm, private GDP over time.

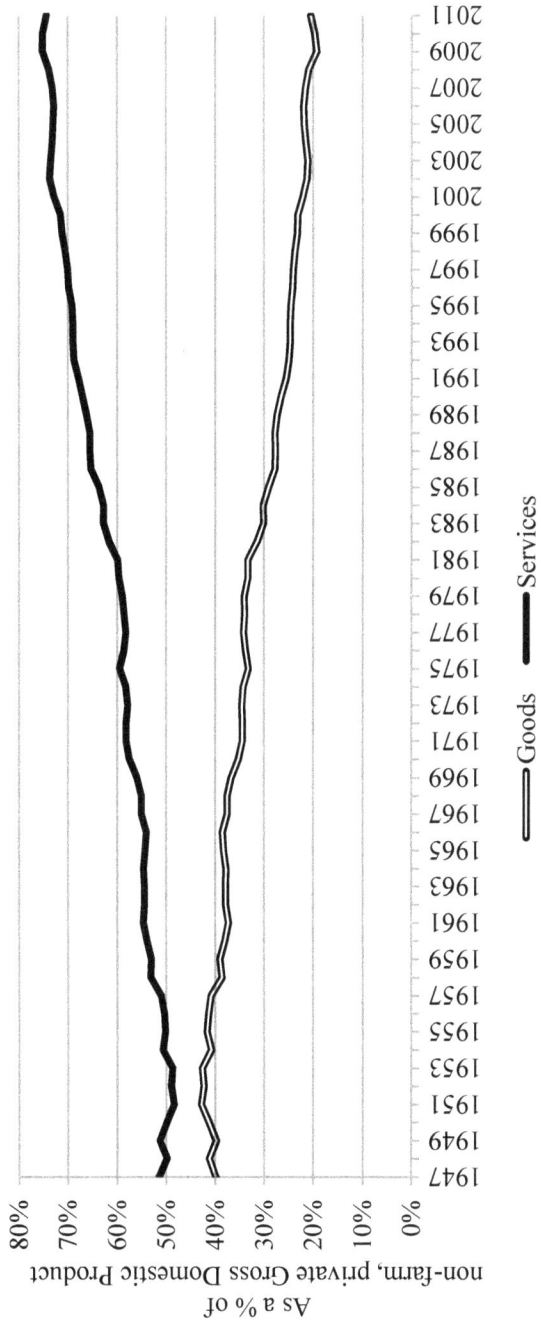

Chart 3.7
Goods & Services as a % of Non-Farm, Private GDP
Source: Bureau of Economic Analysis

As a % of non-farm, private Gross Domestic Product

Goods ———— Services

The classification of industries for GDP purposes is per the North American Industry Classification System (NAICS). Appendix IV shows the value contributed by each industry to GDP in 2011 based on NAICS classification, as well as coding to show which industries produce Goods and which produce Services both for the purpose of BEA GDP classification and the graphs in this chapter.

The graph shows a long-term structural change in American business. In 2011, Goods represented 20.4% (of which Manufacturing was 14.3%) and Services 74.3% of GDP. Looking back over the decades, one can understand why some conclude "America doesn't make anything anymore."

The composition of GDP is confirmed in the composition of employment (Chart 3.8). For 2011, Goods represented 17.5% (of which Manufacturing was 11.3%) and Services represented 78.0% of total non-farm private employment. Goods-producing industries received compensation greater than their share of employment as shown in Chart 3.9: employees in Goods-producing industries received 20.5% of compensation while representing just 17.5% of total employment; on the other hand, Service-producing industries received 74.5% of total compensation but had 78.0% of employment. These statistics appear to confirm the belief that manufacturing jobs (13.7% of compensation compared to 11.3% of employment) are better jobs in terms of pay (nevertheless, there is at least anecdotal evidence that manufacturing jobs no longer pay what they used to, particularly at the low end, which encourages workers to move into the service sector as discussed below). Note that the shares of compensation for Goods and Services in total are almost identical to their contributions to GDP, but Manufacturing contributes more to GDP than its share of employee compensation. The reason for this is that more capital must be added to labor when producing manufactured goods.

Chart 3.8
Goods- & Private Service-Producing Employment
Source: Bureau of Economic Analysis

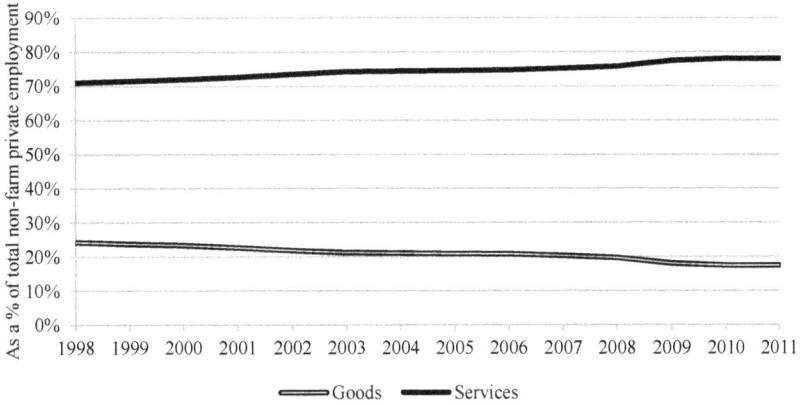

Chart 3.9
Goods & Services Compensation to Total Compensation
Source: Bureau of Economic Analysis

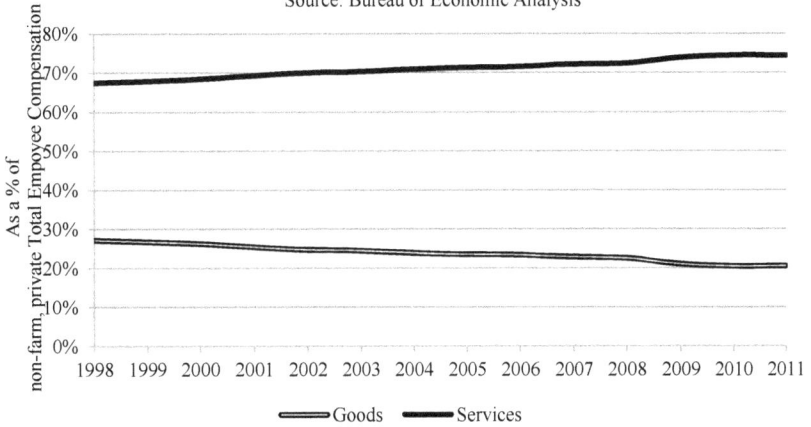

Many explanations have been offered for this structural change by economists, commentators, and others. Following is a bird's-eye view of some of them, but the variety of explanations is too numerous for all to be detailed here.

Demand for services reflects a growing, richer economy. From this perspective, service sector growth should be viewed as natural. At the beginning of the time series in Chart 3.7, the American people had emerged from the Depression of the 1930s and World War II. The Great Depression was a period of great privation. While World War II was better in terms of both employment and wages, consumer goods were rationed as production shifted to building the war machine. After World War II, Americans were able to experience a period of greater normalcy, real incomes rose, and they began to feel better off. As it became easier to fulfill basic needs, demand for additional services emerged as Americans now had higher disposable income. It was thus only natural for the service sector to grow larger. This pattern has been seen in other mature, developed countries in the decades following World War II.

Consumer preferences have driven demand for certain services on which improvements in technology have little bearing. Service segments such as restaurants, house-cleaning, security services, and home healthcare are highly dependent on personal service. Non-college-educated workers have moved into these segments because they have offered higher real wages than other low-skill jobs available to them (whether those jobs are offered in manufacturing or elsewhere). Indeed, wage levels in manufacturing have remained stagnant as job growth has been restrained by automation, so it was only natural for workers to move out of the manufacturing sector. From this perspective as well, growth in the service sector is seen as only natural.[46]

Technology and automation have made it possible to produce more with fewer people. This is, in a way, the obverse of the explanation in the prior paragraph. This explanation suggests that we focus on productivity rather than jobs because that is what matters. This explanation appears to argue that we should not worry too much about the growth in service employment because it is "natural" in a somewhat different way. The argument can be better seen through quotes attributed to Daniel Ikenson, director of Trade Policy Studies at the Cato Institute:

> He says he would take a Facebook (valued at $50 billion [sic]) over a Boeing (valued at the same), even though Boeing hires eighty times more employees. "With 2,000 workers…Facebook is 80 times more productive than Boeing, freeing up 158,000 workers for other more productive endeavors." Those workers not at Facebook will go where they are in demand — just as most candle-makers, hand-spinners, and farmers have found different occupations during times of technological growth. In the end customers get a cheaper product, companies get more profit, and the market finds the means to produce the most possible with the fewest resources. "The essence of growth is to create more value with fewer inputs," Ikenson says. Ikenson thinks the goal of public policy should not be to simply employ people, whether in manufacturing or some other industry. If that was the case then creating jobs would be easy: "Instead of bulldozers, mandate shovels; instead of shovels, require spoons."[47]

This quote should not be taken as epitomizing the complexity of this argument. A more apocalyptic view of the subject can be found in a controversial 1995 book entitled *The End of Work*.[48]

The growth of the computer industry together with related technology segments has contributed greatly to the increase in productivity in the goods sector and in the US economy overall. These segments provide higher-paying jobs than the rest of the service sector and did not exist decades ago. This explanation seems to argue that the division of industries between goods and services is somewhat arbitrary because some manufacturing and service industries are inter-

95

dependent. In a different way, it echoes the prior argument about productivity but focuses more on the "newness" of these segments as a positive factor in growth of services.

Large corporations control the goods sector and have focused on capital rather than labor. There are probably hundreds, if not thousands, of structuralist (including Marxist) explanations which fall here and few probably agree with each other. At their heart, they posit control of the industrial sector by monopoly- or oligopoly-like structures and/or political and economic elites which emphasize productivity and return on equity: workers are just another input and have no countervailing power. The result, in some of these explanations, has been globalization and outsourcing, which have reduced wages in goods-producing industries. As jobs and wages have fallen in manufacturing, workers have had no choice but to move into the service sector where foreign competition is less. These arguments would appear to deemphasize demand as a factor in the growth of the service sector. Some of these arguments appear to incorporate, indirectly and probably unconsciously, Marx's theory of a *reserve army of labor* that holds wages down.

The common effect of these arguments is to allay fears that growth in the service sector is perverse and not to be welcomed. Even structuralist arguments focus on issues in the goods sector, not the service sector itself. Many of these arguments seem more aimed at justifying or explaining why things are the way they are than at considering alternative possibilities. In all of these, we hear echoes of the comment heard most often during market bubbles: 'this time is different.'

We believe it is not particularly helpful to speak to goods- and services-producing sectors in macro-terms. While each of these arguments may contain elements of truth, they avoid addressing particular issues that have been uniquely present in the growth of US service-producing industries.

Imbalances in the Service Sector

Let's speak to the individual sectors which have grown. Table 3.1 shows that the service sector grew to 75.0% of GDP in 2010 from 65.5% in 1987. As can be seen in the numbers, three broad segments were most responsible for the growth.

Banking, securities, and insurance together represented 25% *of the change in service sector GDP share.* Most of the growth in the banking industry has taken place over the past 10 years, after its deregulation during the 1990s. Deregulation was in turn followed by a period of rapid consolidation: banks with over $10 billion in assets held 74% of US deposits at 6/30/12, up from 58% at 6/30/02 and 30% at 6/30/94. The industry's share of GNP fell slightly after the 2007 crash but has since grown back to its previous share. The growth of the securities industry was also promoted by deregulation, in particular by the repeal of the Glass-Steagall Act which had separated commercial from investment banking since the days of the Great Depression; as a result many commercial banks moved into the investment banking and securities space. Most of the growth in the insurance industry share, however, took place during the 1990s. One reason for insurance industry growth was a gradual move away from whole to term life, which threatened slower growth for life insurance companies; they overcame this challenge with a variety of annuity products, particularly the variable annuity with results tied to the performance of embedded mutual funds. Another reason for the increase in the insurance industry's share was the rise in medical costs. Health insurance industry premiums have risen rapidly in line with the growth in the health care sector, which we discuss in further detail below. Thus, unlike banking and securities firms, insurance industry growth has been more in line with the concept that the financial sector exists to serve other areas of the economy.

One might argue that, because the US is the largest economy in the world and because New York City is the world's financial capital, growth in the financial sector should be viewed as only to be expected. One might argue that US financial sector growth also mirrors that of the UK, with London being the world's other financial capital. In other words, growth in the financial sector is again only "natural," the theme of the macroeconomic arguments previously discussed.

The UK financial sector grew from to ~8% of GDP in 2007 from ~5% in 1970, the US financial sector to ~8% in 2010 from ~2% in 1950. Some have attributed this growth to greater productivity in the financial sector that has produced a "miracle": nominal returns to the financial sector prior to the recession were better than most other industries. Yet if one reviews the economic carnage of the past few years, this "miracle" was clearly built on taking outsized risk. That outsized risk was accompanied by much higher leverage, both on-

Table 3.1

3 Top Service Sectors

Source: Bureau of Economic Analysis

	% of GDP		
	1987	2010	Difference
Services	65.5%	75.0%	9.5%
Finance, insurance, real estate, rental, and leasing	18.0%	20.7%	2.7%
Finance and insurance	6.0%	8.5%	2.5%
Federal Reserve banks, credit intermediation, and related activities	3.2%	4.0%	0.8%
Securities, commodity contracts, and investments	0.9%	1.4%	0.5%
Insurance carriers and related activities	1.7%	2.8%	1.1%
Funds, trusts, and other financial vehicles	0.2%	0.3%	0.1%
Real estate and rental and leasing	12.0%	12.2%	0.2%
Professional and business services	8.1%	12.3%	4.2%

Professional, scientific, and technical services	4.7%	7.5%	2.8%
Legal services	1.3%	1.5%	0.2%
Computer systems design and related services	0.5%	1.3%	0.8%
Miscellaneous professional, scientific, and technical services	3.0%	4.8%	1.8%
Management of companies and enterprises	1.6%	1.8%	0.2%
Administrative and waste management services	1.8%	2.9%	1.1%
Administrative and support services	1.6%	2.6%	1.0%
Waste management and remediation services	0.2%	0.3%	0.1%
Educational services, health care, and social assistance	5.9%	8.8%	2.9%
Educational services	0.7%	1.1%	0.4%
Health care and social assistance	5.2%	7.6%	2.4%
Ambulatory health care services	2.5%	3.8%	1.3%
Hospitals and nursing and residential care facilities	2.3%	3.2%	0.9%
Social assistance	0.3%	0.6%	0.3%
Total of 3 Sectors	32.0%	41.8%	9.8%

balance sheet and through derivatives. Adjusting returns for the real risk of banks' and others' activities over the past decade, the "miracle" looks, to use the words of one Bank of England commentator, more like a "mirage." [49]

Increased risk-taking has not been the only issue. The introduction of new financial products has clearly contributed to the financial sector's share of GDP. We have already spoken to the rapid growth in both volume and type of derivatives. Investment products have also grown. Added to the usual slate of stocks, bonds, mutual funds have been, for instance, structured products like collateralized debt obligations (CDO) to complement more traditional asset-based products like mortgage-backed securities.[50] Many CDOs performed miserably after the recent crisis. Furthermore, the proliferation of CDOs in the run-up to the crisis was based not only on actual debt instruments: bankers dreamed up "synthetic" CDOs through use of credit default swaps (CDS), which have been discussed. Why? The reality was that synthetic CDOs were easier to assemble than when using real loans and bonds. They were also more lucrative, for the banks that created CDOs stood at the center of the CDS market and thereby stood to reap additional profitability on CDO transactions. There was more than a whiff of self-interest and self-dealing in the creation of the Street's many "synthetic" products, CDO and otherwise.

Another investment product that has gained wide popularity over the past decade is the Exchange-Traded Fund (ETF). The financial sector has manufactured a wide variety of ETFs through which investors can gain direct exposure to virtually any sector of the economy or the world at a cost that is usually lower than using mutual funds. There are presently over 1,500 ETFs. One questions whether investors really understand the dynamics and risk of these products, yet one thing is clear: so many ETFs have been developed that many have failed to gain a foothold with investors. We have recently seen many investment companies shutter ETFs and/or reduce fees in order to improve profitability. Using ETFs as a clear example, financial products in general appear to be in oversupply relative to the market's actual need and demand for them. Many look back over the history of the past ten years and praise the creativity of the financial sector but, from the perspective of 2012 - 2013, it looks like "financial engineers" ran amok.

Ah, one might ask: but doesn't the fact that some ETFs are being shut down show markets at their best? If too many financial products have been created, the ones that do not add value will inevitably fail and so won't demand and supply come back into balance? That is true, but let's look at it another way. We have a huge number of highly compensated individuals inventing, marketing, and trading new financial products because only in this way can they justify what they are earning. But do they provide anything of incremental value? Do we need 20 different ways to trade General Electric? Do we really need 1,500 ETFs and 6,500 mutual funds? What value do all of these really add to GDP? Yes, the economy does benefit from the liquidity effect of having multiple trading vehicles but is liquidity alone sufficient justification for the invention so many of them? We would argue no, not when the incremental value-added to the economy is negligible.

Overall, the growth of this sector appears to be an imbalance that is not sustainable over the long-term. If household incomes are flat, how can the economy sustain the large proportion of value-added currently being absorbed by this sector? As we discussed at the beginning of Chapter 2, the world of finance does not exist for its own purposes. The financial sector exists to serve the rest of the economy but the sector has built a vast edifice to serve itself. It deserves to have higher vacancy rates. Finance can only succeed if other sectors of the economy are doing well.

We believe this *imbalance* is structural in nature and can only be addressed through a long-term decline in financial sector employment, particularly in high-compensation areas. Employment in the securities, commodities, and investment industries grew at 3.6% per annum from 1990 through 2007, exceeding the rate of growth in GDP. Even though they often feel they are being picked on, investment banking and private equity are cases in point. Investment bankers command extremely high compensation because of, among other things, the high value they supposedly produce when advising on mergers & acquisitions (M&A). The fees they earn are absurdly high relative to the time and manpower spent on each M&A transaction. This suggests that corporate CEOs are not paying attention, not doing their jobs, and happy to pass on M&A costs to shareholders. More importantly, repeated studies of the success of these transactions, relative to their supposed benefits at the time they were announced, show the M&A game to be a toss-up.[51] If you are in a sector that focuses on helping other industries make acquisitions and your advice produces success only ~50% of the time, why should you continue to pull down such high compensation?

M&A fees are earned once the deal closes, whereas private equity (PE) actually invests in each transaction. Given that it takes 3-5 years before a PE firm can sell an investment and realize a profit, it is harder to get information on returns and success rates. But it is also harder to understand what value PE really delivers in each transaction. PE would have us believe that they deliver good advice, strong management capability, intense oversight, and additional capital when needed. What is also clear is that PE delivers a much heavier debt burden to its portfolio of invested companies: the foundation of PE rests on having companies to take on additional debt in order to achieve higher investment returns. It might be argued that private equity is not providing anything new of value; rather, it is just shuffling return calculations by leveraging up the capital structure. PE is looking for returns on investment of at least 20-30%; this is achieved by lowering equity and increasing debt. Why should it command higher shares of GNP when, on a risk-adjusted basis, the value of this portfolio to the economy is probably no different from pre-acquisition and often less? Just because it is more valuable to PE because they have found banks to take on more risk (measured in terms of higher Funded Debt/EBITDA) does not make it more valuable to the economy as a whole.

Computer design (and related services), consulting services, R&D services, and a variety of miscellaneous services represented 38% of service sector change in GDP share.[52] Certainly the value produced by the computer industry for both the US and global economies is commensurate with its statistical share of GDP. One might look instead for imbalances in consulting and R&D. Both management consulting and R&D services represent outsourcing of basic corporate functions. Management consulting is used because a corporation or other entity believes it does not have the time and/or expertise to address critical areas of its business. Management consultants tend to be very highly paid (although they work long hours) and so use of their services is expensive relative to internal staff. Services provided by the industry vary widely and we believe customer satisfaction varies widely as well. We believe slower economic growth is likely to place management consulting services under greater scrutiny: more projects may end up being done in-house. Although this may hurt employment to some degree, we believe that consulting, unlike financial services, does not represent a fundamental imbalance, particularly with respect to the overall economy. The reason for this is that the financial sector plays a central role in every nation's economic life whereas management consulting is on the periphery. Although R&D services are an outsourcing product, the cost of these services is usually less than performing R&D in-house; moreover the services are often of higher quality, particularly for high-volume and repetitive applications. Thus we do not see R&D services as an imbalance either. In conclusion, for this overall grouping of services, we do not detect an imbalance.

Health care represents 23% of the change in service sector GDP share. The growth in this sector has many sources: increased use of technology, more expensive drugs, highly trained staff requiring higher pay to compensate for the cost of training, new and more complex procedures, etc. Growth is expected to continue because of an aging population that will have increasing demand for these services. Table 3.2 shows that the US spends more on health care than any large country by a wide margin, but achieves only middling results. These figures must also be looked at with the knowledge that the US had these high expenditures at the same time as 15.7% of its 2011 population went without health insurance.[53]

The US Bureau of Labor Statistics (BLS) projects growth in health care employment as follows.[54]

Table 3.3		
	Actual Growth 2006 - 2010	Projected Growth 2010 – 2020
Health care practitioners and technical occupations	8.4%	25.9%
Health care support occupations	12.5%	34.5%

Table 3.2
US Health Care Rankings

Measure	Statistic	Ranking	Comment
Health care/GDP	17.9%	2	Marshall Islands is #1. France, at 11.9%, is the next highest ranked large country.
Per capital total expenditure on health	$8,364	1	US is the largest. Only Luxembourg, Norway, and Switzerland are close.
Life expectancy at birth (yrs)	79	29	Tied for #29. Japan is #1 at 83 yrs.
Infant mortality rate (probability of dying by age 1 per 1,000 live births)	6	40	Tied for #40. 8 countries tied for #1 at 2.
Neonatal mortality rate (per 1,000 live births)	4	38	Tied for #38. 8 countries tied for #1 at 1.

Source: World Health Organization, for 2009 or 2010, depending on the statistic

Only "Personal care and service occupations," at 26.8%, shows comparable growth. The troubling point about these projections is that they appear to have been made solely on the basis of demand without looking at the ability of the economy to pay for them; one would think growth in GNP and household income would constrain all projections of employment. With stagnant household income and an aging population, how will the US economy be able to support a sector that seems destined to command an ever larger portion of GDP? The growing size of the health care sector relative to the ability of the economy to pay appears to be a major *imbalance*.

At the heart of the issue is physician pay:

Primary care physicians in the United States make $186,000 per year on average versus $131,000 in Germany. Orthopedic surgeon pay ranges from a high of $442,000 in the United States, to $324,000 in the UK, to a relatively parsimonious $187,000 per year in Australia, that according to analysis by the United Health Group Foundation.[55]

In the US health care debate, discussion of physician pay is usually off-limits because it is sure to arouse accusations of "socialized medicine." To be fair, high physician pay in the US is driven by burdens that doctors in other countries do not carry. The cost of medical education is far higher in the US than in other countries (where it is often subsidized) and the average doctor graduates with a heavy personal debt load. Malpractice insurance and the amount of time that must be devoted to paperwork in a reimbursement system dominated by multiple payers also add to physician costs when compared to other countries. Furthermore, although physician pay is at the heart of the problem, one must acknowledge that costs in almost all other segments of health care are growing as well.[56]

How the *imbalance* between growth in the health care sector and ability to pay will be resolved is hard to predict, but it will be resolved and the process will take years. We are already seeing baby steps. The US Government already sets caps on reimbursement to hospitals, which is putting them under pressure and slashing into profitability. Rates of reimbursement from Medicare are already putting pressure on the health care system, to the point where some doctors currently do not accept Medicare patients. One might ask: if a higher proportion of the population is aging and covered by Medicare, how can doctors decide to write off a large portion of the pool of available patients and still remain in practice? Over time, these types of pressures cannot help but slow growth in physician pay. Realistically, physicians will not be able to resist the pressure applied by an economy that cannot cover growing costs.

Breakdown in the US Economic Model

We believe the long path towards resolving the imbalances posed by the financial and health care sectors will result in fundamental changes to the US economic model as we know it. Another market crash and credit crunch will administer the *shock* that accelerates that change.

Yet while finance and healthcare comprise a significant part of the problem, the US services sector in general appears out of balance when compared to other major countries:

Table 3.4				
Goods & Services as a % of:				
		GDP	**Compensation**	**Employment**
Goods	US	20.4%	20.5%	20.3%
	Germany	37.9%	44.0%	31.8%
	UK	28.9%	27.6%	22.5%
	France	24.8%	29.2%	25.7%
	Japan			29.0%
Services	US	74.3%	74.3%	78.8%
	Germany	62.1%	56.0%	67.2%
	UK	71.1%	72.4%	69.1%
	France	75.2%	70.8%	60.8%
	Japan			68.8%

Source: Germany, UK, France, Japan - OECD & ILO
Source: US BEA for GDP, Compensation: OECD for Employment
GDP & Compensation as of 2011; Employment as of 2008
US Employment for 2011 per US BLS was 17.5% and 78.0% for g&s.
US Employment for 2008 per US BLS was 19.5% and 75.8% for g&s.
OECD breakdown between g&s is as per ISIC as adopted by each country
US BEA and BLS breakdown between g&s is as per 2007 NAICS.
GDP = Gross Domestic Product
Compensation = Total Employee Compensation
Employment = Total No of Employees

The figures are admittedly imprecise because of the way OECD aggregates the data and because some countries, including the US, are not using the latest OECD industry classifications. Nevertheless, we suggest that the US concentration in services is 7-10% higher than its peers. Even if we exclude finance, health care, and computers/information technology from these figures, we still believe that the US concentration in services exceeds that of its peers by 4-7%. This cannot be sustained long-term.[57]

This is not a case of reversion to the mean service percentages of other mature, developed countries; rather, we believe America is probably at the breaking point with its reliance on services. Service sector employment cannot go much higher than where it is today. The reason why the service sector is so problematic is that (leaving technology aside) most service-producing industries do not increase American productivity. In other words, unlike the computer industry, they do not lay the foundations for future growth. Rather, they are aimed at meeting personal consumption demand, which continues to represent roughly 70% of GDP. Thus delivery of a large number of services is at the end of the supply chain, at the point where the service is used (consumed). For any economy to grow, there must be a balance between investment and consumption, for only through investment can a country remain productive and competitive into the future.

The US savings rate has been low for decades as shown in Chart 3.10:

Chart 3.10
US Personal Savings Rate
Source: Bureau of Economic Analysis

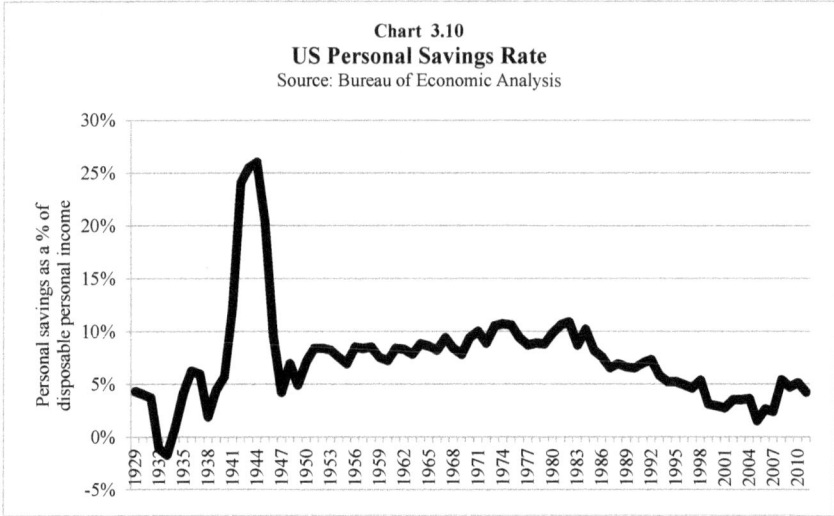

The low personal savings rate has been driven in part by slow growth in household income: it is harder to save if income is not growing. Although the savings rate has recovered a bit in the wake of the recession, the low US savings rate (driven by high consumption which, to repeat, has been met by high reliance on services) has meant that a high proportion of America's needs, both for consumption and investment, have necessarily been funded externally, through foreign debt. Without foreigners' ongoing willingness to purchase US Treasuries, there would have been no way to fund the US consumption binge of the past decades. Given high US budget and trade deficits and in the face of slow growth in household income, the patterns of the previous decades cannot stay the same and another *shock* will ensure they do not remain the same. US consumption must slow, which means growth in service-producing industries must slow.

Growth in services has rested heavily on a US bias towards consumption over investment, compared to other large, developed countries as shown in Table 3.5.[58]

Table 3.5				
Expenditures as a % of 2011 GDP:				
	Consumption	**Investment**	**Government**	**Int'l Trade**
US	71.6%	14.9%	17.3%	-3.8%
Germany	57.4%	18.3%	19.3%	5.1%
UK	64.3%	14.9%	22.4%	-1.6%
France	57.7%	20.6%	24.5%	-2.8%
Japan	60.4%	19.9%	20.7%	-0.9%

Source: OECD

That imbalance must be redressed in order to achieve stronger economic growth over the long-term. Obviously, this will not happen overnight, but it will have to occur. The US must achieve stronger economic growth if it is to produce higher incomes. Can anyone find a large country over the centuries of economic history (we are not talking about countries like Singapore) which has shown strong economic growth with the foundation of that growth based in the service sector? We believe there are none: growth over the long-term requires growth in capital investment.

Our perspective is as follows. The excess compensation earned by the financial sector is unmerited and the excess compensation earned by the health care sector cannot be supported, but excess compensation earned by high-tech sectors appears appropriate. If we set these three sectors aside, the rest of the service sector — and we realize this is a sweeping generalization — is not well paid compared to the rest of the economy and manufacturing in particular. It is the US concentration in these lower-paid service sectors that drags on its ability to produce higher growth in household income. Only higher growth in household income can sustain a vibrant service sector. After the *shock* of a new market crash and credit crunch, we believe that that the current period of low growth will be extended. Furthermore, the outsized service sector will weigh more heavily on the economy because of its inability to generate meaningful growth. Furthermore, as noted, this sector does not lay the foundations of future growth: its products are aimed at current consumption. We believe an outsized service sector, coupled with the forces outlined, has the power to cause a breakdown in the US model as we know it under the force of a *shock*. This will mean dramatic changes in the entire service sector, not just in financial institutions and health care. These changes will lead to job losses.

<u>*Job Losses*</u>

Growth of the service sector over the past decades was built on personal income which created demand. With incomes stagnating, that demand cannot be sustained. Another market crash accompanied by a credit crunch may put the nail in the coffin of our economic structure and point out that how we are operating is unsustainable for the long-term.

With a breakdown in the US business model, the focus must be on the answer to this question: how many more services can we support that are not vital? As an illustration, here are some thoughts on some service occupations that may not stand the test of "need" versus "nice to have." Many Americans are engaged in search engine optimization (SEO). One blog stated that there were over 500,000 professionals with "SEO" listed in their title or description on Linked-In as of July 2012.[59] The test of the value of any occupation is how much clients/customers are willing to pay for the products and services. Today, these occupations have value because of our need to find our way through an ever-growing mountain of data, but if the US business model breaks down, how much value will be placed on skills which direct internet searches to higher rankings on web pages? Will marketing-related skills like these remain a priority?

Here is another thought. Smartphones and tablets are nice to have. When they first appeared, they helped improve productivity. Now, users are pulling down more and more data. AT&T and Verizon are measuring their success by the extent to which they are able to grow average revenue per user (ARPU). But does this growing ARPU mean that smartphones and tablets are vital for productivity, for our daily lives? Or are they just nice to have? As with health care, if household income is stagnant, how can the economy support growing ARPU? To put it clearly: how can you keep buying more and more wireless services if you do not have a good job and rising income? If ARPU growth fades, then employment in telecommunications services will certainly come under pressure.

Here is a third example. A cottage industry of law firms surrounds Wall Street which searches for reasons to bring class action lawsuits every time a stock declines by a material amount or a merger is announced. Company press releases are often accompanied on the same day by notices of lawsuits. These suits are purportedly brought to protect the interests of investors from corporate misconduct or unfairness, a noble cause on the face of it. Yet legal fees far too often represent a huge percentage of the distributions upon final settlement and investors end up with minor amounts. Too often, the purpose of these suits looks like just another way for lawyers to earn a living—we would argue they are analogous to the creation of new products in the financial sector. Indeed, too many of these suits look like harassment or a type of extortion: they are brought in hopes that corporations will pay them off to go away. While we will not argue that corporations are never in the wrong, we believe that the majority of these suits, when initiated, add little incremental value to the country or GDP. If we see a smaller Wall Street in the wake of a shock, there should be fewer opportunities for lawsuits. This means a number of lawyers will have to look for work elsewhere.

To go still further, review the service occupations selected in Appendix V. Without denigrating the worth of any of them today, how do you think employment in these occupations will be able to bear up under a breakdown of the US economic model under pressure from stagnant growth in household income? If the economy remains stagnant, significant segments of the service sector may no longer be sustainable. Many jobs in those segments will consequently "disappear." What we will see is "creative destruction" in action, a term devised by the economist Joseph Schumpeter.[60]

Focus on Value-added

For the US economy to create a new economic model from the ashes of its current one, there must be increased focus on *value-added*. *Value-added*, which is measured only in the eye of the customer, becomes all-important. Per Investopedia, *value-added* is "the enhancement a company gives its product or service before offering it to customers." Companies will be compensated to the degree they add value when compared to competitors. Likewise, individuals will be compensated to the extent that the value they add stands out. Value-added becomes hard to calculate in many service occupations once they come under economic stress. When value-added becomes hard to calculate, then demand for a product or service should fall.

For America to build a new, sustainable economic model, the American worker's value-added must be (a) at least be equal to that of international competitors in terms of both cost and quality (which includes technological superiority) and (b) the American worker's compensation must track the increase in overall value-added for the product or service. If (a) holds true but (b) does not, then the value added by the product or service accrues more to the employer.[61] If employers command the lion's share of value-added in any sector, then household income in that sector cannot grow. This latter pattern, if it occurs across multiple sectors, is a recipe for ongoing stagnation in household income, perhaps your household income.

In the midst of this discussion, one has to ask why there is ongoing anecdotal commentary from many businesses that they cannot find enough skilled workers to meet their needs. These comments are also echoed by those in government who see the issue as one of the biggest challenges to America. What might underlie business's frustrations? Could it be, as they say, that there are not enough applicants with the requisite math, science, and technical skills to meet the demands of these positions? Or could it be that these businesses are not willing to provide attractive wages and benefits to attract qualified individuals who could potentially fill the position away from, say, the service sector? In other words, could it be that business has become mired in behavior towards labor which directly impacts its ability to hire qualified workers? We believe the answers to these questions are "a little of both." Answers to these questions are addressed in more detail in Chapters 4 and 5.

If the current American business

OECD Country	2006
Australia	4.9
Austria	4.8
Belgium	8.3
Canada	6.4
Chile	7.9
Czech Republic	7.2
Denmark	4.0
Estonia	6.0
Finland	7.7
France	8.9
Germany	10.4
Greece	9.0
Hungary	7.5
Iceland	3.0
Ireland	4.7
Israel	8.5
Italy	6.9
Japan	4.3
Korea	3.6
Luxembourg	4.7
Mexico	3.3
Netherlands	4.3
New Zealand	3.9
Norway	3.5
Poland	14.0
Portugal	8.1
Slovak Republic	13.3
Slovenia	6.1
Spain	8.6
Sweden	7.1
Switzerland	4.1
Turkey	10.5
United Kingdom	5.5
United States	4.7
OECD-Total	**6.2**
OECD Average	6.6
OECD Median	6.2
European Average	**7.0**
European Median	**7.0**

Table 3.6
Unemployment Rates
Source: OECD

model is under threat, then you need to consider whether your job will also come under threat.

Early Warning Signs

The market collapse and the credit crunch <u>cannot</u> be used as warning signs of a breakdown in the US economic model. Should these occur, it would already be too late to respond. Changing jobs is a long, slow process—there is no time to react after a market crash. You must position yourself now for any economic distress that the future may bring.

The most fundamental macroeconomic early warning sign of a breakdown in the US economic model will be if unemployment remains over 7% for an extended period of time. We establish this benchmark based on a review of European unemployment rates in 2006, before the onset of worldwide recession. Europe experienced a period of rapid growth after World War II up until the mid-1970s sparked by a need to rebuild infrastructure and industry. European economies had difficulty adjusting to slower growth once the post-war boom ended. This adjustment was in part hindered by the size of the social safety net that had been built on the strength of the boom. In many ways, the reasons for high unemployment in Europe in 2006 are now structural in nature. We believe the imbalance between the US goods- and services-producing sectors is also a structural imbalance. Should the US economy prove itself unable to reduce employment below 7%, then we will probably be looking at a "new normal." That new normal means the US economic model as we know it will be clearly under threat.

There are no other good macroeconomic economic early warning signs besides unemployment. The rest of the early warnings signs below hit closer to home. They ask that you look at your employer and the industry in which you work and determine where they currently stand. We suggest the following:

Employment growth in your industry sector or subsector, and at your employer, lags that of the rest of the economy.

Profitability in your industry and at your employer is flat to down.

Leverage in your industry (non-financial industries only) and at your employer is moderate to high, as measured by the ratio of Funded Debt/ EBITDA of 2.75x or higher.[62]

113

Wall Street stock analyst outlooks for your industry and employer are neutral at best.

All of the above ask that you assess the strength of your employer from a variety of perspectives. Most employees fail to do this. They are happy to have a job and, if they have a good relationship with their immediate bosses, then everything is fine. We need to go beyond what makes us happy today and look to the future. If your analysis of these early warning signs shows weakness, then that means an increased likelihood that lay-offs are on the way. Those lay-offs may not come today, they may not come next year, but they will come as your employer is forced to adapt to a breakdown in the US economic model.

Preparation

A breakdown in the US economic model that has sustained us for so many years will have a major impact on the US job market and potentially, even if you are in a relatively attractive industry, on your job. In any company, the safest jobs are in sales, engineering, and manufacturing; however they might be named, these three general functions are common to every business even if it does not make "things." If you are not in one of these three areas, then your job will be more vulnerable. The reason for this is that direct contact with the product/service and direct contact with the client/customer are usually prized and valued more highly than other jobs. For this reason, jobs in areas like human resources, accounting, purchasing, and administration are generally more vulnerable than sales, engineering, and manufacturing positions. Even if you happen to be in one of the latter three areas, you will still be vulnerable if you are behind the scenes and not on the "front line" where everyone can see you.

You need to be in a growing industry with a growing employer, for it is growth alone that ultimately sustains jobs. If your analysis using the early warning signs discussed points to questions about the future of your employer, you need to consider switching employers or, possibly, industries. The key question is: do you have the skills and experience to make a switch? If you think your skills and experience are lacking, you may need to think about acquiring more training or education. If you are thinking about changing careers, think for the long-term but be realistic. Would you really go back for a degree in engineering if you do not have that kind of aptitude and hate math? It is more important to do something you like than to get the hot job or make a job switch based solely on money. Yet at the same time, you have to make sure that what you will earn will keep you and your family relatively secure.

In addition, just because an industry is considered strong due to high growth does not necessarily make it desirable. As noted, health care is considered a high-growth sector by the Bureau of Labor Statistics (BLS), but if that growth cannot be supported by growth in household income, then employment and wages in that sector will necessarily come under pressure. You must take the likelihood of such pressures into account when considering any new job. Furthermore, even a hot high-tech company with the latest new idea may not be right for you. First, technology obsolesces so quickly that today's darling can easily become tomorrow's dog. Second, today's economic model that is slanted so heavily towards services should cause you to eye some hot companies skeptically. After all, how many more Facebooks, Groupons, Netflixes, Zyngas, and Zillows can be sustained? Will companies like these really be needed after a collapse of the US economic model, or will they be just nice to have around? For if they are just nice to have around, their services will be the first to be jettisoned or cut under the pressure of a shock.

Another issue you will possibly need to consider is what additional skills you may need if the economy continues to deteriorate even further. Think long-term and very basic: what if I had to barter skills in order to live because basic economic functions have, in some way, broken down? In addition to my basic job skills, what secondary skills do I have and/or products can I make that can be traded in a barter economy? Look at skills that are in demand during wartime or within the Amish community to see what is essential for human existence. Do you have something you can offer? If you do not, perhaps it is time to learn something new.

There are no easy answers to these questions. There is no substitute for an in-depth self-assessment, both of where you are today and where you want to go. Once you have completed a self-assessment, then you need to establish a plan for developing skills or repositioning yourself in a new world that will emerge as the economy begins to move towards a new model. Looking at the industries we have marked with a '+' in Appendix III may be a good start. Reviewing BLS's *Occupational Outlook Handbook* may also provide helpful insights.[63] For some, advice from a trusted relative, friend, or employment search consultant may prove valuable. No matter which path you choose, it is critical to be proactive and analyze where you stand. If there are issues with your current job, you need to act.

---

[44] An example is Gallup's Economic Confidence Index which has been net-negative since its inception in January 2008. See http://www.gallup.com/poll/122840/gallup-daily-economic-indexes.aspx (accessed October 31, 2012).

[45] Cassius in Shakespeare's Julius Caesar: "The fault, dear Brutus, is not in our stars, but in ourselves, that we are underlings."

[46] Description of this explanation relies heavily on: David H. Autor and David Dorn, "The Growth of Low Skill Service Jobs and the Polarization of the U.S. Labor Market" (April 2012). Available on-line at: http://www.cemfi.es/~dorn/Autor-Dorn-LowSkillServices-Polarization.pdf (accessed November 1, 2012).

[47] Justin Higginbottom, "Service jobs projected to grow as manufacturing employment continues to decline," *Deseret News*, (January 27, 2012). http://www.deseretnews.com/article/700219853/Service-jobs-projected-to-grow-as-manufacturing-employment-continues-to-decline.html?pg=all (accessed on November 1, 2012).

[48] Jeremy Rifkin, "The End of Work: The Decline of the Global Labor Force and the Dawn of the Post-Market Era," (New York: Putnam Publishing Group, 1995).

[49] The tenor of the discussion in this paragraph is indebted to: Andrew Haldane, "The Contribution of the Financial Sector: Miracle or Mirage?" (Speech given at the Future of Finance Conference, London: July 14, 2010, accessed November 3, 2012 at: http://www.bankofengland.co.uk/publications/Documents/speeches/2010/spee ch442.pdf). Haldane is Executive Director, Financial Stability, at the Bank of England. The content of this speech has been published as a chapter in: Turner, Haldane, Woolley, Wolf, Layard, Kay, Smithers, et.al., *The Future of Finance: The LSE Report*, (London: LSE, August 15, 2010).

[50] A CDO is a security, usually rated investment-grade or issued in tranches with some investment-grade and some non-investment grade, which is secured by pools of bonds, loans, or other similar assets. The term CDO is usually interpreted to mean securities which hold other than mortgages as collateral.

[51] There are a large number of papers, some written by M&A firms and practitioners, some written by academics, that speak to and argue over this issue. A more recent popular article is the following: Robert Sher, "Why Half of All M&A Deals Fail and What You Can Do About It," *Forbes*, (Forbes Leadership Forum, March 19, 2012), http://www.forbes.com/sites/forbesleadershipforum/2012/03/19/why-half-of-all-ma-deals-fail-and-what-you-can-do-about-it/ (accessed November 28, 2012). In fact some conclude that the failure rate is far higher. The question is: how is "failure" defined and that appears to vary paper to paper. Failure does not mean bankruptcy. In our view, it means failure to deliver, in a meaningful way, the results that were originally expected. Given the variance in conclusions, we believe "toss-up" is the best way to describe the success of these transactions. The Financial Times League Tables show fees on M&A transactions for the first 9 months of 2012 of $17.2 billion on $1.4 trillion of transaction value (average fee of 1.22% relative to

transaction value). The important thing to recognize is that these fees were earned by very small deal teams which are highly compensated. See: http://markets.ft.com/investmentBanking/tablesAndTrends.asp (accessed November 26, 2012).

[52] The Administrative & Support Services segment includes a broad variety of services, such as facilities support services, employment services, temporary help services, document support services, call centers, telemarketing, collection agencies, credit bureaus, travel agencies, security services, armored car services, landscaping services, carpet cleaning services, janitorial services, etc.

[53] It should be noted that the 7.0% of GDP spent on ambulatory care services, hospitals, nursing facilities, and residential care facilities is private expenditures only. The WHO figure of 17.9% includes government expenditures on healthcare, which would include both Medicare and Medicaid. In addition, the classification of health care in the WHO statistics and in US GDP statistical reporting may be different so that, in any case, they may not be directly comparable.

[54] C. Brett Lockard and Michael Wolf, "Employment outlook: 2010-2020: Occupational employment projections to 2020," *Monthly Labor Review*, (Bureau of Labor Statistics, p. 84). Available at: http://www.bls.gov/opub/mlr/2012/01/art5full.pdf (accessed November 4, 2012).

[55] Peter Ubel, "It's Physician Pay, Stupid!" *Forbes*, (Pharma & Healthcare post, August 21, 2012). http://www.forbes.com/sites/peterubel/2012/08/21/its-physician-pay-stupid/ (accessed November 4, 2012).

[56] A 2011 OECD report entitled "Why is US Health Care Spending So High?" fails to mention physician pay. Like so many reports, it skirts the issue. This report may be accessed at http://www.oecd.org/unitedstates/49084355.pdf. This report compares the US to Switzerland, Canada, Germany, Japan, and France. It attributes the difference to the following: (1) the cost of in-hospital care is 60% higher; (2) the cost of ambulatory care is 2-1/2 times higher; and (3) the cost of public health administration is 2-1/2 times higher. The report says the US does a good job in cancer care and acute care but a below-average job in primary care.

[57] There is always a temptation to compare the US directly with Germany but the comparison is inapt. Germany has developed a manufacturing sector aimed largely at exports and much of its investment is aimed at that sector. German government policy has aimed strategically at this sector and allowed it to command a larger portion of national income and consumers have not benefitted equally. Due to the size of the US economy, US manufacturing has no need to be centered on exports, nor does the US government play a dominant role in the formulation of US industrial policy. Yet it is clear that Germany invests more than the US. The dilemma for Germany is that its industrial sector, directed towards exports, is suffering in the midst of the current European debt crisis. Europe needs the German consumer to start buying in order to pull the rest of Europe out of recession but switching economic models cannot be made on a dime.

[58] Some might look at the figures and conclude that a portion of the higher government expenditures in other countries has been "commanded" from

individuals who could have used it for consumption; in other words, consumption is understated in other countries because it is the government which is doing it. While this comment may be true to some extent, it ignores the fact that a portion of government expenditures in both the US and overseas goes for "gross investment." Given government's greater role in other countries, it is just as probable that the difference in total private and government investment between other countries and the US is even greater than what is shown in the table.

[59]Nathan Safran, "Demand for SEO Professionals Has Never Been Greater [Study]", *Conductor Blog* (July 11, 2012), http://www.conductor.com/blog/2012/07/demand-for-seo-professionals-has-never-been-greater-study/ (accessed on November 4, 2012).

[60] Joseph A. Schumpeter, *Capitalism, Socialism, and Democracy*, (London: Routledge, 1942, 1994). American business and some on the American right seems to have fallen in love with this term. Obviously, it is hard for anyone else to appreciate the creative side of this process if yours is the job being destroyed, especially when the gap in time between destruction and creation of a new one is often long.

[61] This of course does not address the possibility that the opposite occurs, i.e., that a worker is overcompensated relative to value-added, which we can see in portions of today's financial sector.

[62] EBITDA = earnings before interest, taxes, depreciation, and amortization.

[63] The Occupational Outlook Handbook may be accessed at: http://www.bls.gov/ooh/.

Chapter 4

Painful Transition

Introduction

This chapter assumes that the downward progression that started with the *shock* of the market crash has continued and that we are now in the midst of the structural breakdown discussed in the preceding chapter. Thus Chapters 3 and 4 must be read, in a sense, hand-in-hand. What will be the impact of this structural breakdown?

Adapting in Place

To help us think from a broader perspective, we would like to start with a subject which may at first seem off-topic: immigration to the US. We are fond of saying that immigrants came to the US in search of a better life and in search of freedom, and that is all true. Yet what is equally true is that the economies and societies in their countries of origin failed them. The major waves of US immigration occurred prior to World War I. Let us look at some of them.

	Table 4.1
Country	**Reasons for Emigration**
Ireland	Irish immigration has occurred throughout US history, but the period of greatest immigration was after the potato famine of the 1840s, which produced a *shock* that caused many to starve and altered Irish society. With much of the land in Ireland in the hands of English landlords, many saw a bleak future. Waves of immigration have occurred ever since as Ireland has failed to produce sufficient jobs for its young people. Many returned to Ireland during the Celtic Tiger period of the 2000s but, with the collapse of the real estate boom, net emigration has begun once again.
Scotland	Scottish immigration has occurred throughout US history but the period of greatest emigration began after the Battle of Culloden in 1746, which suppressed clan uprisings aimed at placing the Catholic James VII of Scotland on the throne of

	England. In part to undermine the basis of the clans' strength, the English government supported a program of land enclosure under which both Scottish and English aristocrats began clearing the land of population to pave the way for an economy based on sheepherding. Note that most Scottish farmers were tenants and so had no right to farm their land. The aristocrats termed this program of land clearances "improvements." Many Scots were forced off their lands into small communities on the coast where they fell into poverty. Many emigrated to Nova Scotia and the US. In the mid-19th century, Scotland experienced its own potato famine accompanied by a cholera epidemic. Many emigrated then as well. The Scottish economy has remained sluggish since the *shock* of the land clearances, even up until the present day.
Germany	The majority of immigration from Germany came prior to its unification in 1871, which was the triumph of Bismarck's years as Chancellor. The Thirty Years War of 1618-1648, a religious war with political dimensions, was trans-European with much of it fought on what is now German territory. The Treaty of Westphalia of 1648 put an end to the sclerotic remnants of the Holy Roman Empire, leaving a crazy-quilt of German states in its place. Some of these were Protestant, some Catholic. While outright warfare had ended, oppression on the basis of religion continued state-by-state. The devastation of the War created great human suffering, with population in the German states estimated to have fallen by 25-40% over the thirty years (percentage-wise, far greater than the impact of World Wars I and II combined). This suffering caused many to leave their native lands for other states which welcomed their co-religionists, but many found themselves landless as a result. It is not possible to point to a shock as prominent as famine and land clearances as a reason for German emigration (furthermore, there was no "wave" as there was for the Irish), but the aftermath of such a devastating war was certainly very important. German emigration slowed after unification, presumably because life for the average German was then more stable.
Italy	Much of southern Italy was agricultural during the 19th century and there was a shortage of land relative to its growing population. Similar to Germany, Italy prior to 1861 had been ruled by city-states, with many of those ruling poorly. Southern Italy and Sicily fought against Garibaldi and Victor

	Emmanuel II, but the latter won and achieved unification in 1861 (*il Risorgimento*). Unification brought harsher rule to the south because it had chosen the losing side. Unification was the *shock* that led to increased emigration. The greatest wave of Italian emigration to the US came during the period 1880-1920, with the central government in Rome actively encouraging emigration as a solution to overpopulation in the south.
Russia	The greatest wave of Russian immigration took place in the late 19th and early 20th centuries. Harsh oppression, starting with the pogroms of 1881-1882, was encouraged by the Tsar and caused Russian Jews to flee. A schism within the Russian Orthodox Church also caused emigration. Although the serfs had been freed in 1861, they still had no land: landholding was still concentrated within the aristocracy. Lack of land and the backwardness of the Russian agricultural sector were undoubtedly contributing factors, but religious oppression was the *shock* which caused people to leave.
Poland	Prior to World War I, the Poles were an oppressed minority, divided under the rule of the Russia, Austria-Hungary, and Prussia following the defeat of Kosciousko in 1795. Many departed Poland in the early 19th century. There were repeated uprisings over the course of the 19th century, which were quickly suppressed. Under Prussia and Russia in particular, active measures were taken to erase Polish culture. The growing Polish population could not be accommodated within the available land. Many turned from being landless farmers to migrant laborers. Religious oppression also contributed to emigration, with Polish Jews under harsh anti-Semitic laws. Russian Orthodoxy also discriminated against Polish Catholics and they emigrated as well. The bulk of the emigration took place in the late 19th century up until World War I, at a time when life for the average Pole was most unsettled and Russian rule the harshest. One can point to many conditions which contributed to emigration but no individual *shock*. The only event of singular importance was the Russo-Japanese War of 1905 and the subsequent social, political, and economic turmoil which led to the 1905 Russian Revolution. The textile and iron foundry industries in and around Lodz, like much of Russian industry, experienced depression-like conditions after 1905, and Polish labor began emigrating to the rest of Europe and the US to find jobs.
China	China experienced years of political and economic turmoil

	during the waning decades of the Manchu Qing Dynasty. The Taiping Rebellion of 1850-1864, which took place in southern China, was the singular *shock*. The Rebellion is estimated to have been directly responsible for 20-30 million deaths. The economy was devastated. The people were in poverty and the government could do little to help them. Under pressure from its large population, available land had always been an issue. Chinese men, mostly from southern China, began to emigrate in the second half of the 1800s in order to find work, many drawn by jobs in US railroad construction as a way to support their families in China. While many of them returned to China at some point, many stayed and married Chinese women who emigrated to become brides. US fear of the "yellow peril" led to repeated acts of racial discrimination starting with the Chinese Exclusion Act of 1882. Normal Chinese immigration was only permitted after World War II.
Japan	The Meiji Restoration of 1868 was a *shock* which created rapid economic change and unsettled political and social conditions. Many did not benefit from this change, particularly in the agricultural sector where availability of land was an ongoing issue. Large numbers of Japanese emigrated to Hawaii and the West Coast thereafter and took up low-skill jobs, particularly in agriculture. The restrictions on Chinese immigration after 1882 helped open the doors to Japanese immigration still wider: US employers still wanted low-priced labor whatever the source, but they preferred labor that was less restive and less likely to be influenced by the nascent union movement. Again due to fear of the "yellow peril," Japanese immigration was limited beginning in 1907. The Immigration Act of 1924 banned immigration for almost all Japanese. Significant immigration from Japan did not resume until new legislation was passed in 1965.

One is struck by the courage of American immigrants and of American pioneers who left the Eastern seaboard for the West. They left parents, siblings, friends, and community behind, knowing they would likely never see them again. One wonders whether courage of similar magnitude can be found in any developed country today given the relative ease of modern life. Yet one is also struck by how bad things must have been for people to pack up and leave. Conditions in each country may have been truly harsh for centuries but, suddenly, the various *shocks* which weave through Table 4.1 made them unbearable. Even in those countries where we cannot discern a single shock, some tipping point must have been reached even if we cannot make it out. Also weaving through Table 4.1 is land. The world of the 19th century was largely agricultural, with wealth and sense of well-being usually measured in terms of landholding. Yet much of the population did not own land. Most were tenant-farmers, some under conditions little better than slavery. The US offered a path of escape from unbearable conditions at home. More important, it offered the prospect of a brighter future: the Homestead Act of 1862 provided free land to those who could meet its conditions. The attraction of free land was irresistible for farming households who had never owned any. Added to free land was the prospect of public education in many cities and towns, something unheard of in many of the countries of origin.

We have assumed the US economy has experienced a *shock*. With the possible exception of Canada, no large country in the world today welcomes immigrants the way the US did in the late 19th and early 20th century. Thus, there is nowhere Americans can go to escape the aftereffects of a shock and seek a better life. Even if Canada opened its doors freely, there is based on its population of ~35 million clearly a limit on its ability to absorb immigrants from a country as large as the US. The "safety valve" that the US offered countries of origin 150 years ago no longer exists. There is no way for the US economy to "let off steam" in terms of exporting its "excess" work force even though a breakdown in the US economic model would mean that it has failed to provide for the welfare of a significant portion of its citizens, just like the countries of origin of the past. Even if a "safety valve" were available, it is not clear that Americans will have been beaten down enough to want to leave; while the future may look negative through our eyes today, conditions in America are nowhere near as severe as during the era of immigration. In the end, it appears that American workers are stuck in place and so must adapt to a new economic model in place. Furthermore, there is nothing so spectacular as free land or free public education that points to a brighter future elsewhere. There is no "greener grass."

Many Americans and Canadians moved to Detroit during the 1920s when Henry Ford started offering $5 per day. That period saw great mobility within the US labor force but Chart 4.1 shows a far less mobile America today.[64] Part of this is undoubtedly due to two-income households that were touched on in Chapter 3. A *shock* will likely change US mobility patterns. If Americans cannot emigrate, then they will at least have to become more open to moving within the US if they want to attain a better future for their families. Without moving, Americans will be tied to local economic conditions which, due to the breakdown in the US economic model, may no longer be able to sustain household income. A greater openness to relocation is probably the first change we will see in the American lifestyle in the aftermath of a shock. In this small way, America in the midst of an economic breakdown may resemble the age of immigration.

Chart 4.1
US Geographic Mobility, 1948-2011
Source : US Census Bureau

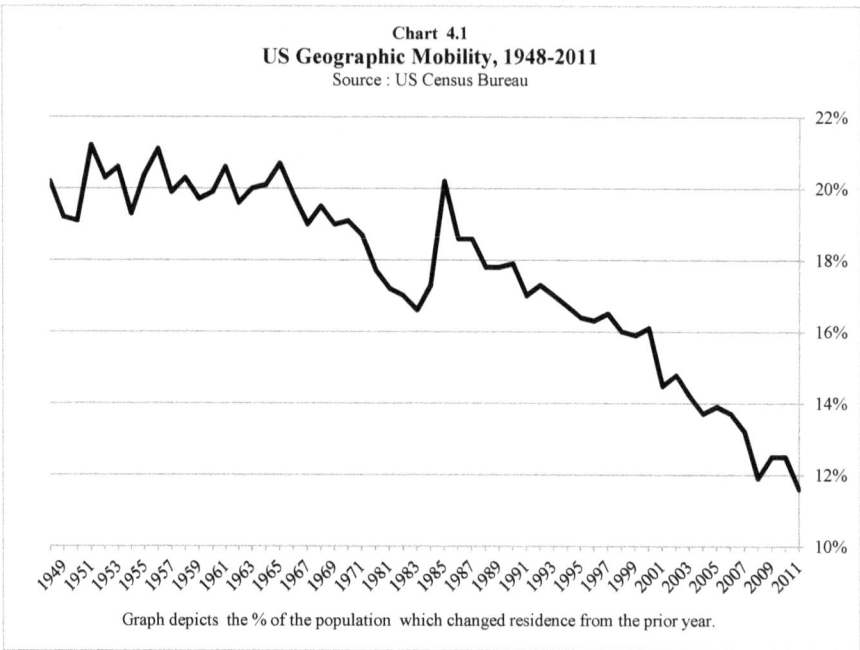

Graph depicts the % of the population which changed residence from the prior year.

Decline in Jobs and Wages and the Possible Emergence of Deflation

Chapter 3 forecasted decline in service sector employment in the wake of a shock. This means there will be a large number of individuals whose skills will no longer be in demand. Those individuals will now compete for those jobs which remain but there will be fewer of those because so many sectors of the economy will be struggling. Let us be very clear: a breakdown in the US economic model will look like economic collapse in the eyes of many. Any period of heavy job loss feels like economic collapse even if the economic statistics might say otherwise.

124

Competition for jobs will directly affect wage rates and household income growth will remain sluggish. Pressure on wage rates, coupled with industrial malaise, has the potential to bring on deflation, which will produce a further fall in asset values. As during Japan's Lost Decade, it is very difficult to recover quickly once deflation has begun. Under deflation, every actor in the economy hesitates to spend, hesitates to invest. The thought process works like this: why should I lay out my precious dollars and buy something today when I can buy it cheaper a few months from now? Breaking a deflationary mindset takes years. If it has taken decades and multiple shocks to break the US economy's reliance on consumption, then we cannot expect to overcome the deflationary mindset easily, for this mindset will almost certainly accompany a breakdown in the US economic model.

Japan and the Lost Decade

Some might ask whether it is appropriate to use the Japanese experience as a standard of comparison. We have already spoken a number of times about Japan's Lost Decade (1991-2000). The reader might ask: was it really that bad? Based on the Charts 4.2 – 4.5, some might argue that the Lost Decade was indeed "not that bad." Perhaps the reader was expecting conditions like the Great Depression. The Lost Decade was clearly not that. We note 1.1% CAGR in GDP, .9% CAGR in per capita GDP, and 1.0% CAGR in non-energy, non-food CPI over the period. Yes, unemployment did climb, from a low base of 2.1% in 1990, but it still remained lower than current US unemployment rates.[65]

Chart 4.2
Japan: Annual Real Growth in GDP
Source: OECD

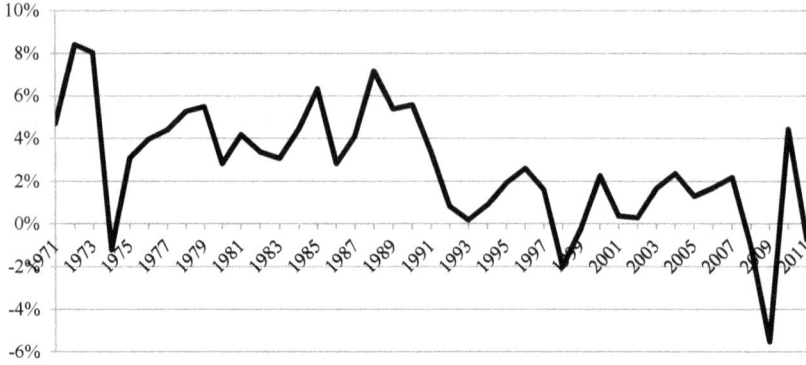

1.1% compound annual growth for the Lost Decade, 1991-2000

Chart 4.2
Japan: Annual Change in Consumer Prices
Source: OECD

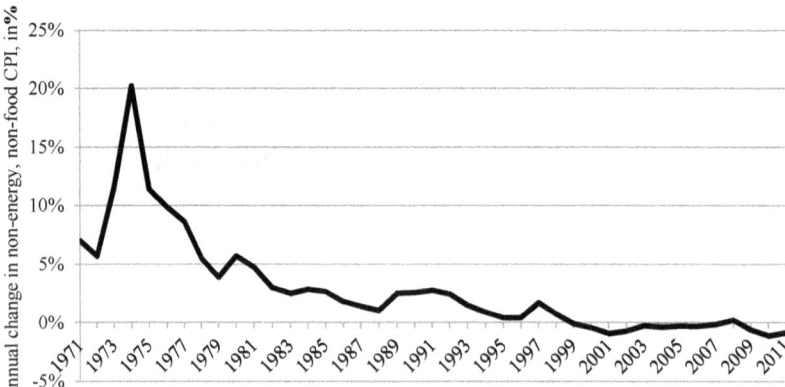

1.0% compound annual change, for Lost Decade, 1991-2000

Chart 4.4
Japan: Unemployment Rate
Source: ILO

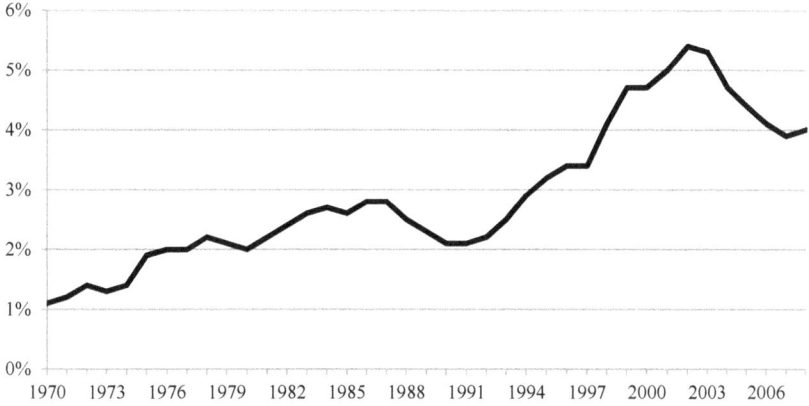

Chart 4.5
Japan: Real GDP Growth Per Capita
Source: OECD

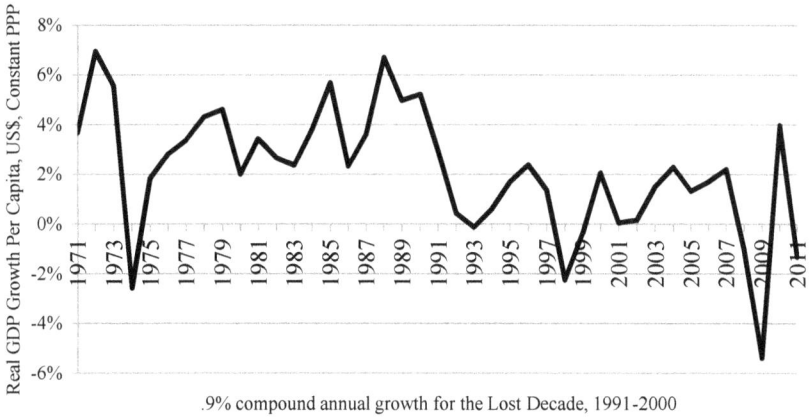

.9% compound annual growth for the Lost Decade, 1991-2000

Even so, these figures are clearly mediocre. It is hard to call them "not that bad" whatever one had expected to see. Furthermore, what the graphs do show is that the phrase "Lost Decade" is a misnomer, completely misleading. What the data in fact shows us is a Lost Score, a lost 20 years. For the period 1991-2007 (before the worldwide recession and the Japanese tsunami), GDP CAGR was just 1.1%, GDP per capita CAGR was just 1.0%, and CPI CAGR was just .4%. In fact, consumer prices had a compound annual rate of decline of -.5% from 2000 to 2007. Thus the real period of deflation was subsequent to the Lost Decade and the deflationary mindset remains a threat to Japan that hinders its ability to grow even today. Only unemployment showed a dip from its 2003 high but it was still only slightly better than 2000. The conclusion is that the period of adjustment after the collapse of Japan's large bubble has been extremely long. The Lost Decade and its aftermath were not an economic depression. Rather this was a period of lost opportunity impossible to recoup.

The real cost of the Lost Decade was thus opportunity cost, not direct economic losses: Japan's vigor had already been spent during years of fevered speculation. When that speculation broke, its economic model was literally drained, and it has spent the last 20 years trying to get back on its feet. Surely one can point to errors in Japanese fiscal and monetary policy that made recovery much harder than it should have been. One can even argue with good reason that the US economy is much more flexible than that of Japan and so may be able to avoid many of its mistakes. Nevertheless, based on Japan's experience, and although no one can predict with accuracy how long US adjustment to a new economic model might take, we need to consider the possibility that it will take a very long time. The reason for this is that the US reliance on consumption and the service sector has grown over many decades and we, like pre-1990 Japan, have squandered many opportunities. It is hard to believe we could switch gears to a new model in just 2-4 years after such a long period of imbalance.

Wage rates will stop falling when supply equals demand and when—equalized for the quality and productivity of the labor force and the value-added it produces—they are in rough balance with other countries. This is of course a great statement in economic theory which is hard to prove empirically. We lack the detailed data to make real-time analyses of what will be happening; rather, we can only make conclusions about 2-3 years after wage adjustments have already taken place—and then they may already be in the process of adjusting further. During the age of immigration, the labor force in one country was isolated from every other because international trade was a minor component of global production. Today we have a global economy in which imports and exports are extremely important. In the age of immigration, labor had to move physically in order to find decent wages and working conditions. Today, given the internet, a sophisticated international telecommunications infrastructure, and a dynamic intermodal shipping network, many services and (sometimes) goods can theoretically be provided from any corner of the world. It is no longer necessary for workers to emigrate to get a decent job. American workers thus face more direct competition today than at any time in the past. Quality of the labor force in any country was never particularly important when each country produced in relative isolation. Quality of the American labor force is now critically important because against India, China, and other emerging markets, the US worker cannot win based on cost alone. The US must focus on the quality of its labor force, which includes technological superiority, in order to overcome cost differentials with other countries. A high quality labor force is the key to making the transition to a new economic model.

The Importance of Education

Quality of the labor force starts with education, even for those who are already working. Much concern has been expressed over the past decade about America's falling position relative to other countries. Rankings on the 2009 PISA test given to 15 year-olds, as shown in Table 4.2, are the best known. As the Table shows, the US ranked 17th in reading, 31st in math, and 23rd in science, a mediocre performance given a level of education spending which far exceeds OECD averages. Furthermore, 42% of the 15-year olds in 2009 failed to attain Level 3 on the 2009 PISA reading test, which means they are theoretically not qualified for upper secondary or college education. A level of 42% means that these 15-year olds may face a fundamental barrier to attaining higher skilled jobs or performing well in college. While 42% is close to the OECD average, some countries do far better. China, Korea, and Finland have ratios of just above 20%.

Of greater concern is the percentage of American students which fails to graduate from high school. Chart 4.6 shows that the US graduation rate ranks 21st, reflecting a drop-out rate of 23.6%. Drop-out rates in inner city schools far exceed 23.6%.

A third area bears watching. The US ranks in the top 5 for the percentage of its adult population that has attained a college degree; at 41%, its percentage exceeds the OECD average by 11%. This advantage rests on the high percentage of older US citizens which has a college degree. Yet the US is the only country where attainment levels among those just entering the labor market (ages 25-34) do not exceed those about to leave it (ages 55-64). The US ranks #15 among 34 OECD countries for attainment of a college education among 25-34 year-olds. We suspect that this is because of the increasing cost of earning a US degree, far more than in other OECD countries.[66]

Many use statistics like those outlined to question whether the US can remain competitive. They effectively doubt our ability to make a transition to a new economic model. Far too often, these questions bleed into fears that the US is declining, falling behind, particularly with respect to China. Many are disturbed by the fact that Chinese GDP is likely to eclipse US GDP in the near future, while ignoring the fact that the US is far richer with per capita GDP seven times that of China. The theory of US decline has been grist for the mill of numerous books over the past decade, many pointing to China as a threat. One cannot help but sense an erudite, but still racist, undercurrent similar to the "yellow peril" lurking among many of these.[67] One is also struck by the similarity in themes between these books and those on Japan prior to 1990.[68] One has never seen waves of books with textures like these written about European nations. One ventures to say, but with some hesitation, that even books written about the USSR prior to the fall of the Berlin Wall, do not have the same feel as books about China today or Japan during the 1980s.

Table 4.2
RANKINGS IN READING, MATH & SCIENCE

| | On the overall reading scale | On the reading subscales | | | | | On the mathematics scale | On the science scale |
		Access and retrieve	Integrate and interpret	Reflect and evaluate	Continuous texts	Non-continuous texts		
Shanghai-China	556	549	558	557	564	539	600	575
Korea	539	542	541	542	538	542	546	538
Finland	536	532	538	536	535	535	541	554
Hong Kong-China	533	530	530	540	538	522	555	549
Singapore	526	526	525	529	522	539	562	542
Canada	524	517	522	535	524	527	527	529
New Zealand	521	521	517	531	518	532	519	532
Japan	520	530	520	521	520	518	529	539
Australia	515	513	513	523	513	524	514	527
Netherlands	508	519	504	510	506	514	526	522
Belgium	506	513	504	505	504	511	515	507
Norway	503	512	502	505	505	498	498	500
Estonia	501	503	500	503	497	512	512	528
Switzerland	501	505	502	497	498	505	534	517
Poland	500	500	503	498	502	496	495	508
Iceland	500	507	503	496	501	499	507	496
United States	**500**	**492**	**495**	**512**	**500**	**503**	**487**	**502**
Liechtenstein	499	508	498	498	495	506	536	520
Sweden	497	505	494	502	499	498	494	495
Germany	497	501	501	491	496	497	513	520
Ireland	496	498	494	502	497	496	487	508
France	496	492	497	495	492	498	497	498
Chinese Taipei	495	496	499	493	496	500	543	520
Denmark	495	502	492	493	496	493	503	499
United Kingdom	494	491	491	503	492	506	492	514
Hungary	494	501	496	489	497	487	490	503
Portugal	489	488	487	496	492	488	487	493
Macao-China	487	493	488	481	488	481	525	511
Italy	486	482	490	482	489	476	483	489
Latvia	484	476	484	492	484	487	482	494
Slovenia	483	489	489	470	484	476	501	512
Greece	483	468	484	489	487	472	466	470
Spain	481	480	481	483	484	473	483	488
Czech Republic	478	479	488	462	479	474	493	500

131

Country								
Slovak Republic	477	491	481	466	479	471	497	490
Croatia	476	492	472	471	478	472	460	486
Israel	474	463	473	483	477	467	447	455
Luxembourg	472	471	475	471	470	472	489	484
Austria	470	477	471	463	470	472	496	494
Lithuania	468	476	469	463	466	462	477	491
Turkey	464	467	459	473	461	461	445	454
Dubai (UAE)	459	458	457	466	461	460	453	466
Russian Federation	459	469	467	441	453	452	468	478
Chile	449	444	452	452	444	444	421	447
Serbia	442	449	445	430	433	438	442	443
Bulgaria	429	430	436	417	429	421	428	439
Uruguay	426	424	423	436	426	421	427	427
Mexico	425	433	418	432	423	424	419	416
Romania	424	423	425	426	423	424	427	428
Thailand	421	431	416	420	418	423	419	425
Trinidad and Tobago	416	413	419	413	415	417	414	410
Colombia	413	404	411	422	414	409	381	402
Brazil	412	407	406	424	411	408	386	405
Montenegro	408	408	420	383	417	398	403	401
Jordan	405	394	410	407	408	387	387	415
Tunisia	404	393	393	427	405	393	371	401
Indonesia	402	399	397	409	400	399	371	383
Argentina	398	394	398	402	399	391	388	401
Kazakhstan	390	397	397	373	392	371	405	400
Albania	385	380	393	376	375	366	377	391
Qatar	372	354	379	376	373	361	368	379
Panama	371	363	372	377	374	359	360	376
Peru	370	364	371	368	373	356	365	369
Azerbaijan	362	361	373	335	362	351	431	373
Kyrgyzstan	314	299	327	300	319	293	331	330

Statistically significantly above the OECD average

Not statistically significantly different from the OECD average

Statistically significantly below the OECD average

Source: OECD PISA (Program for International Student Assessment) 2009 database. 500 is the OECD average, standard deviation is 100.

132

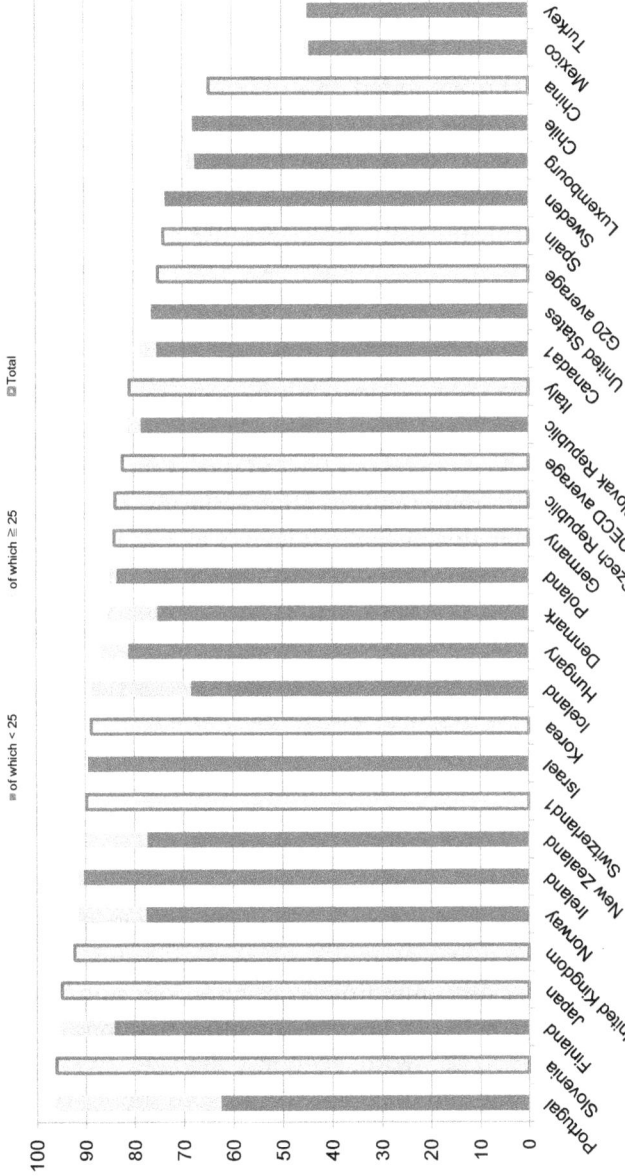

Chart 4.6 Upper secondary graduation rates (2009)

■ of which < 25 ☐ of which ≧ 25 ☒ Total

1. Year of reference 2008. <25 = less than 25 years of age at graduation. >= means 25 years of age or older at graduation.
Countries are ranked in descending order of the upper secondary graduation rates in 2009.
Source: OECD. China: UNESCO Institute for Statistics (World Education Indicators Programme). Table A2.1. See Annex 3 for notes
(www.oecd.org/edu/eag2011).

In spite of the fears about the strength of its education system, the US stands ahead of the world in science, technology, engineering, and mathematics (STEM), whether in industry, education, jobs, or R&D. Per the National Science Board:[69] (1) knowledge and technology-intensive industries (KITI) represented 30% of global economic output in 2007; (2) US KITI represented 38% of GDP in 2007 (note that this figure is not comparable with the presentation in Chapter 3) versus 23% for China; (3) US share of global KTI was 34% in 2007 versus 5% for China; (4) the US has a 33% share of the $1.1 trillion spent on R&D worldwide in 2007, versus 13% for Japan and 9% for China; and (5) STEM continues to represent about 25-33% of undergraduate degrees. The world also recognizes US superiority in STEM post-graduate education: foreign students represented ~24% of US STEM masters degrees, ~33% of US STEM PhD's, and ~57% of those who undertook STEM post-doctoral study in 2006. While some look with alarm at these statistics and use them to allege American weakness in STEM, about 75% of foreign students studying for PhDs said they intended to remain in the US after graduation. Thus America stands to benefit from immigrants just as it always has. While it is true that America's international trade in KITI products has fallen into deficit (with China moving into surplus), it is hard to find hard evidence of American decline here.

Many of those arguing for American decline see the global economy as a zero-sum game: the rise of China means an inevitable decline in the US. This viewpoint is simplistic. While the US certainly has political, economic, and social issues to address, the overblown rhetoric makes it seem that other countries, and particularly China, have almost none. Furthermore, far too much of the analysis is written from a trendline, as if the Chinese economy will grow to the moon. We have already spoken to the danger of reliance on trendlines and at the same time ignoring that growth is normally up-and-down for all countries and especially emerging economies.[70] In sum, we do not see why the _relative_ growth of China or any other nation is necessarily negative for the US. If the world economy manages to keep growing and the US participates in that growth…ah, but there's the rub.

To restate where we are: we have posited a new market crash accompanied by a credit crunch. We have posited a consequent breakdown in the US economic model with a long period of readjustment thereafter. We have posited that the US labor force must adjust as well. During this period of readjustment, it is likely that US economic growth will remain sluggish. We have said that the key to making that adjustment is remaining competitive, by producing high value-added goods and services, and that the major factor in remaining competitive is a well-trained work force. Americans are presently focused on quality of education and certainly, with increased focus, many of the well-known problems discussed can be addressed, particularly in the better school systems around the country.

There is one education barrier, however, which will be very difficult to overcome in the wake of a shock: high school drop-outs and the percentage of Americans as a whole whose education and technical training remain inadequate relative to the needs of today's economy. Continued high drop-out rates will slow a transition to any type of new economic model. Surveys show many reasons for why people drop out. In some cases it is the outright rigor of the curriculum for which they were not prepared in earlier grades; furthermore, there is usually little assistance available to help them catch up. An equally important reason is lack of motivation: students see nothing of value coming at the end of four years of high school and so see no need to stay. College is rarely presented as an option. The importance of technical skills is not emphasized. The higher income available to those earning a college degree or attaining proficiency in technical skills is not made clear. Furthermore, the attitudes of family, friends and even teachers are not supportive and problems in some families often weigh heavily on student ability to stay in school. Though no one explicitly says so, students come to believe there is no better future available through school, so why not start working right now?

Drop-outs are thrown into a world of low-wage, low-skill jobs with little opportunity for growth or advancement. The Bureau of Labor Statistics showed the following unemployment rates by education level for October 2012.

Table 4.2	
Education Level Achieved	**Unemployment Rate**
Less than high school	12.2%
High school graduate	8.4%
Some college or associate degree	6.9%
Bachelor's degree or higher	3.8%
Overall	7.9%

Schools with high drop-out rates are failing both children and their parents. By whatever measure one uses, the future of high school drop-outs will be very difficult. Most of today's drop-outs go into service jobs. If the US economic model breaks down, many of those jobs will disappear. Unemployment among those without a high school diploma can be expected to move above where it stands today. Furthermore, those who remain employed will continue to be poorly paid.

There is already a wide gap in earnings between the high school graduate and the college-educated. A breakdown in the US economic model risks widening that gap. The ramifications of such a development can only be negative for the rest of the economy and for society as a whole. Much has been written about income inequality in the US. OECD data shows a US Gini coefficient (which measures income dispersion) of .38 versus an OECD average of .31; only Chile, Mexico, and Turkey have higher coefficients. Sweden, Denmark, and Norway had the lowest coefficients, ~.24 -.25 (a coefficient of 0 means that all segments are equal, a coefficient of 1 that segments are "perfectly" unequal).[71] In the absence of a path for those at the bottom to move ahead, income inequality is likely to grow. This risks creating a two-tier society, with the one on top doing fairly well and the other a permanent underclass many of whom will lack a high school diploma and technical skills. A two-tier system will probably bring dramatic change to the American way of life. Americans have always held to the myth that they live in a classless society. A breakdown in the US economic model will likely shatter that myth forever, with outcomes indeterminable.

Only the US and two other OECD countries spend less on disadvantaged students than on advantaged ones. In addition, good, experienced teachers have little incentive to move to inner city schools. Note as well that the average US teacher earns just 65% of his or her degreed counterpart in private industry, as compared to 85% in other OECD countries; thus there are few financial incentives to take on demanding educational tasks. Without adequate support, there is little way for inner city and other disadvantaged students to find a path to the future under a new economic model. While there have been many successful experiments and projects in inner cities which have improved quality of education in localized settings, the drop-out rate in inner city schools still exceeds the national average. Solving this issue requires more than one-time projects that benefit only a few but, when the subject is raised, many respond that 'throwing money at the problem solves nothing.' Rather they are quick to blame parents, the students themselves, and a so-called culture of poverty. While there may be elements of truth in these accusations, there is a certain inner peace that comes with playing the blame game: they can justify doing nothing and still go to church each Sunday with a clear conscience.

It is hard to believe that the US can create a new economic model if it leaves significant portions of its population behind. Some may cynically state that the poor will always be with us and so sit on their hands, yet if the goal is to achieve satisfactory growth in household income, then that means all or most households, not just a few. Households struggling along at the bottom not only hurt the statistics. They hurt overall economic demand and so drag on the rest of the economy. Moreover, they have the highest demand for government services and thereby make it harder to close government deficits. It is surely less costly over the long-term to support a path towards decent jobs than to leave people on public assistance.

Quite frankly, it is probably too late for the 47 year-old maid or the 53 year-old construction worker without high school diplomas to be retrained. They themselves know it. But even they, contrary to some of the rhetoric, want better lives for their children. If parents see a sincere effort to provide better education for their children, they will buy in to it and be supportive, but if they feel the effort is half-hearted, focused on standardized testing and little else, they will sit on their hands. Nobody said it was going to be easy but, if we are going to retool America, we have to start with basic blocking-and-tackling, making sure education is the path of opportunity for all Americans, the same path which served immigrants so well years ago. Indeed, if "education means opportunity" were stressed during every school day across America, the mindset towards education in this country would change dramatically just because of the rote repetition. Chinese, Koreans, Japanese, Indians, Israelis, and others understand the linkage of education to personal and macroeconomic success all too well. We can at least match them there.

Leaving the issue of high school graduation and education as a path to opportunity aside for the moment, one subject must be raised that some will find controversial. We continue to hear commentators say that American-born students are deliberately trying to avoid math and the sciences except when required. Even though the data shows that 25-33% of all undergraduate degrees are in STEM subjects (and only a small percentage of STEM <u>undergraduates</u> is foreign), this belief persists, perhaps in part due to the concentration of foreign students in STEM <u>graduate</u> programs. Although we have heard many anecdotes, we know of no data that can substantiate the contention of STEM-avoidance. Nevertheless, we are willing, for the sake of argument, to consider the proposition.

The reason why we believe it may be true is that today's generation of parents and the baby boomers have been beneficiaries of a revitalization of the US economy after World War II. We believe most have had it relatively easy when compared to the generations that preceded them. Since they have had it relatively easy, they have often found no reason to set extremely high expectations for their children. After all, they had been able to find jobs fairly easily; why wouldn't their children? They were willing to provide their children a good deal of choice in both field of study and other areas because they believed jobs would be readily available, whether in manufacturing or the service sector. Now that proposition is fraying around the edges for many families and it will be in tatters in the wake of a shock. Many surveys report that many American parents do not believe their children will be better off than they are.

Americans need to begin thinking of how to add a bit more structure to their children's lives. Education means opportunity as much as for those in the suburbs as it does for those in the inner city. Children must be guided to understand this. They need to understand that well-rounded education means being grounded in a wide variety of subjects. Even if a child has no interest in pursuing STEM after graduation from high school, he or she must still be guided to get exposure to those subjects. The American educational system is generally praised for its ability to create analytical, creative thinkers, unlike some other countries where rote learning plays a greater role. Analytical, creative thinking rests on having a good base of fundamental knowledge. Even if your child is going into non-STEM areas, he or she needs to understand that the world of today is technologically far more complex than even a decade ago. To address the world successfully, every child must understand the basics of math, science, and technology. Moreover, whatever the profession, a child needs to understand that success means developing skills, skills that help one stand out from others. Knowing how to navigate from screen to screen on an iPad is not a real skill. Furthermore, and especially for those children bound for STEM professions, parents must encourage good writing skills. All high school graduates, STEM and non-STEM, must understand that the ability to communicate well, both orally and in writing, is critical to success in every job.

Early Warning Signs

These early warning signs should provide information that will enable us to determine whether the current economic model is spent in order that we can begin transitioning to a new economic model. Nowhere in Chapter 3 or in Chapter 4 to this point did we highlight in detail how a breakdown might look. These warning signs provide a stark picture of what we might see.

Growth in household income shows no sign of improvement.

Employment in non-technology service sectors remains flat or turns downward for more than three consecutive quarters.

Poverty rises, as shown in US Government statistics.

Demand for unemployment insurance, food stamps, and Medicaid rises materially above current levels.

Default rates on credit cards, mortgages, and other types of consumer debt begin to rise. Default rates on high-yield debt also begin to rise.

American cities experience increased stress, as indicated by greater budgetary issues and other evidence that they cannot serve their citizens as they did before. There is rising incidence of unrest in cities.

Preparation

In Chapter 3, we focused on your job in preparation for a breakdown in the US model. Here we focus not on the workplace but on the home. We ask that you examine how you want to live your life in the midst of this transitional period that promises to be very difficult.

It is all about choice and the choice has to be right for you personally. At one end might be a choice which attempts, if possible, to insulate you and your family from the economic trauma. This choice is only possible if you and your spouse's jobs are relevantly immune from the restructuring which will have to take place. At the extreme, this choice may look like a "gated community" in which you carry on as before as if nothing were going on outside. In order to preserve values and a way of life, some may even choose to remove themselves to separatist communities, religious or otherwise. Making the latter choice would often require that you and your family relocate. That, in and of itself, is a wrenching decision, not to mention having to adapt to what may be an entirely new lifestyle.

On the other hand, you may choose to try to engage in life as it is currently lived. If you make this choice, a number of questions immediately arise. How do I maintain a satisfactory way of life and at the same time engage? If I am one of the ones suffering the brunt of this transition, how do I engage? If I remain well off in relative terms, how do I engage? If I need to relocate to take advantage of opportunities that exist, where will I go and how will I adapt to the new community I am moving into? If I see no need to move, how do I remain engaged with the community I live in?

The feel of American life has changed as Americans have moved to suburbia since World War II. In small towns, people knew each other and, for the most part, interacted with each other. Now in 21st century suburbia, just as in cities, people often do not know their next-door neighbors. Even if they know them, they likely do not interact with them. During a few years while I was growing up, we lived in a small town of 7,000. Large portions of its citizens knew each other. Today that town has grown to 14,000 and become a bedroom community. Even at 14,000, the town is now too big for many to know each other. Furthermore, the composition of the population has changed. Back then, a substantial portion of the population was engaged in farming. Many of those farms are now gone.

The late 20th and early 21st centuries are the era of the so-called nuclear family. Since the founding of the American republic, there have always been two points of view competing for our attention: individualism and community needs. In many ways, individualism appears to be currently in ascendance. Certainly individualism is a theme that unites many of the views of those on the right. Yet even those in the center or on the left do not reject individualism, for

140

celebration of individual opportunity and individual achievement appears to be part of every American's DNA. And those on the right do not reject community needs either. Indeed, much of our current political and social debate centers on how to balance individual and community rights and needs.

For at least three centuries, the underlying premise in political, social, economic, and even scientific thought has been that man and his world both experience and are capable of ongoing progress. This premise has been deduced from man's observation of inventions, rises in industrial production, advances in scientific learning, and rapid technological change and their impact on his way of life. Most history and philosophy has been written from perspectives that look for evidence of progress. The emphasis on progress has been strengthened by the scientific contributions of Charles Darwin, many of which have bowdlerized for popular consumption. He would certainly be surprised to see his theory of evolution conflated with the view that progress is always onward-and-upward. Yet onward-and-upward is the major theme which unites most of Western thought. Any recession, war, or other negative phenomenon is usually viewed as just a bump in the road of inevitable human progress.

Americans have been fortunate in many ways. No war has been fought on American soil since 1865. America somehow survived the Great Depression intact and moved forward. Less than 175 years after its founding, it found itself the strongest military and economic power in the world. It is difficult for Americans to look at history and, despite the many contra-tendencies to which one can point, not see progress as a particularly American theme.

Certainly there have been many dissenters from this theme, starting with the abolitionists and moving on to labor organizers, civil rights advocates, anti-war marchers, and populist movements of every stripe. Yet somehow their voices have been subsumed within the ideal of progress. The view from the rest of the world is more nuanced. War, privation, dislocation, radicalism, the emergence of new nations, the collapse of others, and a history longer than that of the US have given the rest of the world a different perspective. While the rest of the world still believes in progress, the voices of dissenters are much louder in Europe and carry more weight. Perhaps they are just less naïve than Americans. For at least 200 years, Europeans have accused us of being naïve. Maybe a shock of the magnitude we are talking about will cause many Americans to agree with them.

141

A *shock* may cause many Americans to call the whole "progress narrative" into question. The average individual, who presumably does not read political and social philosophy, experiences the shock empirically, first-hand, and wants an answer to one simple question: will my children be better off than me? Negative answers to this question will bring profound changes in how an American engages with his or her world. For some, negative answers even have the potential to veer off into radicalism, a subject which will be addressed in Chapter 5. These negative answers will be looked at as mere bumps in the road for adherents to the "progress narrative," but for Americans who have to live their lives every day, hearing that everything will come out alright in the end provides little comfort. Churchgoers too may be comforted by the vision of an afterlife but they too want better lives today for both themselves and their children.

Americans faced with a question like the one in the previous paragraph may begin to ask other questions. Can I really cope with what is happening all on my own? Or do I need to work with others? Is it reasonable to think I can build a better life for my children all on my own? Some will answer, yes, I can do it by myself because I am sure I can do it. The force of the *shock* will cause others to answer to the contrary. From those individuals, a new sense of community may emerge that will help people adapt during the transition to a new economic model.

What will this new community look like? Let us first say what it cannot be. It cannot be just talking to each other and being nice to each other. Most people think only of these things when they hear words like "sense of community." The times we are talking about will call for far more than this. There must be action, not just discussion. We believe the severity of the times have the potential to push many Americans in that direction.

Those who choose to work with others to address the issues confronting them always face one major dilemma. What can I do? I am just one person. Will what I do make any real difference in the face of such daunting problems? But if you have determined that you cannot manage through this crisis on your own, then you are saying you believe you somehow have to make a difference, even if it is difficult to see the way forward. So it is time to act on that belief. Here are some very basic thoughts about what you can do.

Teach. Everybody knows something. Communicating what you know can strengthen those around you. Teaching others skills they do not know directly addresses the transition so many are facing.

Learn. Everyone needs to bring their knowledge and skills up-to-date, even if they are mundane, day-to-day skills. Learning of any sort refreshes the mind and gives new perspectives. New perspectives are the key to adapting to a new economic model.

Get involved. Schools, churches, local government, and community organizations can be a source of strength in enabling citizens to adapt. Your active participation strengthens them.

Reach out to those you have never spoken to before. Get out of your comfort zone. Understand what others are facing. By understanding what they are facing, you will better understand overall community needs, as well as your own. With this understanding, you can help formulate better plans and "make it happen."

The heart of all this is: do not assume others will do it for you. The modus operandi for many Americans for far too many decades has been: (a) let others do it because we are too busy and our time is much too valuable and then (b) criticize them like hell when we do not like the results, acting like they are boobs, incompetent, and dishonest, using every pejorative phrase we can think of. There is little moderation in today's America. Many of us like to stand on the sidelines and kibbitz. The force of the *shock* will be pulling us into the game. For the sake of our children and future generations, we cannot resist.

Some might accuse this chapter of being mere feel-good pap, pure Mom-and-apple-pie. While that may be true, that does not make it necessarily wrong, particularly for a time of transition to a new economic model. Criticism of this chapter may reflect where people are today, but does that criticism really understand what people will need to survive and move forward? Criticism like this may instead reflect the 2012-2013 mindset: attack first, think later. For it is in times like these, a downward spiral, that we find out what we really believe in. Maybe we really do believe in Mom-and-apple-pie. And what is wrong with that?

[64] Note that gaps in the annual data exist from 1972-1975 and from 1977-1980. Also note that the US Census Bureau has changed the way it has conducted its survey over the years, which means that year-to-year changes may not be directly comparable during certain periods.

[65] One must be very careful when comparing certain statistics like the unemployment rate between countries. We would suggest that it is not the absolute unemployment rate that matters. What matters is the change in unemployment over time. At an unemployment rate of ~2%, Japan had become used to virtual full employment, much of it based on a system of so-called "lifetime employment." We think of "lifetime employment" as descriptive of life throughout Japan prior to 1990. To the contrary, this system prevailed mostly among larger companies. Working life was more tenuous for the rest. Arrival of the Lost Decade brought real change across industrial Japan. Lifetime employment, while not gone, covers fewer companies today. All companies have begun resorting to temporary or contract employees who are not covered by lifetime employment. Larger companies have begun outsourcing functions to smaller companies which are not covered by lifetime employment. Unemployment rose to 5.0% by 2000 and we suggest that was a huge change within the context of Japan. Furthermore, this statistic does not reveal the extent to which workers are now underemployed or have shifted to jobs where they are earning much less than before. In addition, the statistical methods for counting the unemployed tend to vary between countries so that it is hard to say if the US and Japanese unemployment rates are apples-to-apples. Lastly, some have pointed to the high savings rate in Japan as somehow cushioning the fall and have concluded that the average Japanese household was able to survive satisfactorily over the Lost Decade. This comment ignores the fact that they had little choice: the Japanese social "safety net" is far smaller than in the US and Europe. The Japanese had no choice but to rely on their personal savings through a grinding period of slow growth. This is partially confirmed by Japanese household holdings of financial assets (after deducting life insurance reserves): for the 5-year period 1994-1998, household savings were flat-to-down. The reason for lack of growth was either people were not saving or that people were drawing down what they had. We suggest it was more the latter.

[66] OECD, *Education at a Glance 2011: OECD Indicators*, http://www.oecd.org/edu/highereducationandadultlearning/48678896.pdf (accessed November 13, 2012). The reasons why 25-34 year-olds are getting fewer degrees are many. One contributor is the high cost of an American college education, the highest among all OECD countries by a fairly wide margin. Slow growth in household income and uncertainty in the job market has probably caused many to look more closely at the value of post-secondary education. The average American college graduate in 2011 exited school with a debt load of $27,000, a daunting burden in an era of slow job growth. Some have speculated on whether there is not a "higher education bubble" within the US but great controversy surrounds this contention. Yet college tuition and fees have doubled since 2000, this at a time of little growth in household income. Most of this has been

due to rapidly rising salaries and benefits for professors. While they may have been underpaid at one time, it is hard to make this contention today, particularly given the tenure system and the fact that many universities subsidize health care insurance premiums to a greater degree than private industry.

[67] While the author has not read all these books, one is struck by the titles: Matt Buttsworth, *China versus the US: The Chinese Challenge to the World Trading System*, (Buttsworth Books, May 24, 2011). Robert Ross, Oystein Tunsjo, and Zhang Tuosheng, *US-China-EU Relations: Managing the New World Order*, (New York: Routledge, 2011). Martin A. Smith, *Power in the Changing Global Order: The US, Russia and China*, (Malden, MA: Polity Press, 2012). Dambisa Moyo, *Winner Take All: China's Race for Resources and What It Means for the World*, (Toronto: Basic Books, 2012). *Russell Ong, China's Strategic Competition with the United States (Routledge Security in Asia Series)*, (New York: Routledge, 2011). Aaron L. Friedberg, *A Contest for Supremacy: China, America, and the Struggle for Mastery in Asia*, (New York: W.W. Norton & Co, 2012). Rosemary Foot and Andrew Walter, *China, the United States and Global Order*, (Cambridge: Cambridge University Press, 2010). Toshi Yoshihara and James R. Holmes, *Red Star over the Pacific: China's Rise and the Challenge to U.S. Maritime Strategy*, (Newport, RI: Naval Institute Press, 2010). Angang Hu, Cheng Li, and John L. Thornton, *China in 2020: A New Type of Superpower (The Thornton Center Chinese Thinkers Series)*, (Washington: Brookings Institution Press, 2010). Patrick J. Buchanan, *Suicide of a Superpower: Will America Survive to 2025?* (St. Martin's Griffin, 2012).

[68] While the author has not read these books, one is struck by the titles: Jack Seward and Howard van Zandt, *Japan: The Hungry Guest: Japanese Business Ethics vs. Those of the U.S.*, (Tuttle Publishing, 1986). Daniel Burstein, *Yen: Japan's New Financial Empire and its Threat to America*, (New York, Simon & Schuster, 1988). David Halberstam, *The Reckoning*, (New York: William Morrow & Co, 1986). *Japan: A New Kind of Superpower?* (Princeton: Woodrow Wilson Center Press, 1984). There were many more like these published during the 1980s.

[69] National Science Board, Science and Engineering Indicators 2012: A broad base of quantitative information on the U.S. and international science and engineering enterprise, http://www.nsf.gov/statistics/seind12/ (accessed November 13, 2012).

[70] An interesting article on this subject is: Ruchir Sharma, "Broken BRICs: Why the Rest Stopped Rising," *Foreign Affairs* (November/December 2012), p.2. "BRIC" is a newish abbreviation for Brazil, Russia, India, and China.

[71] OECD Economic Surveys: United States, (June 2012). http://www.oecd.org/eco/surveys/Overview%20Eng%20US%20%282%29.pdf (accessed November 13, 2012).

Chapter 5

Onset of Political and Economic Turmoil

Introduction

The previous chapters have shown things getting progressively worse. In Chapter 3, we asked you to address your position in the job market in anticipation of this deterioration. In Chapter 4, we asked you to address how you might respond personally to the stress. Chapter 4 ended on a fairly upbeat note. It gave the impression that confronting the problem and hard work can turn things around. What we have not yet addressed are countervailing pressures, pressures that may make it harder to maintain both your job in the way you envision it and a positive outlook. This chapter takes into account the probability that some will respond to the economic crisis in entirely different ways, ways you may not like to imagine for yourself.

Radicalism

Chapters 3 and 4 show fairly benign responses to the economic crisis facing America, responses which may fit well with your current outlook. On the other hand, the stress of the crisis may radicalize the disaffected, particularly if they find voices in charismatic, powerful leaders. This chapter has its genesis in the last chapter's comment that the *shock* may cause some to veer toward radicalism. This radicalization has the potential to spiral us further downward.

Is there anything necessarily wrong with radicalization or radicalism? Let's start with an anecdote. I had a colleague once who was extremely cynical about everything. He could get cynical about something as simple as a cup of coffee. When we tired of this and called him on it, he would always respond, "Cynicism is just a heightened sense of reality." I do not know if this quote was original (I cannot find it anywhere else), but should we not consider the possibility that radicals might have better insight into the problems and their solutions than our consensus world-view? Echoing what we have said in Chapters 1 and 2, we believe it always makes sense to ask: what if I am wrong? It should be noted that his chapter does not examine the particulars of any radical viewpoint; rather it focuses on the challenges such viewpoints pose to other Americans and the risks that come from not giving them a modicum of respect.

With some notable exceptions, radicals have been on the fringe of American society and not been taken seriously. Organizations like the Black Panthers, the Simbianese Liberation Army, and the Weather Underground may have grabbed headlines but they had no real influence. Three possible exceptions were John Brown, the Ku Klux Klan (KKK), and radicals within the labor movement.

John Brown was on the fringe of the abolitionist movement prior to the Civil War. Most Americans, even if they were against slavery, found abolitionist views too extreme. The purpose of his raid on the federal arsenal in Harpers Ferry, West Virginia in 1859, undertaken with fewer than 25 men, was to arm the slaves so they had the means to rebel. The raid failed miserably and Brown was executed. However quixotic his quest may have been, the raid shocked both North and South. The South became ever more fearful of the Northern intentions and of what abolitionists might do. The North tended to focus on the "nobility" of Brown's quest (presumably forgetting the 1856 Pottawatomie, Kansas massacre) and he was seen as a martyr by many (though others thought he was crazy). His radical action had the effect of moving many in the North closer to abolitionist views, thereby making it easier to consider confrontation with the South as a solution to the slavery issue. Thus one might argue that John Brown was one of many who helped pave the road to the Civil War. If effectiveness is judged by results, it might be argued that he was the most effective radical in US history.

The KKK has had three incarnations. It began after the Civil War but was superseded by other organizations after Reconstruction ended in 1877. It was revived again in 1915. Its heyday came in the early- to-mid-1920s when it had 4-6 million members across the United States, not just in the South. It is estimated that at one point 15% of "eligible" (whatever that means) American men belonged to it. It had real political influence during the 1920s but membership fell to 30,000 by 1930 under the weight of in-fighting, criminal behavior on the part of its leaders, and external opposition. The third version of the Klan gained strength in opposition to the civil rights movement of the 1950s and 1960s yet, at that point in its history, it was more effective at attracting media attention than building a real movement. Throughout its existence, the KKK was, at heart, a nativist group that wanted everything "100% American" (to use the words of Confederate General Nathan Bedford Forrest, its first leader). With no real philosophy, it stood in opposition to anything or anyone that seemed "un-American": blacks, Jews, Catholics, labor organizers, Socialists, Communists, immigrants, and even "wets" during the Prohibition era. At the height of its strength, the KKK put members in political office and fomented violence to meet its objectives; to that degree one might argue it was effective. The question is: was it really radical or did it just reflect the views that many around them held but were afraid to espouse openly?

Over the course of American history, ideas which were at one time considered radical have moved into the mainstream even if our national discourse still does not support all of them: the eight-hour day, the five-day work week, overtime, interracial and same-sex marriage, integration in schools, gays in the military, voting rights for minorities and women, environmentalism, ordination for women, civil rights. Radicalism implies being out of the mainstream, but in the South prior to 1960, many of its core views did not differ in substance from many, maybe the majority of, whites. One might ask whether the KKK really led and had influence during its periods of ascendance or whether it was used by those who found it useful. That it has risen and faded so quickly three times tilts us more toward the latter view.

Anarchists have been on the fringe of the labor movement from its beginnings but many of them have been larger than life: Albert Parsons, Big Bill Haywood, Joe Hill, Mother Jones, Emma Goldman, Sacco & Vanzetti, etc. Rightly or wrongly, anarchists have been associated with some of the great labor struggles in American history: the Great Railroad Strike (1877), the so-called Haymarket Riot or Massacre (1886), the Homestead Strike (1892), and the Colorado Labor Wars (1903-1904). However much their activities were covered in the press, it is hard to decide, in retrospect, how much of an impact they really had. While their writings and speeches set a tone, it is not clear to what degree the rank-and-file absorbed their views.

The most successful quasi-anarchist union was the Industrial Workers of the World (the IWW or the "Wobblies"). Founded in 1905 with Big Bill Haywood as President and Eugene V. Debs one of its many famous founders, it boasted 100,000 members by the early 1920s and claimed to be able to influence even more. It was suppressed after the Red Scare of the early 1920s but it had been fairly effective at union organizing up until then. Nevertheless, it remains a footnote in US labor history.

During its later history, the US labor movement has moved away from radical political action to focus on wages, benefits, hours, and working conditions. It never took the same path as in other countries and many workers moved into the middle class during the latter half of the 20th century. Socialism, in particular with Debs, was a major stream of thought in the union movement during the early part of the 20th century, but it was swept aside under combined pressure from government and business which employed the supposed threat of communism to demonize it.

Today's unions are far from radical, they are supporters of the way things are. In some ways, it is not surprising that labor unions have lost membership over the last few decades. Focusing solely on bread-and-butter issues may meet the needs of workers but is hardly inspiring. Charismatic labor leaders have passed from the scene, replaced by bureaucrats. Indeed, we speculate that many of them would feel just as comfortable at a desk in the Labor Relations Department of General Motors as in a suite at United Auto Workers headquarters across town. Looking back over the last 150 years, one may easily conclude that radicalism — and socialism if one wants to stretch and call it a form of radicalism — has never played much of a role in American life.

American Exceptionalism

The reasons why socialism and more radical political ideas have never taken hold in America, even in the depths of the Depression when one would think workers would have been most receptive to them, has kept academics (and socialist writers who have been astonished to find in the US an exception to the doctrinal "inevitability of socialism") employed for decades. Furthermore, the US is the only major country which has never had a powerful labor or socialist party.[72] Much of the analysis of this subject to date appears to have been written from the viewpoint of "American exceptionalism." One hesitates to use this word because it has become overused and taken on political dimensions. Although it is hard to define, we believe the word is fitting for what we want to say here. Wikipedia defines it as:

> …the proposition that the United States is different
> from other countries in that it has a specific world
> mission to spread liberty and democracy. It is not a

notion that the United States is quantitatively better than other cultures or that it has a superior culture, but rather that it is "qualitatively different." In this view, America's exceptionalism stems from its emergence from a revolution, becoming what political scientist Seymour Martin Lipset called "the first new nation, ... other than Iceland to become independent," and developing a uniquely American ideology based on liberty, egalitarianism, individualism, populism, and laissez-faire. This observation can be traced to Alexis de Tocqueville, the first writer to describe the United States as "exceptional" in 1831 and 1840.

Here are some of the exceptionalist arguments for why socialism in particular and perhaps radicalism in general (whether from the left or the right) have not been able to put down roots in America:[73]

Lack of class structure. The US never went through a feudal period or had defined aristocratic and working classes that divided one citizen from another. On the contrary, egalitarianism and social mobility are long-held American ideals. This argument implies that the ground is most fertile for development of socialism where there is class consciousness.

Influence of religion. Even though the US has never had a state-sponsored religion, Americans are more deeply religious than citizens of other countries. Socialism in its many guises has an anti-religious or anti-clerical element. This argument thus implies that socialism could not co-exist with Americans' spiritual views.

Electoral democracy. The US is the world's oldest electoral democracy. American workers had access to the ballot box earlier than workers in other countries which gave them the sense that they were participating in creating their own future. This argument implies that socialism rests on discontent and that discontent rests on the existence of centralized, powerful, non-representative governments which are unresponsive to workers' needs. Also in this view, because the US has a federal system of government, the central government is not all-powerful and so must listen more closely to citizens' concerns.

Ethnic and racial diversity. This argument appears to argue that socialism has a better chance when it addresses a homogeneous population which will hear its message in much the same way. It is much harder for it to gain footing if it must tailor its message to different groups who interpret its message based on their own particular backgrounds and experience. A corollary to this argument may be that many Americans look on anarchism and socialism as <u>foreign</u> imports incompatible with American life because they have been created by Europeans of various stripes. Implicit in this argument is that many anarchist and socialist labor organizers were unsuccessful precisely because many were foreign-born and were thus seen as un-American. Their backgrounds and experience thus meant they could not deliver the message of socialism or anarchism to the average American.

Meritocracy, self-reliance, individualism. These are core American ideals. Americans believe one can get ahead based on imagination, creativity, skills, and hard work. Under this argument, the "leveling" concept inherent in socialism conflicts directly with Americans' ideals.

Lack of ideology. Under this argument, Americans see themselves as a pragmatic people who take pride in being non-ideological, in contrast to Europeans. Under this view, socialism cannot make headway in the US because it conflicts with Americans' fundamental worldview. Many using this argument also point out that US socialists in the past put far too much emphasis on ideology and party-organizing without paying enough attention to labor-organizing, thereby squandering precious opportunities to strengthen the labor movement. Obviously, this argument also seems to think that American exceptionalism does not rise to the level of being an ideology.

Populism. America has seen a myriad variety of populist movements since its founding. Although the powerful may often co-opt these movements for their own ends, most Americans see change starting from the grass-roots as one of their better traditions. Socialism, on the other hand, is seen as a top-down solution imposed by others without the people's consent. The US worldview thus has an anti-government, anti-statist stream of thought running through it which provides poor soil for the seedlings of socialism.

Success of the US economic model. The US economic model, based on capitalism and free enterprise, has delivered better lives for all Americans, including workers. This argument implies that socialism and radicalism can only gain adherents when an economic model is failing its citizens.

These arguments all contain elements that are true but seem less sturdy when one looks at the facts, the stubborn facts of history. Incorporating the facts into the narrative of American exceptionalism often requires using very tortured logic. Beating the drum of American exceptionalism so loudly can cause one to ignore explanations that may carry weight equal to those discussed.

An Alternative Explanation

There is one possible alternative explanation: socialism and radicalism have failed in the US because they have been repeatedly suppressed by the united force of the state and big business every time they tried to make headway. It was not only that socialism and radicalism failed. Labor organizing itself, even when detached from ideology, has been repeatedly thwarted and the construct of relationships between business and labor that has been built over the past century remains with us today.

We would like to consider three threads of this alternative explanation but, before doing so, we ask the reader to consider first the meaning of the word "worker." Before reading further, stop for a few seconds and ask yourself: *what images arise when I hear this word*? Now proceed. Do you see a blue-collar worker on the factory floor? Is he or she necessarily a member of a union? Do you hear Karl Marx speaking, as in "Workers of the world, unite"? If perhaps you have a white-collar job, does the word "worker" have anything to do with you? If you are in middle or even upper management, is "worker" the antonym of your role in the business world?

"Worker" is freighted with so many meanings. Use of the word elicits predictable reactions depending on context. Those reactions rise from three general sources, the history of the labor movement, Western response over the past century to the Russian Revolution, and day-to-day political rhetoric.

During the period from ~1865 to ~1930, labor's organizing efforts were usually depicted by politicians, business, and newspapers of the time as us-versus-them, with "them" being the workers. The legacy of this divisive depiction remains even as all of us have benefitted from labor's efforts in ways we now take for granted, e.g., the 8-hour day.

The focus shifted after 1917. Most Americans, except for some like Thomas Jefferson, were appalled by the French Revolution's bloodshed; thus Americans usually saw the differences between French and American revolutionaries in sharp relief. Americans, particularly the well-to-do, watched events like the Revolutions of 1848 and the Paris Commune of 1871 with trepidation, particularly in light of America's nascent labor movement. Then, all of sudden a revolution, supposedly aimed at elevating the working class into a position of power, succeeded. This produced a counter-reaction in the US also depicted in us-versus-them terms. The "them" in this case were Communists who espoused a way of life anathema to most Americans. The American labor movement has had to tiptoe very carefully through this minefield ever since in order to accomplish its goals. In the white-hot political atmosphere post-1917, labor had to abandon any political aspirations it may once have had in favor of wages, hours, benefits, and working conditions. Yet when we hear "worker" today, many of us still hear "communist" whispering in our ears due to this legacy.

"Worker" seems to have dropped out of fashion today, particularly in our political rhetoric. The US Presidential campaign of 2012 saw both candidates target their messages toward the "middle class." The poor were rarely mentioned. "Workers" or "working class" were rarely used. Why? First, political operatives believe every American aspires to be a member of the middle class even if he or she is poor. The candidate compliments the voter if he acts like every citizen is already a member. Furthermore, it is easier to target the electorate with one big blanket message instead of slicing-and-dicing it for various constituencies. Second, "workers" and "working class" are not often used by politicians because business and some on the right have successfully conflated these terms with socialism, communism, class warfare, and even un-Americanism — not explicitly but with the tone of their anti-union, anti-labor rhetoric and positions which also serve to promote an us-versus-them view of the world. Each of our own views of life in America today has been in some way shaped by the current state of political discourse.

In the discussion that follows, we will use words like worker and labor frequently, often but not only in a union context because of the history. *Yet we do not mean to suggest that worker = union member.*

154

Rather we ask that the reader remain open to the broader idea that the term can include most of us under its umbrella. For do not most of us work? And how many of us have real power to change conditions in the workplace? This is not a call for worker solidarity. It rather calls for us to recognize that lay-offs can hit any of us, blue-collar or white-collar, union or non-union. Whether you are hourly or salaried, on the factory floor or in middle management, you are not immune to lay-offs, you are not immune to sudden changes in wages, benefits, hours, and working conditions. Even most members of senior management can experience the same trauma that the rest of us do: loss of regular wages, loss of health insurance, and difficulty in finding new work (in part due to age discrimination). Only those at the very top who are usually awarded generous employment contracts stuffed with golden parachutes and world-class benefits (at the same time as they automatically reject the idea of employment contracts for anyone else in their organization except union members) seem truly immune.

The issue is not the term "worker." The stagnation in household income discussed in Chapter 3 is not limited to those on the assembly line or in foundries. It affects all of us, even those at the top, because tepid consumer demand for goods and services saps America's ability to grow. It affects those who own small- and medium-sized businesses in exactly the same way. Thus we all have an interest in ensuring that the American economic model works for all of us, all of us who work. That we discuss unions or labor relations at points does not detract from the general interest all of us should share. Labor unions are the only entities we have that can negotiate worker issues with management on relatively equal terms. To the extent that they fail or succeed, they affect how the economic model for the rest of the country evolves, for they are usually at the forefront of changes in the relationship between business and labor. Thus it is on America's business model that we need to focus. Us-versus-them must be pushed to the side. Now we return to the thread of the alternative explanation.

According to a 1969 study, the US has had the bloodiest and most violent labor history of any industrial country.[74] It is ironic that every time we discuss this subject we use the term "labor violence." It is as if strikers alone were the only ones who did wrong. Without denying the fact that workers bear their own responsibility for events, focusing on labor as the supposed sole cause of violence ignores the fact that the state, which has deployed the police and National Guard, and businesses, which have deployed thugs, have been far more violent. Have not the state and big business won nearly every major labor confrontation in the US? How could they have done so had they not been more violent? Who lost more lives in this violence? And why did labor feel they had no recourse except strikes and, sometimes, violence? No one wants to talk about the history of state-endorsed anti-labor violence in the US. No one wants to talk about the treatment of workers for a century prior to World War II. None of this fits today's view of who we are—or of the benign view of business that it has foisted upon us. The media has been useless in all of this: they either sat silent or actively encouraged suppression in the past and they sit largely silent today.

The US is the most conservative of all large OECD countries. The Democratic and Republican parties are both conservative when compared to many large countries in the rest of the world. Business, and in particular big business, has a very large influence over economic, social, and labor policy. In general, politicians' views of the world, regardless of party, do not deviate far from those of big business; indeed they rely heavily on big business for political funding. The result has been labor legislation that very much does big businesses' bidding. Various studies and surveys have shown that the US ranks near the bottom in measures of labor protection, i.e., protection of permanent workers against individual dismissal, specific requirements for collective dismissal, regulation of temporary forms of employment, difficulty of hiring, difficulty of firing, etc. Studies like these provoke immediate charges that they were prepared by those with socialist or anti-American views. These charges are supposedly confirmed by the fact that Scandinavian countries, which are supposedly "socialist," often land at the top of these and similar rankings. Yet even the conservative Heritage Foundation's 2012 Economic Freedom Index ranks the US #10 overall (the ranking is higher if one excludes small countries) but #1 in terms of Labor Freedom. Here is how the Heritage Foundation looks at labor freedom within the context of its Index:

> The ability of individuals to work as much as they want and wherever they want is a key component of economic freedom. By the same token, the ability of businesses to contract freely for labor and dismiss redundant workers when they are no longer needed is a vital mechanism for enhancing productivity and

sustaining overall economic growth. The core principle
of any market is free, voluntary exchange. That is as
true in the labor market as it is in the market for goods.

State intervention generates the same problems in the
labor market that it produces in any other market.
Government regulations take a variety of forms,
including wage controls, hiring and firing restrictions,
and other restrictions. In many countries, unions play
an important role in regulating labor freedom and,
depending on the nature of their activity, may be either
a force for greater freedom or an impediment to the
efficient functioning of labor markets. In general, the
greater the degree of labor freedom, the lower the rate
of unemployment in an economy.[75]

All of these rankings and indices agree on the same truth: the
current US economic model that allows businesses to cast off labor "at
will" provides them greater flexibility in responding to economic
downturns than in other countries. Business celebrates this. Others
question the trade-offs we have to make.

Charts 5.1 and 5.2 show the shares of profits and labor as a
percentage of real gross value-added (GVA) for the past decade.
Corporate profits have captured a higher percentage of GVA even
allowing for the recession. Workers have captured an ever smaller
share. As an aside, it should be noted that wages show a trend opposite
to profits during recessionary years because unit labor and non-labor
costs remain relatively stable whereas profit (what is left over after
deducting all costs) suffers most in down periods when sales are flat-
to-down. The charts deliver the same message as the discussion of
household income in Chapter 3: average Americans are not benefitting
from our current economic model. For an economic model to be
successful, it must deliver for everybody. When it does not deliver—
and it is not delivering today—we risk alienating portions of our
population. Alienation is what places the US at greatest risk. One
would think those who most celebrate the US economic model would
be the most concerned that it is not showing benefits commensurate
with the supposed value that labor force flexibility gives to employers.
One would think they would be concerned that the data does not

match their rhetoric. One would think all would be concerned about future implications of the imbalance that the current data shows.

Contrary to the rhetoric of the Heritage Foundation, big business and large employers do not really believe in free enterprise, in free and voluntary exchange, except for themselves. That is not what they practice. Every small- and medium-sized business has great misgivings when it enters into a relationship with a large company. Just ask one. These relationships are out-of-balance from the start. Both parties understand well who has the power in the relationship. Even if the large company does not engage in illegal acts, even if it does not engage in unethical behavior, both parties understand that it can get what it wants by sheer power, by requesting favorable treatment with the small company fully comprehending the consequences of failing to respond. Is this truly free and voluntary exchange? Freedom for whom?

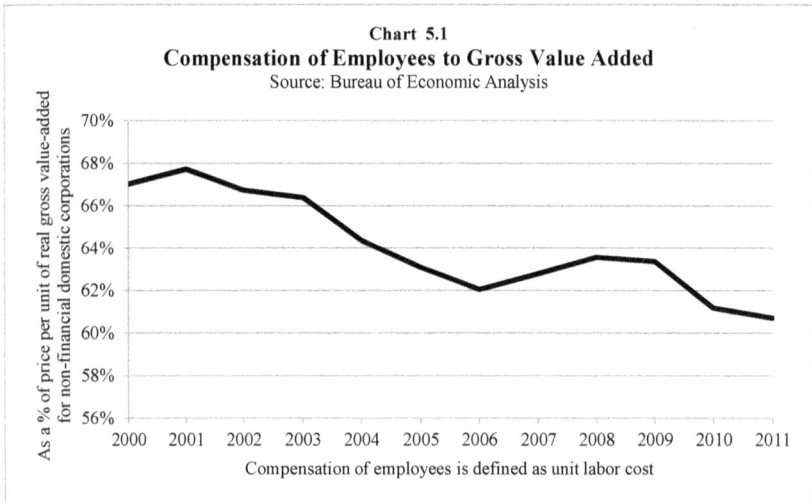

Chart 5.1
Compensation of Employees to Gross Value Added
Source: Bureau of Economic Analysis

Compensation of employees is defined as unit labor cost

Chart 5.2
Pre-Tax Corporate Profits to Gross Value Added
Source: Bureau of Economic Analysis

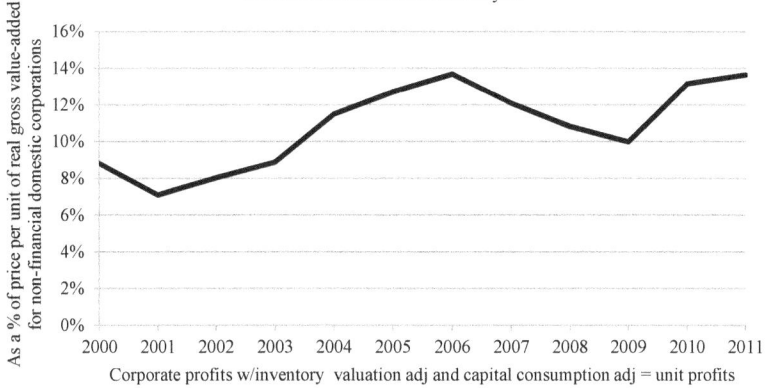

As a % of price per unit of real gross value-added for non-financial domestic corporations

16%	
14%	
12%	
10%	
8%	
6%	
4%	
2%	
0%	2000 2001 2002 2003 2004 2005 2006 2007 2008 2009 2010 2011

Corporate profits w/inventory valuation adj and capital consumption adj = unit profits

For the most part, large companies are not innovators. They have already built their business models. Their future success now rests on defending their cash flow against all comers. True competition is an afterthought. Many, particularly in technology sectors, defend their cash flow with an army of lawyers aimed at protecting patents, trademarks, and processes. Litigation is a legitimate tool of competition in the hands of large companies. Woe to the small- or medium-sized company that crosses their paths, for they do not have the resources to match their firepower, legal and otherwise.

Labor is in a similar position, particularly if non-unionized. Business and government together have built a legal structure which is anti-worker and anti-union. The US is party to multiple international treaties which guarantee freedom of association but continues to apply measures that thwart unionization. The Taft-Hartley Act (1947), an anti-labor piece of legislation, rolled back labor protections instituted for the first time during the New Deal and put numerous obstacles in the way of union organization. Corporations can form at will but union organizers must jump through hoops and comply with legal strictures on solicitation, communications, organizing locations, card-signing, elections, and recognition. Certain industries are prohibited from unionizing and, as the recent actions of Wisconsin Governor Scott Walker show, the drive to limit freedom of association remains powerful even when it does not gain momentary success. Is it not paradoxical that Americans, who have a strong anti-government streak, are willing to sit back and watch government tell people whom they can associate with? Would Americans accept such laws in any other area of their lives?

Once a union is formed, corporations have multiple avenues to thwart union effectiveness: limitations on picketing, work stoppages, and strikes, union- and strike-busting measures such as lockouts, termination of employment for union organizers, threats of dismissal for others, and replacement of strikers. Rarely does a corporation lose when its actions are challenged in court. The language of the Landrum-Griffin Act (1959) is so vague that employers can act as they will; indeed, an army of consultants has arisen which advises employers on how they can engage in anti-union tactics and still remain in compliance with the law.

The Taft-Hartley Act also permitted so-called "right to work" laws which are in fact anti-labor laws that have been enacted in 22 states to make it harder for unions to organize. That the media continues to use the word "right to work" instead of calling these laws what they are, anti-union legislation, shows how pro-business rhetoric has invaded our national narrative without being challenged. Words matter almost as much as action. Euphemisms for actions against workers which really hurt—downsizing, creative destruction, labor synergies, outsourcing, offshoring—have entered our vocabulary as if there is nothing wrong with them. Yet none of these other terms mask malicious intent as much as "right to work" and "labor freedom."

Adopting businesses' preferred verbiage directly affects how Americans think about labor. Shouts of "class warfare" are heard any time one dwells too much on fairness or on workers' salaries, benefits, and rights. Many Americans, even some on the left, are quick to blame labor in any dispute, especially when a strike disturbs the comfort of their daily lives. The media, mostly controlled by large corporations, sits by silently and does little to challenge this verbiage.

All of this is not to say that the criticism of union activities of the past has been off-base. There have been incidents in the past of Mafia infiltration, corruption, poor leadership, and wrong-headed and/or illegal tactics to include violence. No one can deny that. Yet it is the height of hypocrisy for business to oppose unions on the justification that they are protecting workers. What about the actions of Enron, Bernie Madoff, MCI Worldcom, Tyco International, MFS Global, BP, and Halliburton in Iraq? What about price-fixing? What about bribery? What about violations of anti-trust law? There is no end to

160

tales of outright corporate incompetence. There is no end to the stories of failure of corporate stewardship, breach of fiduciary responsibility, and corruption. These stories exceed those of union malfeasance by a ten thousandfold—not that numbers make union malfeasance any less wrong. And what of the behavior of the financial sector during the real estate bubble? From whom do we really need protection? In the end, it is up to members and regulators to police union leadership, just as it is up to boards of directors, shareholders, and regulators to police corporate leadership. Neither is an easy task but it is their own responsibility to address. For corporations to say that they will protect their workers from the depredations of unions is patronizing and self-serving.

Business will answer that it is not union depredations they are worried about. Labor unions are blamed for raising costs and making US business uncompetitive. In the public sector, they are blamed for extracting concessions from state governments to which they somehow cannot say no. We will not argue that there are not bad contracts, but some are bad for management and some are bad for labor and some are a series of trade-offs that make sense to both parties. Competition in the labor markets, and any market, is a two-way street. Unions do not force management to enter into contracts with guns at their heads but business acts as if this were true.

Collective bargaining is a process of negotiation and mistakes can be made on either side that jeopardize either business results or jobs. Yet major mistakes are made in business all the time, not just in collective bargaining. The future guarantees nothing, to neither management nor labor. Both must make an informed and accurate analysis of their respective best interests and act accordingly. If they find they were wrong and that mistakes have been made, it is up to both parties to find an acceptable method for correcting them, just as with correcting any other business misjudgment. And no one said it was going to be easy: truly competitive accommodation between business and labor is always going to be give-and-take and both sides must get used to it.

What it all comes down to is what we said at the beginning: deep down, big business does not believe in free enterprise except for itself and it does not believe in competition. It does not like any situation where a customer, a supplier, or a worker is in a position of strength. In the case of workers, unlike customers and suppliers, business has the legal tools to ensure it remains dominant in the relationship. Should Americans wake up in the aftermath of a *shock* and find themselves facing another ten years of grinding stagnation, the backlash against big business and those allied with it could be harsh.[76] And we are not talking about something as ineffective as the *Occupy Wall Street* movement. For the truly disaffected, alienated, and angry, who will want real action, the "be-in" atmosphere of the *Occupy* and anti-globalization movements will offer little.

In the end, labor unions by themselves are not the answer. There is nothing special about labor unions as a solution to the problems that face us. There are many, many fine employers who treat their employees well, whether unionized or not, and they should be recognized. Yet what it comes down to is this: workers cannot rely on anyone—neither employers nor government—to protect their interests and to ensure that working conditions are equitable. They must stand up for themselves, whether in a union or not. Workers must first empower themselves, with education and skills, so they are valuable to any employer. They must also figure out the best way to build a life for themselves, whether the setting is union or non-union. And in the end, they must speak up, whether in a union setting or not, if they find things wrong or unfair. And they must work with other Americans to roll back the wave of anti-worker (not just anti-union) practices that currently blights American life. Efforts like these should not be thought of as purely anti-business, although we acknowledge some will go to those extremes at times. The objective should be to achieve greater balance between the interests of business and labor, something that does not exist today.

Let us think about balance. Look back over the past twenty years. One sees a steady erosion of workers' (both union and non-union) rights, benefits, pensions, and well-being. This erosion has taken place in large part due to business's contention that it can no longer afford high costs and benefits and that labor must be competitive. Looking at Charts 5.1 and 5.2 and the charts in Chapter 3, one has to say that workers have done about all they can. The question now before us is: can we afford the costs of a business model focused solely on capturing maximum compensation for top management and shareholders without taking other American stakeholders into account? Can workers afford to lose more ground over the next ten years given all they have lost over the past twenty? Admittedly, addressing these issues will be difficult but no one ever said life would

162

be easy. And will workers find it any easier if they repeatedly back down?

A Further Digression on Balance

Okay, we want to achieve better balance, but you will undoubtedly ask: what does that really mean in practice? The word is very vague, as noted in our discussion of "imbalance" in Chapter 3. Let us start with an anecdote. I have been fortunate to work in Asia for a long period. In two countries, it is common for people (even those you do not know) to ask, "How much money do you make?" An American faced with this question is flummoxed. Like politics and religion, it is a subject most of us avoid. We do not feel comfortable discussing it with others, even with father and mother, brothers and sisters. Indeed, workers in some US companies must sign a pledge not to disclose their salaries to others. In Asia, I would always try to avoid answering this question with some smooth response like, "Well … um … uh … we don't really talk about that." Often the questioner was stunned. Back would come, "Why not?" I can assure you I produced an equally smooth response, a dissertation on the social and cultural history of the United States. Indeed in those two countries, salaries are discussed between family, friends, co-workers, and sometimes even slight acquaintances as a matter of course. No one thinks anything of it.

And another anecdote. I worked for one non-unionized company which held regular meetings with its employees. From time to time, they would say something like, "We just have completed another review of our wages and benefits. We are proud to say we offer a wage-and-benefits package competitive with those offered by comparable companies. In fact, we feel our package is more competitive than the average comparable company." On occasion, a naïve employee would raise his or her hand and ask, "Can you give us a copy of the review?"
The response would always be: "We're sorry, that's proprietary information. We cannot give that out." In other words, trust us.

We contend that balance starts with education, forming an accurate assessment of the labor market and one's place in it. Making that assessment is far easier in a union setting. A union has a staff devoted to labor relations. It has specialists who regularly survey wages, benefits, and working conditions across the industry. It keeps track of changes in the work environment across the country. This provides it the data needed to make the assessment which will form the core of its negotiating strategy with management.

The task is far more difficult if you are not in a union. Your knowledge of what constitutes competitive wages and working conditions is spotty, often based on what you hear and read in passing. Business has taken a deliberate divide-and-conquer approach with respect to non-union labor. By isolating one worker from another, it can deal with each worker from a position of power. It is a fundamentally uncompetitive relationship, regardless of all the talk about labor freedom.

Balance can only come from greater competition. And greater competition can only come when a worker knows where he or she stands in the labor markets. And, again, knowledge can only come through education.

So here's an idea—call me crazy—of one way to gain knowledge so as to achieve greater competitive balance between business and workers. Why not require every that company with more than, say, 25 employees provide a detailed table which classifies and stratifies its entire work force by salary, skills, age, education, location, and years of service and shows <u>actual</u> wages and compensation for the past 12 months. Furthermore, require that this data be publicly available. In order to forestall business attempts to provide gobbledegook designed to be impenetrable, maybe the government should provide a format. Would this not provide workers with the knowledge needed to provide a more informed choice? Would not any worker feel his or her relationship with management was more balanced with this type of information in hand? Do you think workers in the Asian countries noted feel more or less empowered because of the knowledge they possess?

We can hear the screams now. Our responses:

Another report, more bureaucracy, more expense! But you already have this data in hand. You already do this stratification for internal purposes. There is no additional work. All you have to do is disclose what you already have. Moreover, you are already disclosing this type of data in blind studies to HR consultants.

We already provide information on pay grades and salary ranges! Pay grades and salary ranges are an HR creation deliberately designed to obfuscate the entire issue of compensation. We want to know what workers actually earn today, not what they might theoretically earn some day in the far-distant future.

Right to privacy! But don't you disclose the compensation of top employees in proxy statements? And everyone knows what union members make. We do not need to disclose the names of individual employees in a report like this. All we need is the data, however grouped.

This information is proprietary and will disclose our cost structure to our competitors! But do you think General Motors does not have a very good idea of the union and non-union cost structure at its competitors? And the data will go both ways, GM will have access to Ford's compensation and Ford will have access to GM's.

Ford and GM may conspire to fix pay for non-union workers based on this information! But isn't price-fixing a violation of federal law? As an aside, we question all of the so-called "blind" studies hosted by HR consultants through which corporations share data on wages, benefits, hours, and working conditions. Although we are certain they are structured so as to avoid violation of current law, one might ask if such studies do not achieve price-fixing of wages and benefits through the back door. Indeed, no corporation would escape prosecutorial attention if it began sharing pricing information on its products and services with competitors through an intermediary. Maybe someone should look into all these HR blind studies. And anyway, if this type of data is already being shared with HR consultants, why can't employees see it?

This disclosure will create upward pressure on labor and benefits! We guess you are saying you are worried about workers being in a more competitive negotiating posture. In some cases, workers will see that they are underpaid relative to others and so will seek more competitive wages and benefits. Yet others may be surprised to find they are overpaid relative to the industry. Will not this not temper wage and benefit expectations? On a company-by-company basis, it is hard to know what the impact of greater knowledge will be on labor costs. But it will definitely serve to strengthen the negotiating position of the individual worker, something that business wants desperately to avoid. Again, business has no real interest in competition when it comes to workers.

***This will worsen employee morale through envy and
backbiting!*** Do you mean to say that envy and backbiting about salary,
benefits and all sorts of other issues do not exist today?

Okay, so you do not like the idea of corporate disclosure. Why
then can't employees create their own off-site database off-site into
which employees can voluntarily input (with individual names
confidential) all data that business might disclose in the type of report
noted. We suppose that business might try to oppose such an idea on
the grounds of confidentiality or that employees are conspiring to fix
prices. Both of those contentions are very weak. But if you do not like
this idea, why not have the government sponsor a database into which
workers can voluntarily input data?

As you can see, the issue of balance — particularly for non-
union workers — can be approached from multiple angles, and not just
in the area of knowledge which we have focused on here. The goal
again is to achieve a more equal competitive balance between labor and
management. As we have noted, we believe that balance can only be
achieved through greater knowledge and understanding on the part of
all workers, both union and non-union. Think through this issue and
see if you can come up with better ideas than what we have laid out
that will help achieve the same goal.

A Return to the Spiral

Even if the arguments outlined under the rubric of
"exceptionalism" correctly explain why radicalism and socialism have
not made headway in America, one must still ask whether they apply
today. After all, the Depression began over 80 years ago. Is it not
possible that things have changed since then? Throughout this book we
have continually cautioned against the risk of overreliance on
trendlines and patterns to forecast the future. We must always ask
ourselves: will the future really look like the past? Is America truly the
exceptional country? We have posited a downward spiral and a
breakdown in the US economic model in the aftermath of a *shock*. Do
we not have to consider the possibility that Americans, particularly the
disaffected, the alienated, and the angry will act differently this time
around because of the related stress?

The response from the exceptionalists will be that numerous
Americans both left and right (including groups like the Tea Party) are
terribly unhappy with the way things are. Apart from the anti-

166

government views of some, they will argue that most are unhappy about slow job growth and the stagnant economy. They will also argue that, no matter how unhappy they may be, we observe no action beyond trying to win control through use of the ballot box. They will point out that no radical solutions are currently being proposed and that no radical organizations are rising to propound them. The exceptionalists will claim that this shows that Americans are fundamentally satisfied with how our current economic model works even as, at the same time, they have grievances. The exceptionalists thus posit a great American apathy, a great American disinterest in fundamental change even as American household wages and income stagnate. In this book, we want to maintain an open mind towards other possibilities. We look back to the discussion of immigration at the beginning of Chapter 4 for an alternative view. People suffered for decades if not centuries in their countries of origin and did nothing, but *shocks* emerged which caused them to act. After having already experienced a decade of stagnation, what will happen if Americans experience another new, severe *shock* and see the prospect of another long period of painful adjustment ahead of them? Could it not be that Americans will act in ways which do not fit the exceptionalist narrative?

American Unity & True Believers

Contrary to the rhetoric of American nationalism and American exceptionalism, there is no reason of necessity that any country, and particularly a country as large and diverse as the US, should hold together. In fact, we have seen many large countries fall apart. Leaving aside countries which have fallen apart under the impact of war waged by external parties, here are examples of large countries which have fallen apart or which continue to have separatist movements:

Table 5.1	
Country	**Comment**
USSR	Collapsed into separate states in 1991.
Russia	Strong separatist movements remain in the Caucusus.
China	The country has united and divided multiple times during its 5,000-year history. Separatist movements remain in Tibet, Xinjiang, and Inner Mongolia.

UK	A referendum on Scottish independence is scheduled for 2014.
Spain	The movement for Catalan independence appears to be gaining strength.
Canada	The Quebec separatist movement has lost strength since the 1960s and 1970s but a separatist minority remains.
Belgium	Increasing centrifugal forces appear to be separating the Flemish and Walloons.
Indonesia	East Timor seceded in 2002. A significant separatist movement remains in Aceh.
Pakistan	East Pakistan (Bangladesh) gained independence in 1971. Pakistan faces a separatist movement in Baluchistan and does not exercise effective governmental control over many of its federally administered tribal regions and territories.
Turkey, Iraq	Movements for Kurd separatism, autonomy, or independence exist in both countries.

The reasons why these countries fell apart or still face separatist movements vary from country to country. No one theme seems to unite them. The point is: there is no reason why any country must necessarily stay united. There always exist forces which, left unaddressed, can threaten to pull a large country apart, particularly in the aftermath of the kind of *shock* discussed in this book.

Unlike what 20-20 hindsight and nationalism would tell us, the experiment that began with the founding of the United States was not destined to succeed. The Founding Fathers did not have great self-assurance in what they had established. They knew what they were trying was brand new and that the path to the future was not clear. They knew that every step they took established a precedent for the future and so many steps were subsequently surrounded with great controversy. Uncertainty about the future of the republic only seems to have dissipated sometime after the War of 1812 (but note the New England secession convention of 1814-1815) and with the arrival of Andrew Jackson. Only with Jackson did America become more confident and self-assured because at the same time it had become larger, more powerful, and more dynamic. It was thus less dependent on England and France and so less worried about whatever trouble they might cause.[77]

The Constitution was stitched together through an awkward accommodation with slavery which kicked the can down the road. Although most, both North and South, seemed to have had worries about this accommodation, no one foresaw that a war would be fought over slavery 70 years later. On the contrary, most seemed to think (when they bothered to think about it) that the ban on importation of slaves (which was enacted in 1808, the earliest date permitted under the Constitution) would somehow cause slavery to die on the vine. No one foresaw that, over the decades, the country would become ever more divided over slavery and that the gap between viewpoints at signing of the Constitution would eventually turn into a chasm. The Founders did not reckon on the power of the "true believers" who would rally to slavery's defense.[78]

Political, social, and even economic discourse today is dominated by the "true believer." Few pay attention to quieter voices. Our 24/7 media extravaganza prizes the sound bite and rewards strident rhetoric. Many say that political rhetoric is the worst it has ever been, while ignoring the fact that political campaigns during the 19th century were usually far viler in terms of language and accusations. What distinguishes us today is a 24/7 news cycle that bombards us with this rhetoric. While citizens were bombarded with vile rhetoric during the 19th century, it was limited to newspapers and magazines, and many were illiterate. It is hard to believe that the average citizen took heavy doses of this rhetoric except at election time—and they did not have election campaigns which lasted years as they do today. Furthermore, with the right to vote limited in so many ways, it is hard to believe that the average citizen was heavily distracted from work and daily life by this rhetoric. What is different today is that a large percentage of the citizenry has imbibed this rhetoric, which has led to national polarization. Many are "true believers." While there is no issue as threatening as slavery before us today, the rhetoric wants the listener to believe that every issue, e.g., federal debt, rises to that level of importance.

The result of polarization, whether in the US or elsewhere, is to demonize one's opponents, to see them as "the other."[79] History teaches hard lessons about societies which see other nations, parties, movements, races, ethnicities, or religious groups as "the other." One wonders whether the descent into economic breakdown posited here does not have great potential for us to relearn such lessons, for us to face a descent into even greater political turmoil and, yes, even political violence.

Turmoil

Based on a review of history, it is not unthinkable for a second civil war to occur if polarization continues. A second civil war will likely come long after we are all dead, but we would not be surprised to see one if current trends continue. Then again, it might not take long given how quickly things move today. One is struck by the fact that, in the midst of hyperinflation and economic catastrophe, it took the Nazis just seven years to gain a majority in the Reichstag after their 1923 Beer Hall Putsch uprising had been suppressed by the German Government. The lesson is that things can move much quicker than we might expect. Most will answer that America is exceptional, far different from the Germany of the 1920s. Maybe that it is true, maybe not, but who can define with certainty what will result from an economic breakdown?

A rise in radicalism, a rise in extremism from either the right or the left, may indeed be consequences of a breakdown. Some of their analytical insights may even have merit, some of their solutions may indeed be worth considering, but it is doubtful, in today's atmosphere, that anyone except the like-minded will give them a respectful hearing. Rather these solutions and the people who sponsor them will likely be labeled: socialist, communist, reactionary, fascist, etc. More likely, especially given the use of language in America since 9/11/01, is that the word "terrorist" or "potential terrorist" will applied to these people, just as anarchists were conflated with trade unionists during the 19th and early 20th centuries. Use of the word "terrorist" generates a kneejerk reaction from the average American.

Yet it is not just radicals who will be so labeled. Designation of "the other" will cover more citizens than just radicals and extremists. The smear will compound all political opponents. Those who are currently termed liberal, progressive, pro-labor, pro-choice, and pro-civil rights will be lumped together with radicals and extremists, because that serves the objectives of the labelers. Those who are currently termed fiscal conservative, social conservative, pro-life, pro-business, and anti-tax will be lumped with another set of radicals and extremists, because that serves the objectives of the labelers. Those at the forefront of the labelers — some politicians, some commentators and various others who could emerge as leaders in the midst of turmoil —

170

will often have purposeful, malicious agendas and smears to further their agendas.

One important issue for consideration in all this is that a large portion of America is armed. It is very hard to get an accurate handle on private gun ownership in the US. The National Rifle Association estimates that there are 300 million privately owned firearms in the US of which 100 million are handguns; it estimates that the number of firearms rises by 4 million annually. It estimates that there are 100 million gun owners in the US of which 40-45 million own handguns. It estimates that 40-45% of US households own firearms.[80] This data is partially confirmed by a 2011 Gallup Poll which found that 47% of American adults have a gun in their household or on their property.[81] The growth of guns in private hands is also partially confirmed by ATF data which showed 6.1 million firearms manufactured and sold for domestic consumption in 2011, an all-time high by a wide margin; this figure presumably includes firearms sold to law enforcement, so growth of 4 million per annum (which would also include imports) may be in the ballpark.[82]

One has to wonder: why do Americans buy another 4 million new guns every year, particularly when they know existing guns will last for decades if well-maintained? What is driving this growth? Although a large number of these weapons are used in hunting, the justification for the others is either sport or self-defense. Although some say there is nothing wrong with guns and that only criminals use guns, why is this great store of weapons being built? Is the number of criminals in the US really skyrocketing? Might it not be that normal concerns about self-defense are changing into fear, fear of others one does not know or understand, fear of "the other"? If even just *some* gun owners saw individuals becoming increasingly radicalized due to the state of the economy, it is not unthinkable that self-defense might morph into preemption, i.e. alleged threats from those who have been labeled radical or extreme, "the other," justify a preventive attack. It would only take a small portion of the nation's gun owners to adopt this view. That is where it may start. That is when political turmoil spirals downward into political violence, and political violence has the potential to tear this country apart.

Where will the states and the federal government stand in all this? They have almost always sided with capital against labor during the past 150 years. Yet capital versus labor may be too simplistic a construct to apply to the new world we are talking about after a *shock*.

"The other" is unlikely to be the labor organizer; as noted, the labeling will likely encompass a much wider swath of the American populace. And there is another thought beyond capital versus labor: may not concern about "the other" lead to the emergence of paramilitary organizations which we do not see today? Who will support these organizations? How many people? And another thought: what about all the weapons sitting in state armories across the United States? In a crisis, who controls them? Can paramilitaries steal them or will someone open the doors and let them walk in? Again, we are talking about a period of severe crisis. During a crisis, we have to remember that those who believe in violence as a solution are unlikely to put limitations on their own actions. We have to recognize that a rise in violence is a possible consequence of turmoil that may come with a breakdown in the US economy. In Chapter 1 we said that the outcome of any war is unpredictable. The outcomes of violence, once it starts, are just as hard to predict.

Early Warning Sign & Red Flag

It will be difficult to distinguish the loud voices we expect to see as a normal part of the democratic process from those that point in the direction of turmoil that has the potential to tear America apart. That we begin to hear more untempered opinions from ordinary Americans after a *shock* should not necessarily disturb us. Americans have never been afraid to speak their minds. That radicals on the right or the left stake out extreme positions in the midst of a downward spiral should not, in and of itself, be viewed as an early warning sign. Radicals, even if ineffective, have always been with us and it has been part of the strength of the fabric of America that our belief in the First Amendment has accepted their rights to free speech, even if grudgingly. That we may see increased evidence of strikes and demonstrations, whether from the right or the left, should also not necessarily be viewed with alarm, even if accompanied by occasional disorder. The use of the streets and other public venues to express political views, even views opposed by the majority, is part of the US democratic tradition. Even riots and other acts of random violence in which it is hard to discern a cause beyond the desire to destroy are not necessarily an early warning sign. Riots too have always been with us and, even as average Americans have recoiled from this violence, the fabric of America has remained intact.

What we will be searching for is a change in the way people express themselves. Normal dissent and radical opinions should be expected but when we see many people begin advocating, even if only artfully and subtlely, the use of violence to accomplish political goals or, alternatively, to defend themselves against the "other," then everything changes. A line is crossed once someone begins advocating violence as a political tool. Clearly, the occasional crackpot who takes such stands should not be viewed with particular alarm but if the rhetoric seems to be building from multiple sources and if people seem to be taking it seriously, then it must be viewed as a clear early warning sign (both in this Chapter 5 and Chapter 6 which follows). Talk of this sort is likely to generate turmoil the likes of which we have never seen in America. This talk will almost definitely accentuate perceived differences between Americans. What it will also do is increase political turmoil to heightened levels which threaten the loss of national and social cohesion and thereby speed the swirl of the eddying downward spiral.

Once this type of rhetoric appears, we must begin to look for the formation of paramilitary organizations as a red flag. Although state-sponsored violence against citizens, as in today's Syria, is a phenomenon seen at times throughout history, we believe that the probability of such violence in the US is very low. Furthermore, random, disorganized violence (like a riot) should not be overanalyzed even as much as we may condemn it. Rather, organized violence poses the greatest threat to our national cohesion. What we should be looking for are political parties or movements which now find it necessary to form their own militias or security forces. The tiny ultra-extremist militia movements we see today should not bother us. It is only paramilitary forces swelling from the ranks of ordinary Americans that we should designate a red flag.

There are no signs today of either substantive political rhetoric advocating violence or of growth in paramilitaries. Although there are no current signs that point to a higher probability of turmoil and violence, we believe it is foolish to act as if they will never appear. The political atmosphere today is far too heated for us to ignore the possibility that it can rise to a boil under the force of a *shock*.

173

Preparation

Clearly the scenarios we are describing in this chapter would have horrific outcomes. Preparing for events like these is a difficult task. Making choices in the face of turmoil and/or violence is difficult to think about today, but the purpose of this book is to think about the unthinkable and develop a plan. In this case, one cannot have an exact plan. Rather it is about forming a clear view of how you want to act and how you want to live your life, and of the legacy you want to leave for future generations. Your choices will be determined by multiple factors, to include your personal belief system, socio-economic status, physical location, and family situation. Only you can make these choices, and you must chart a personalized plan that flows from those choices.

---

[72] There have been many European parties with "socialist" in their name but their actions while in power look anything but socialist (at least socialist to the extent they conform to socialist political theory). We see François Hollande and the French Socialist Party proposing strong action to reform what they see as an uncompetitive business model. These steps will directly affect all workers. We see the Nazis of the past co-opting the word. One wonders whether parties now use the word just because it sounds good.

[73] This paragraph relies partially on: Seymour Martin Lipset and Gary Wolfe Marks, *It Didn't Happen Here: Why Socialism Failed in the United States*, (New York: W.W. Norton & Co, 2001).

[74] Philip Taft and Philip Ross, "American Labor Violence: Its Causes, Character and Outcome," *The History of Violence in America: A Report to the National Commission on the Causes and Prevention of Violence* (ed. Hugh Davis Graham and Ted Robert Gurr, 1969).

[75] Ambassador Terry Miller and Anthony Kim, "Defining Economic Freedom," 2012 Index of Economic Freedom, (The Heritage Foundation: 2012), http://www.heritage.org/index/book/chapter-1 (accessed November 17, 2012).

[76] The Republican Party is most often seen as the party of big business but support within the Party is by no means uniform. A meaningful cross-section of the GOP remains deeply suspicious of big business power. Nevertheless, it is likely that all members of the GOP will be tarred with the same brush during a backlash because of the Party's historical stance.

[77] These two books provide an excellent overview of America's first 60 years: Gordon S. Wood, *Empire of Liberty: A History of the Early Republic, 1789-1815 (Oxford History of the United States)*, (New York: Oxford University Press USA, 2009) and Daniel Walker Howe, *What Hath God Wrought: The Transformation of America, 1815-1848 (Oxford History of the United States)*, (New York: Oxford University Press USA, 2007).

[78] We would argue that "true believers" have been at the heart of every major political cataclysm over the past 500 years. Review for example the history of the English Civil Wars (1642-1651) to see the effect of "true believers" on both sides. A good history of the Wars is: Michael Braddick, *God's Fury, England's Fire: A New History of the English Civil Wars*, (London: Allen Lane, 2008). The turmoil which led to the English Civil Wars was important for the US because the Puritans, also "true believers," fled England to establish a colony in the New World. This fine book speaks to the impact of their beliefs on American thought: John M. Barry, *Roger Williams and the Creation of the American Soul: Church, State, and the Birth of Liberty*, (New York: Viking, 2012).

[79] "The other" is used in the sense first used by Edward Said in describing Western views of the Middle East. See Edward Said, *Orientalism*, (New York: Vintage Books, 1979).

[80] NRA Institute for Legislative Action, Firearms Fact Card 2012, http://www.nraila.org/news-issues/fact-sheets/2012/nra-ila-firearms-fact-card-2012.aspx?s=&st=&ps= (accessed November 19, 2012).

[81] Linda Saad, "Self-Reported Gun Ownership in U.S. Is Highest Since 1993," October 26, 2011, http://www.gallup.com/poll/150353/Self-Reported-Gun-Ownership-Highest-1993.aspx (accessed November 19, 2012).

[82] Annual Firearms Manufacturers and Export Reports, 1998-2011, Bureau of Alcohol, Tobacco, Firearms and Explosives, http://www.atf.gov/statistics/ (accessed November 19, 2012).

Chapter 6

Breakdown in Social Cohesion: Hitting Bottom

Introduction

Whether or not the political and economic turmoil discussed breaks out into violence, whether or not the US as we know it breaks apart, the net result of economic turmoil will be an increase in mistrust and fear.

In commercial markets, a long-term relationship between a single buyer and a single seller rests on trust. When relations break down, it is usually because trust between the two has been shaken. Once shaken, it is hard to reestablish. All markets, financial and otherwise, rest on a foundation of trust. Trust rests on rule of law, a sense of what is both fair and ethical, and the sense that other market participants should be given the benefit of the doubt when forming business relationships until proven otherwise. Political and economic turmoil would likely undermine that foundation.

Let's take a simple example. Shipping of goods between businesses rests on five assumptions between buyer and seller: (1) that the goods being shipped by the seller will meet the specifications of the purchase order and will be of good quality; (2) that they will be shipped and received by the date specified in the purchase order; (3) that the buyer is reasonably creditworthy such that prepayment or advance deposit is not required; (4) that in fact the seller is willing to extend some degree of trade credit and is willing to accept payment, say, 30 days after invoice date; and (5) that the buyer will make payment when due and will not raise illegitimate defenses against payment. Political and economic turmoil, by increasing mistrust, have the potential to upend all this. When these five conditions do not exist, then other arrangements must be made. In the international arena, banks stand as intermediaries between buyers and sellers under letters of credit (L/Cs). L/Cs are used precisely because there is lack of confidence that these five conditions remain true when dealing overseas.

The inevitable reaction to lack of confidence and mistrust is to do business only with those one knows well. During a period of constant political and economic turmoil, would a seller ship to New

York City if he were based in Mississippi? Would he ship to Maryland if headquartered in Los Angeles? We contend that buyers and sellers will, almost naturally, search for relationships closer to home, with companies they can physically contact. This shift will only be human: during a period of stress, people seek out others with whom they feel the most comfortable.

The breakdown in business relations will have its counterpart in a breakdown in social relations. Those engaged in "rabble-rousing" or political violence will of course not associate with those they demonize as "the other." They will not even want to talk to them.[83] As with businesses, individuals will likely stay close to home. They will interact and form communities with those with whom they feel a common bond. This will cause a shift towards regional or smaller communities. We use the word "small" in this context as shorthand to contrast with American life as we know it today and there is no necessary cap on population. "Small" will typify more insular, inward-looking communities; at the smallest, these communities may self-identify on the basis of separation from other Americans. Smaller communities will appear most often in rural and suburban life, for it is difficult to maintain insularity within the confines of cities which are, by nature, diverse. Nevertheless, regional communities may have cities at their centers.

We make no attempt here to characterize the nature of these communities. The smallest might be socialist, utopian, survivalist or religious. Regardless of their nature, many of the smallest communities are likely to reject outsiders and will want to remain separate from them. Even communities based on geographic regions are likely to be less welcoming to outsiders. The reason for this will likely be suspicion of and antipathy toward the recent political and economic turmoil and of what has developed in its aftermath. A breakup of the United States as we know it, if it happened, could well see a confederation of New England, New York, and New Jersey on the east coast, California, Oregon, and Washington on the west, an independent Texas, and a variety of other combinations in between. If separation on a regional basis were to occur, one would expect some degree of hostility between the regional groupings.

Regional and smaller communities will likely be *autarkic* when compared to American towns and cities as we know them today. An autarkic region or community is one that stresses self-sufficiency and self-reliance. Autarkic communities will, by definition, deemphasize and, in some cases, turn away from economic relations with other parts

178

of the region or country. Autarkic communities have the same general needs as any other community: food, clothing, housing, water, sanitation, energy, transportation, and education. Yet they have less ability to fill those needs because their population is limited in both size and skills. Due to these limitations, small communities will prize skills that contribute to fulfilling basic needs. Service-sector skills will be less highly valued.

A shift to regional and smaller communities will lead to a breakdown in regional and intra-national (assuming the US as we know it remains intact) relations. Furthermore, the strength of economic activity will lessen. The reason for this is that the decline in intra-national trade and the move towards autarky means the US and its regions will have lost the benefits of comparative advantage that come with production on the basis of specialization. With a significant portion of production now shifted more to a regional or smaller community model, value-added per worker will be lower because workers in the community will, in effect, have to replace those who are far more skilled and productive at certain tasks but who live outside the community however defined. Furthermore, capital to be paired with labor in regional or smaller communities will be less available. Not only will sources of capital like private equity and hedge funds make less capital available for investment, but all, including banks, will be less willing to take on risk. All of this argues for economic stagnation.

Today's exemplar for *autarky* is North Korea. Cambodia under the Khmer Rouge was another extreme example. Mercantilist thinking dominated nationalist economic models during the 17th and 18th centuries; under such models, global economic activity was viewed as a zero-sum game with imports evidence of economic, military, and political weakness. Even after outright mercantilism waned, the history of the past two centuries has seen quite a few countries that pursued autarkic policies in varying degrees. Like North Korea and Cambodia, these autarkic economic policies often, but not always, went hand-in-hand with varying degrees of authoritarianism and political oppression.

Below the national and regional level, we see many examples of autarkic small communities. Many are religious communities of various types like the kibbutzes in Israel or the Hutterites in Canada. The US has seen many similar types of communities since its founding, most utopian, most short-lived. The most famous and arguably most successful was the Oneida Community in Upstate New York. Leaving these communities aside, we can see communities of larger size based on religion which have been far more successful, starting with the Amish in Pennsylvania and the Lubavitch Jewish community in Brooklyn.

For some, the emergence of an autarkic community represents the fulfillment of a dream.[84] We would suggest that much of this is just wishful thinking, maybe a delusion. Not only, as discussed, will economic performance be worse. We see a strong possibility that a move toward regional or smaller communities will generate anti-democratic forms of political governance inconsistent with our current ideals. The experience of nation-states with autarky appears to confirm this.

Anti-democratic structures may arise from new communities' antipathy toward others. This can easily morph into strictures on contacting other communities and from there, to greater regulation of daily life. New regional communities would likely emerge based on the leadership of charismatic individuals or groups whose visions for society may sometimes be fundamentally at variance with the America of today. It will be from these new leaders that anti-democratic and even oppressive rule may arise.

Based on this, it is possible that the economic breakdown will move us toward communities that do not fit one's current outlook and world-view. We do not attempt to describe the communities that will result. Indeed, as noted, a "community" could conceivably cover a fairly large geographic region. What is important to us is one undeniable fact: a loss of social cohesion will almost definitely accompany a loss of political cohesion. We think that loss of cohesion can manifest itself in a wide variety of ways, none of which need necessarily resemble the types of communes or other small communities that today exist on the periphery of American life. All must prepare for very real change.

Early Warning Sign & Red Flag

Same as in Chapter 5.

Preparation

Preparation for this stage of the spiral must focus on ensuring you can provide the basics for you and your family: food, clothing, housing, water, sanitation, energy, transportation, safety, medical services and prescription drugs (if needed), and probably education. Each person must assess his or her specific situation, to include (a) projected shortfalls between demand for the basics and available supply and (b) concerns about turmoil that may potentially impair one's ability to meet basic needs. A plan should be developed for how to meet those needs, preferably in advance of the emergence of early warning signs. There are many resources available on the internet and elsewhere, the details of which go beyond the scope of this book, which can assist you in developing such a plan. Whatever plan you develop, only you can decide how you want to live your life and your plan must reflect your own goals and values. The plan will also have to take into account that you will likely be living in a regional or smaller community, at least in character different from where you live today. Over the medium-term, achievement of your goals and at the same time maintaining your values will rest on the success of such communities.

Once regional and smaller communities have begun to emerge and gain some modicum of success, we will likely have reached the end of the downward spiral. Post-apocalyptic movies like *The Road*, *The Postman*, *Waterworld*, *Planet of the Apes*, and *Mad Max* would have us returning to some quasi-Stone Age. That is not reality, that's Hollywood.

The key point is: <u>we are still capable</u>. The knowledge of how to do things, or at least of how things should be done, still remains in our heads, in our books, and on our computers. There is no Dark Age during which all knowledge disappears into monasteries. Our resources may have been depleted during the downward spiral. We may not have the physical and/or economic capacity to do everything we need to, but we are still intellectually capable of doing so given the resources.

Though we are still capable, many, if not all, will succumb to depression. This depression will impair the ability of many to act. This depression will result from a type of post-traumatic stress resulting from the years of political and social turmoil after an economic breakdown.[85] This depression will cause some to resort to alcohol, drugs, or other means of escape. It is possible that a great lassitude, a great inertia will emerge in these new regional and smaller communities which prevent them, at the beginning, from functioning to their full potential. The reason is that many will be unable to envision a way forward from the way things used to be. There may be a way forward, but it will require inching toward it, baby-steps. Most will be impatient, most will want speed.

Some may theorize that this lassitude and inertia will make the mindset of these new regional and smaller communities like that of the residents of slums both in the US and around the world. They perhaps have images of people sitting on stoops all day long staring into space— bored, unwilling to work, depressed, stoned. But are these images really true? Certainly for some, but will they reflect reality?

Just as overreliance on our powers of reason seems to be built into our DNA, we believe it is difficult for humans to go forward without hope. It is hard to believe humans can live long without hope. The writings of concentration camp survivors show that people somehow have hope in even the most unimaginable circumstances. That hope may have been unrealistic, it may have been tiny, but it is hard to believe they could have gone on without it. Maybe it is the hope given by religion, the belief that you will survive and be rewarded in the end even if you have gone through hell on earth. This religious view may be comforting to many but we suspect it is not enough. People need some semblance of hope on earth as well. One is struck by the level of hope in Katherine Boo's narrative of life in one of Mumbai's worst slums.[86] Its people were suffering the most abject poverty but were, for the most part, still trying to move forward with their lives. We all have negative images of the poor and destitute. Yet it is probable that these are wrong to some degree (especially when we know that some people aim to distort our images of the poor for political advantage). Yes, there are times when they are depressed, but they move forward. We suspect that residents of regional and smaller communities will also find a way to emerge from depression and build new lives. Furthermore, if individualism and self-reliance are indeed part of the American character, then hope combined with character would seem to play right into the needs of regional and smaller communities.

At some point, things hit bottom, just as the US housing market hit bottom and struggles upward. This does not mean regional and smaller communities hit bottom and bound upward. They can skitter across the bottom for quite some time. But they do hit bottom and so there is the prospect of moving upward.

Signs of a Way Forward

What does the bottom look and feel like? First of all, there is no further drop in economic performance because there is nowhere deeper to go. At some point, people move forward. At some point, regional and smaller communities find a way to function and succeed. Everything likely has a different feel than before the market crash but people are making do with what they have because they are capable and have hope. Without turmoil and given some level of freedom, people find their own way. Even in the midst of turmoil they somehow find a way.

This is not some phenomenon of the American spirit, some sort of American exceptionalism. It is the strength humans have shown time and again in the face of adversity. There is no way to prove this but history and journalism can point to thousands of examples. If we read history to learn, how can we not learn this? Academics can argue over methodology, ideology, causation, and the like, but we have yet to see anyone argue against the position that man is resurgent. Someone arguing against this would have to adopt the position that people are delusional, that they ignore the possibility that they might fail again (as my colleague cited earlier might have argued using his definition of cynicism). Yet we think people understand all too well that there is risk and that they might fail. They have doubts, they lack confidence at times, they get depressed now and then, yet they move forward, they still try. Communities are built on this striving. What other characteristics of communities will we be able to find that show there is now a way forward?

The level of violence, if it was present, will have fallen, particularly in the environs of the specific regional or smaller community. The community will have established an adequate level of security and policing, a sense of safety.

Regional and smaller communities will have been able to meet the needs of most of their citizens. Furthermore, in line with the earlier discussion of hope, people will have plans to build both homes and businesses because they see opportunities to improve their lives. They will now have the confidence to want to take advantage of them. Communities as well will have plans to improve infrastructure and other services to meet the needs of their citizens.

People will have been able to work together for the most part although there will always be some disagreement. People are people, with all their myriad strengths and weaknesses.

There will a viable political structure with which people are generally satisfied. Citizens are able to participate in the political process.

There will considerable intellectual give-and-take as people try to make sense of their lives. People generally listen, even if they do not always agree. They try to evaluate the news from the "outside world" as it makes its way through to them.

Religious and similar organizations will be recognized as supportive of and adding strength to community life. They are not tearing it apart by emphasizing particularity and insularity.

Preparation for an Upturn

We are at an inflection point. Before now, we have always been planning for the worst. Now we have to be ready to take advantage of an upturn. Planning for an upturn should resemble your planning process in advance of a market crash, except with a much more positive outlook.

The focus of your planning should be on taking advantage of opportunities. Planning for a market crash and credit crunch stressed downside protection and credit quality. Now you need to look carefully at what we believe will be a variety of opportunities. By this we mean opportunities for which you have skills and experience and the requisite enthusiasm. Some of these might be job opportunities because of businesses or projects that are being built in your community. Others might be business opportunities. With respect to the latter, conditions in the aftermath of a market crash and credit crunch make it much harder to for entrepreneurs to find funding. Once things hit bottom, people with assets may be willing to go "risk on" and take a chance at funding good business ideas. Presumably there will be fewer private equity, hedge fund, and investment bankers in the market yet depository institutions will still be present even if their lending standards are tight. Yet even they may be in the process of becoming more accommodating. In looking at opportunities and potential sources of funding, take a second look at your financial and other assets. Ask yourself to what extent you can monetize assets that you own in order fund new opportunities.

Redo your skills assessment. Are you positioned for an upturn? Is there anything you need to do differently? What do you have to offer?

There should be no need to change your lifestyle. After surviving the rigors of the downturn, the way you want to live your life is probably set. The only thing you must guard against is spending beyond your means if your new opportunities turn successful. Spending beyond our means was a major contributing factor to the economic collapse outlined in this book, so why would you choose to start this all over again?

---

[83]Look, for instance, at the titles of Ann Coulter's books at www.anncoulter.com. If you believe what she is saying, why would you even want to associate or talk with "the other"?

[84] An example of this thinking can be seen in the following blog post: Matthias, "What is all this autarky buzz about?" (August 2, 2010), http://ma.juii.net/blog/what-is-all-this-autarky-buzz-about (accessed November 22, 2012).

[85] An interesting book that comments on the depression of a people after a period of stress is: John W. Dower, *Embracing Defeat: Japan in the Wake of World War II*, (New York: W.W. Norton & Co, 1999, Chapter 3 ("*Kyodatsu*: Exhaustion and Despair").

[86] Katherine Boo, *Behind the Beautiful Forevers: Life, Death, and Hope in a Mumbai Undercity*, (New York: Random House, 2012).

Chapter 7

Reaching Out, Rebuilding Markets, Rebuilding Consensus

Introduction

We have seen a downward spiral through Chapter 6. At the end of Chapter 6, we forecast that a bottom would be reached, as well as some of the signs that would indicate we are at a bottom. Now we want to look at conditions to be met for the pattern to reverse, for Americans to emerge from their regional and smaller communities, to reestablish regional and national markets, and to rebuild national consensus. This all assumes that there is still one United States. If there is not, the consensus will refer to the regional entity we are part of.

Markets

A mammoth library exists of works on economic history, business history, and economic development. These have been written from a variety of perspectives. Academics can spend an inordinate amount of time defining what a market is, how it works, and its characteristics. Without trying to be flip, we will take the position that we know a market when we see one. We discussed financial markets in Chapter 1. That these are markets is most evident from stock exchanges and other formal venues where financial assets are bought and sold. Yet a market also clearly exists in real estate even though it is so varied and fractionated that it is hard to describe. And markets exist for the endless variety of products and services that make this country run. In other words, when people start to call it a market or think it about it as a market, then it is a market. The market may be dominated by oligopolistic buyers and sellers. That a market does not match pure economic theory or the writings of Adam Smith does not make it any less a market. That a market consists of thousands of participants does not make it any more of a market. What defines a market is that buyers and sellers are willing to trade goods, services, and assets.

Markets are evolving all the time. New sellers enter, some exit, new buyers enter, some exit. New products enter the market, others disappear. Economists and economic historians have the ability to

187

describe the dimensions of a market empirically, how it works, and how it has grown or faded over time. Such work can demonstrate how the actions of individual market participants, as a totality, have affected the market and how those actions have multiplied (or not) to help markets grow. After analyzing individual markets, the next analytical step is to compare one market with another, to seek out similarities and differences. We believe this is the way markets and the history of markets should be explored. We believe analytical results are more defensible if analysts are willing to leave *a priori* statements and ideology at the door. Building an analysis from the ground up seems to make far more sense when we have so much data on various markets. Furthermore, they should be far more believable than those which spend so much time on framework and ideology before proceeding to the detail. In other words, we are increasingly frustrated by stale, Ivory Tower constructs in this area of economics and economic history.

We believe most will agree, regardless of perspective, that presence of the following will characterize healthy markets that develop and achieve their full potential:

Trust and confidence. This is the one of the key themes that run throughout this book and has been commented on elsewhere throughout.

Rule of law. Law sets an appropriate framework which sets minimally acceptable expectations for buyers and sellers. It also establishes an alternative path for resolving issues when trust has broken down and negotiation has been unsuccessful. Buyers and sellers both feel they have equal access to the courts and will receive fair treatment regardless of size, wealth, or power.

Recognized means of payment. A currency exists in which all transactions are denominated. Buyers and sellers have a good level of confidence in the value of the currency and are willing to offer and accept it as legal tender without reservations. In most cases, this implicitly assumes there is a Federal Reserve Bank, or similar monetary authority, charged with regulating the money supply and that it is recognized for performing its functions effectively. A variety of means to make payment exist as an alternative to cash, ranging from check, and credit cards to wire and electronic funds transfer. An economic system based largely on barter would generally fail to meet this test of a market.

Surplus capacity or surplus product. A market cannot develop if one's working day and total productive capacity are directed toward meeting one's own needs. To use the most extreme example, a subsistence farmer does not have the time to do anything else; his every working hour is spent on growing enough to feed himself and his family. There is little left over, for what is left over must be stored away to sustain the family over the winter, spring, and summer months before the next crop comes in. The subsistence farmer has nothing left over to buy "extras" from a market; he does not even have extra labor time that he can barter. Markets only develop when participants are so productive that they produce more than they need for daily life. This surplus can then be made available to a market. If other market participants see value in the surplus, then they are willing to pay for it. A surplus can also mean surplus time instead of surplus product. If someone can easily meet all of his own needs, he could decide to offer his unused capacity or time to the market. Again, others may be willing to pay for this. Payment received for surplus product or surplus capacity will be directed back to the market (or perhaps a different market) because the payment can usually not be spent at home.

Evolution. Once a participant is exposed to a market, his or her production is directed to serving market demand. This usually results in specialization, customization, inventions, and innovations in order to meet market needs. As production grows larger, moving from the household to the community level, standardization is possible, which both improves quality and reduces costs. As markets grow even larger, opportunities may arise to buy products and services which are not available in the local community. In the early stages, this sometimes means that the surplus sold in markets is used directly to purchase goods to bring back to the local community for resale. This is likely to mean that a few early movers dominate relations with outside markets.

Competition. As interaction with outside markets grows, more are likely to see increased opportunity to advance their prospects and early movers will face increased competition. For the first time, the community as a whole comes to be exposed to increased competition. For the first time, it begins to experience real winners and losers. The early movers will perhaps have created barriers to competition that protect themselves but, over time, those barriers fall under the pressure from supply and demand.

Location. Location of the market is key. It must be convenient to all who want to use it. It must be relatively easy to get there which means that strong infrastructure, including roads, is extremely important. Communications also becomes critical as the market evolves: buyers and sellers need to have a sense of supply and demand before they arrive at market. If the product is heavy and bulky, then transport is required and transport costs become an issue, particularly if the market is too far away. If the product is perishable or will not be used for some time, the market must offer warehousing facilities. Furthermore, it must likely have access to many markets, i.e., farmers markets of today probably do not meet the criteria we have laid out here. Failure to meet any of these points will make it less attractive to buyers and sellers and limit its ability to grow.

Ancillary services. More developed markets have ancillary entities like credit institutions, shipping agents and brokers. These entities do not engage in production, buying, and selling but assist in the process. In addition, a market hub will have services like shops, hotels, and restaurants to accommodate those coming to market. As ancillary services grow, the market hub itself will create its own demand instead of just acting as an intermediary between local markets in outlying cities and towns.

These factors are what cause markets to develop based on a review of economic history; however, it is not as if the members of our regional and smaller communities have no memory of what a market looks like. Markets might have been astounding and thrilling to farmers carrying their produce to towns during the Middle Ages. Market day was an event. They will not be astounding to members of new regional communities. What probably will be astounding to them is how they could have broken down, how things could have gotten so bad.

Here again, everything depends on perspective. We have made no comment on how long it has been since the US economic model collapsed and how long political and social cohesion has broken down. We have not predicted how long it will take to move from the market conditions as we see them today to the bottom of our downward spiral. This is essentially unknowable. Theoretically it could take just a few years, though we doubt it. On the other hand, it could be decades.

Since members of our community generally know what a market is supposed to look and feel like, presumably the path toward rebuilding markets will be shorter than after other periods of crisis in economic history. Based on the signs of a way forward, confidence in our regional and smaller communities would probably greater now than at any time in the recent past. People probably feel good about themselves, better than they have felt in a long time. What has to happen for the insularity of our regional and smaller communities to change?

Signs of a Way Forward

It probably all starts with communications. We presume that telecommunications technology remains relatively unchanged since the market crash, even though there may have been disruptions. We also assume that the internet still exists as we know it. People hear intriguing things about what is happening elsewhere. They develop some trust in the content—it is not all internet spam. People become interested in exploring things further. Conversations within the community repeatedly return to what is going on outside the community.[87]

People begin to think about and identify opportunities that may arise from participating in different, new markets. Entrepreneurs and others venture forth and dip their toes in the water to find out what is going on for themselves. They report back. Maybe they hear that the "other" they were all worried about never really existed. Maybe the source of all the turmoil is no longer there or, if so, it is much weaker. People begin to sense that the previous threats to public safety and personal well-being are much lower than before. Confidence, a key component to everything discussed in this book, rises as people sense diminished risk. The rise in confidence is the foundation on which all can move forward.

Preparation

If people are going to move into new markets, they need to put aside some of their previous ideas and misconceptions. They must become truly open. Are you really open to looking at new ideas, to having someone challenge what you have always thought was true? Or are you stuck in the past? As in Chapter 3, we believe education is critical.

Education is the only way to ensure that both present and future generations are exposed to the past and its shortcomings. Will we have a clear view or will we distort the past to suit our own needs? Or to make ourselves feel good? Will we ignore the ugly side of the past? We suggest that only by looking at the parts of the past we are not proud of can we move forward and make real progress. We must remember, and remember accurately, which is difficult because there is always the human tendency to sweep things we do not want to see or talk about under the rug.[88]

Education is the only way to ensure that both present and future generations have as clear a picture as possible of the rest of the world. We must make every effort to discover the world as it is. We must remember that the world is incredibly complex and always changing. We must resist those with agendas who try to simplify everything for us by creating "silver bullets" that will supposedly cure our ills. Only through education can we analyze and evaluate the competing narratives that appear before us every single day. Many Islamic terrorists have limited educations and so find it hard to resist the "silver bullets" offered by extremist religious leaders. Anti-globalization activists, while educated, have allowed their limited knowledge about how business works to accept without challenge "silver bullets" offered by economic crackpots. The uneducated majority in pre-Revolution Russia accepted Bolshevik solutions for their poverty, oppression, and lack of progress because of charismatic leadership and messianic texts without understanding what the Communist ideology really had in store for them. The followers of Jim Jones, though presumably educated, followed him to ultimate disaster and death. How can this be? There appears to be no end to the human yearning for simple solutions to life. Given this, there appears no end to the folly that hucksters can perpetrate. Maybe a sucker truly is born every minute. Educating ourselves and our children is the only thing that stands in the way of being taken in. Admittedly, there is no guarantee — even the well-educated with multiple degrees make grievous errors — but education is the best protection we have.

Better education can help people stop harping on differences and look for ways in which people are alike. Hopefully, greater openness will cause people to start dismissing the caricature of the "other."

Education may cause people to want to reach out, to want to learn about other people directly instead of through the media and word-of-mouth. Many may become more open to traveling outside of their communities.

If we see progress—we are looking only for progress, not utopia—on the above, then it is more than likely that many of the conditions, especially trust, which underpin healthy markets can be met. If trust can be reestablished, then markets will have a foundation for growth and our regional and smaller communities can grow along with them. How markets develop cannot be forecast here. Markets are inherently dynamic and will adapt to meet the needs of buyers and sellers.[89]

One question must still be answered. Do growing markets contribute to national consensus or is national consensus a prerequisite to growing markets? The political turmoil we have posited was a contributor to the breakdown in markets and contributed to the loss of social cohesion. Individuals retreated from contact with others because they were unsure and afraid. What brings them back again?

What brings them back is need. As noted, confidence and trust are the cornerstones of every market. For local and regional markets, trust and confidence are relatively easy to establish because we can meet the other participants directly. What must happen if one needs to go beyond the local or regional market?

To consider possible answers to this question, it may be helpful to look at our own American experience. Why did the colonies see a need to unite? Each of the thirteen colonies was established under a different charter and was sponsored by different groups/companies in England. Each had a different character, different economic base, different goals, and different outlooks. Their citizens had different religious, economic, and class backgrounds. If each colony was slightly different, why could they have not gone on as they were? Much has obviously been written on this subject but these were probably the two most important reasons:

Taxation. Taxation without representation was the issue which bound the interests of the colonies together because all felt they needed common relief. All felt taxes, however levied, were too high.

Restrictions on self-government. New English laws reversed the political processes established in the original charters in each colony. Royal governors took control. In reaction, provincial congresses were established in each colony, in defiance of the Intolerable Acts. Concerns about taxation and self-government went hand-in-hand.

Taxation was most important to the propertied because the tax burden fell most heavily on them. They, not the working classes, were the ones who felt common bond across the colonies and they were the ones who led the American Revolution. This was not a revolution from below. There was no guillotine, no spasm of bloodshed. A good deal of writing about the Revolution emphasizes Americans' desire for freedom as its cause. While this is true to a point, we believe it is overdone. Without the economic issues and the way they affected the leaders in each colony, we doubt that freedom in the abstract would have been enough to cause a break with England. Some of the most prominent leaders of the Revolution were very conflicted about separating from what they saw as the mother country. Historians have estimated that loyalists constituted 15-20% of the population during the Revolution. Without the economic issues, we venture to say that loyalist sentiments might have been held by more than 15-20% and that the Revolution may have been averted.

Once united, why did each colony find the method of governance under the Articles of Confederation unsatisfactory? The reason was that Congress, like the Continental Congress before it, had no power over taxation and trade. Those powers remained with the states. In fact, most powers remained with the states: Congress could only accomplish what the states would permit. Again, just as before Independence, we see economic issues predominating. The economic situation was unmanageable. The post-Revolutionary period saw economic turmoil. The states compounded the problem by refusing to print paper money and then began pursuing unpaid taxes in order to pay off war debt. Debtors, in the depth of a post-war economic crisis, resisted. Some states then began issuing paper money which they used to pay off war debt, which aroused creditors who found their assets effectively "annihilated" (per General Knox in a letter to George Washington). Shays Rebellion, supported by farmers who wanted debt relief, broke out in Massachusetts. The Rebellion alarmed all American leaders.[90] They realized that they had to change the Articles in order to address the economic problems at issue. This paved the way to the US Constitution and a stronger central government.

Economic issues appear to have been central, fundamental in forming "a more perfect union." We believe that people who want to see markets grow will demand government which can provide the stability needed for market confidence. As with the American experience under the Articles of Confederation, we believe a demand for better government will arise from a demand for strong markets and this has the potential to create a new national consensus. We doubt that the process works the other way around. For consensus to arise without roots in economic demand would appear to imply that citizens have noble interests they want to pursue because they are troubled by the divisions that plague the country. We tend to believe that people vote their pocketbooks. People will be most willing to address the problems they face when those problems pinch their pocketbooks.

National consensus will grow stronger once people become more open to change. Seeing others as "the other" will no longer be acceptable to the vast majority. Yet, based on history, we doubt that consensus can be attained until people begin demanding it. The major reason they will begin demanding it is the need to standardize economic relations that span a wider geography than the regional and smaller communities. When people understand that standardizing economic relations requires working together, consensus will grow and the conflicts of the past will hopefully subside.

---

[87]See Howe in fn. 77 for a good discussion of how newspapers, roads, and waterways helped bind the US closer together.

[88] An interesting book of varied essays/articles that speak partly to this topic from a US and Japanese perspective is: John W. Dower, *Ways of Forgetting, Ways of Remembering: Japan in the Modern World*, (New York: The New Press, 2012).

[89] The writings of some academics, especially some economic historians, overstress the institutional side of markets. It is as if markets stand almost independent of buyers and sellers, without acknowledging that buyers and sellers create them. This is an unfortunate overemphasis perhaps stemming from government's role in helping markets develop during the Middle Ages. These narratives must be better adjusted to the state of markets as they stand today.

[90]A side issue for speculation: would the US Constitution have come into being without the *shock* of Shays Rebellion to propel American leaders forward?

Afterword

We have laid out a downward spiral through six chapters followed by a discussion of the basis for recovery in the seventh. This spiral plunges the US into the depths of an agonizing loss of economic, political, and social cohesion. The question of course arises: is the downward spiral inevitable? At its foundation this question has two parts. First, can the *shock* that starts the spiral be averted? And second, can the spiral, once it starts, be stopped before it reaches the absolute depths described in Chapters 5 and 6?

A *shock* <u>will</u> occur at some point in the future. It cannot be avoided. The world is too complex. Complexity means that imbalances will inevitably arise. Adam Smith's "invisible hand" cannot sweep all of them away. Some will be left to fester, some like a market bubble will build unnoticed. They will always be with us. An unexpected or misperceived event will burst "out of nowhere," shock our political and economic system, and expose the most severe imbalances for what they are. The market crash and the credit crunch are the economy's initial attempt to adjust to the imbalances. If, however, the imbalances are intractable, structural, mere changes in market pricing and practices cannot eliminate them.

If a *shock* is inevitable, the best course would seem to lie in delaying it as long as possible. The longer we can delay a shock, the more likely we will be stronger than we are today. The downward spiral in Chapters 1-6 is most likely to arise as we remain weak from the collapse of the real estate bubble which burst in 2007-2009. That we are still weak today makes us more vulnerable, our adjustment to the force of the shock more difficult. Strength means that we can adjust more quickly and easily. Delay also means we have a better chance to uncover and address imbalances <u>before</u> they become a major threat. Yet how can we delay a shock? Isn't this just wishful thinking?

Let's look at China. China has tremendous imbalances within both its economy and society but has not imploded. What has enabled it to avoid tremendous economic and social pain has been strong economic growth, 7%+ in 2012, over 8% in the five years prior. We suggested in Chapter 1 that slowing growth was the biggest threat to China because it would then no longer have the breathing room to deal with imbalances. We suggested that in the possibility of lower growth lies greater potential for a *shock* not only to China but to the global economy.

Table A.1 shows that US growth over the past decade has been far lower than that seen in the prior fifty years.

Table A.1	
Annual Growth in Real GDP	
1951-1961	3.0%
1961-1971	4.3%
1971-1981	3.1%
1981-1991	3.0%
1991-2001	3.5%
2001-2011	1.6%
Compound annual rates of growth by decade	
Source: Bureau of Economic Analysis	

The reason why US debt and government deficits seem like such a threat is that lower economic growth means insufficient government revenue. The Congressional Budget Office (CBO) projects 2.1-2.3% annual real GDP growth through 2022 (under various scenarios), far below the historical averages seen in Table A.1. It is on the basis of projections like these that many have raised the alarm about the unsustainability of current debt levels and deficits.

Harping on debt and deficits looks very much like extrapolating from the current trendline. It assumes that economic growth over the next decade will look very much like the past ten years. Extrapolating from the current trendline is the reason why so many are assuming that America is in decline.[91] Much of the analysis of debt and deficits arises from an attitude of pessimism, in some cases extreme pessimism. We are sure the reader is sick of this but we will make the point one more time: humans are overly prone to forecasting the future based on historical patterns and trends. They have difficulty considering alternatives not embedded in the current trendline. Clearly a return to GDP growth of 3.0-3.5% or higher over a period of years would mean a sea-change in both our fiscal picture and mental outlook. Yet analysts and commentators appear unable to consider this alternative possibility even though they have 50+ years of data sitting before them. We will not attempt to readjust CBO's estimates of federal deficits under higher economic growth rates—without access to CBO's economic model, the task is far too hard because there are too many path-dependent scenarios for tax rates and spending—but it is clear that higher growth would result in much lower deficits. And higher growth gives us greater flexibility for dealing with the imbalances which exist today as we delay a *shock*.

Do we truly believe we will never see 3.0% growth again? Are we dwelling too much on the difficulties of today and not putting things in perspective? The harsh political rhetoric of today makes it appear that America now sits in the worst position it has. This is clearly ludicrous. Too many seem to have forgotten the debate over slavery, the Civil War, economic and labor strife during the latter half of the 19th century, World War I, the Great Depression, the rise of communism and fascism, World War II, and the global military, political, and economic crises of the Cold War period. Surely no one can say that the crises of today, however critical, measure up to those of the past which threatened our very existence. And yet in the midst of all this turmoil during the second half of the 20th century, the US was still able to achieve average GDP growth of 3% or better.

To focus only on our problems is to ignore America's strengths. Let's reacquaint ourselves with those strengths, which we classify under three headings:

Size & Position. For all the talk about China, it is easy to forget that the US is the third largest country of the world in terms of population. More important, that population is a source of relative strength in spite of the aging of the baby boomers. Europe, China, and Japan all face greater challenges due to aging populations than we do. While US birth rates have declined, they remain higher than in other developed countries. Furthermore, in spite of our inability to establish a workable policy in this area, the US still remains more open to immigration than other countries. Immigrants have also proven to have higher birth rates than native-born Americans and thus have been an ongoing source of demographic strength. In addition, the US population is dispersed across a great land area, unlike much of the rest of the world. This means that geography does not present a limitation on growth. One often hears the words "population is destiny." If this is true, then the US is in a very strong position.

The US also has the largest economy in the world. Not only is it large, but it is far more vibrant and varied, in spite of the current malaise, than any other country. The breadth and depth of the US economy provides it incredible strength that others, whose economic activity is less diverse, cannot match.

Although the US clearly faces issues, everyone looks to the US for leadership, militarily, politically, and economically.[92] It has been said many times that the US is the irreplaceable, the indispensable nation. While one might say this is hyperbole—no one is irreplaceable—one sees no other nation rising to replace us. First, countries like China and India clearly have no interest in international leadership except on a few side issues. Europe, mired in solving its own problems, cannot lead. Russia, still in the process of adapting to the fall of the Soviet Union and overly dependent on energy for its future, is at the moment too inward-looking to do much on the world stage. Second, in spite of natural resentment over US dominance and disagreements over US policies, most nations are comfortable with the US position in the world. Few will say so on the record but they can see no one else taking our place. Moreover, they would probably have great distress if countries like China or Russia were to have greater weight in world affairs. The reason why most are comfortable with US leadership is that we are a known quantity, we are dependable. They have a very good feeling of how we will react to crises and of how we will lead. Our leadership keeps the world on a path towards greater democracy, freedom, and human rights and insists that a pro-trade, anti-protectionist economic system remains critical to the well-being of all; it thereby blunts centrifugal forces that pull in other directions. Yes, we may be arrogant at times, we may disregard others' views, we may make mistakes, and others may suspect our motives, but most know we will ultimately try to do the right thing—even if we veer off onto side-paths and it sometimes takes overly long to get there. This position of leadership, even as it adjusts to changing circumstances, is unlikely to change for a very, very long time. This is a clear position of strength that no other can match.

Productivity. The US exceeds almost every OECD country in virtually every measure of productivity. The US is the world's leader in technology. It has the finest research universities. It spends more on R&D than any other nation. Its high-tech companies lead the world wherever one cares to look: hardware, software, information technology, telecommunications technology, biotechnology, medical technology. It has produced more technical advances and inventions than any other country by a wide margin. US technological superiority has driven great advances in productivity over the last three decades — not just for the US but for the world — by delivering the power of computing and information technology to the desktop and the factory floor. Today, it is very hard to remember how we used to function without the desktop/laptop/tablet computer, cellphone, and internet. They are all due to the US. This technological leadership is clearly a source of strength. While one cannot forecast whether technological superiority will bring a new surge in productivity over the next decade — one cannot predict where the next breakthrough will come from — one would not want to bet against it. The US economy rests on the best technological foundation of any other country which gives us the wherewithal to maintain our lead in productivity.

Competitiveness. For all its faults, the US economy is the most business-friendly of any country in the world. It is easier to start a business here. The rule of law provides great stability. The market is huge, which makes it the best place to test any new idea. Corruption is low. The workforce is generally skilled. Moreover, American workers appear to be more flexible and adaptable than in other nations. Our high-quality, challenging business schools, which no other country can match, turn out graduates for whom starting their own business is often a personal dream. This contrasts sharply with other economies dominated by large companies and elites in which it is hard to get ahead on one's own. The US clearly values entrepreneurship more than other country and does more to foster an environment in which small- and medium-sized businesses can succeed. Yet it is not only in entrepreneurship, flexibility, and adaptability that the US stands alone. The US is in the midst of an energy revolution based on development of new sources of oil and natural gas (including from "fracking"). These have the potential to reduce our costs of energy relative to other countries and make the US even more competitive. Indeed, as this revolution proceeds, we may see companies, both US and foreign, seeking to build more plants in the US because of advantageous energy cost differentials and the other strengths the US market offers.

Given all this, is it not possible that size & position, productivity, and competitiveness will combine to provide us stronger growth than currently forecast? Granted, it is hard to achieve strong growth with Europe currently in recession, but the US has clear strengths which can cause one to be optimistic even as we remain mindful of the challenges we face. Even so, we know there are no guarantees that growth will improve. What can we do to allow us to better utilize our strengths and thereby achieve stronger growth? Here are some thoughts:

Focus on growth, not ancillary matters. We must not let ourselves get side-tracked on debt and deficits. Only growth offers the US a brighter future. Austerity is a short-term band-aid for current deficits but provides us no path to the future; in fact, it will undermine our future, just as it is doing in Greece and Spain. Thus budget cuts must be approached with a scalpel, not a meat-axe. Likewise, tax increases must be approached in a reasonable fashion. While one may question the wisdom of the Bush tax cuts, they are with us and so cannot be overturned overnight. On the other hand, many of the well-to-do have done quite well solely as a result of those tax cuts, not because they were wondrous "job creators" as rhetoric might have us believe. It is probably time to talk about paying their paying more, particularly when the combined federal, state, and local tax burden on US citizens is lower than it has been in a very long time.[93]

Reward capital expenditures aimed at growth. Investment spending helps the economy today and establishes the foundations of future growth. Capital expenditures ("capex") should thus be encouraged. Tax cuts, including cuts in capital gains taxes, are a mantra, the first idea one hears when discussing encouragement of investment; yet there is no data that proves that the proceeds from across-the-board tax cuts will go towards new capital equipment. Thus they are inefficient with respect to the growth we need to achieve. Many cite the Kennedy-era investment tax credit of 1962 as giving a real boost to the economy. One questions whether one-time measures like that really boost long-term growth; in the end, they may merely front-load capex that was going to occur anyway. We need a targeted policy that supports capex and which is stable over the long-term, not just 1-2 years.

There are two types of capex. Maintenance capex ("mcapex") is "required" in order to keep cash flow at current levels; it is required because, without it, cash flow will diminish. A machine that wears out must be replaced; if it is not, productive capacity falls. Note, however, that no growth results—mcapex merely enables a company to stay where it is. What we want to reward, perhaps via a tax credit, is growth capex ("gcapex"), capex which either expands capacity or reduces production costs such that cash flow can grow. Businesses that are spending for gcapex should be rewarded, others not. We realize that the US tax code is already complex and that it may be hard to distinguish mcapex from gcapex, but we think it is wise to the make the effort because it points us in the direction we want to go.

Reward spending on technical training and on hiring for STEM jobs. We want to ensure the US labor force meets the needs of business. Consider a 100% tax credit — again, this should be a long-term program, not a short-term stimulus — for any technical training provided by business. Consider a tax deduction, perhaps for one year, equal to a fixed percentage of any salary costs required to hire individuals with existing STEM skills that relate *directly* to a company's business needs. As with rewarding investment in gcapex, these ideas focus on moving us in the direction we want to go. Yes, we acknowledge that these benefits (as well as tax credits for gcapex discussed) may be abused as companies try to squeeze their capex, training, and hiring into categories that qualify for favorable tax treatment, but we believe that the potential benefits of tax policies specifically targeted towards growth should outweigh fear of tax compliance issues. Comparing the two, fostering tax compliance will always be more easily achieved than encouraging gcapex.

Higher growth should provide a way to delay a *shock* which gives us more time to deal with existing imbalances like those discussed in Chapters 1 through 6. We should be much stronger the longer we can delay it but, if one occurs, are there still ways to avoid the depths of the downward spiral? Can we make adjustments without having to go through tremendous pain? Many observers addressing this question focus on America's political will and ongoing polarization in Washington. Many doubt whether we have the will to resolve problems that face us. As with perspectives on future growth rates, the narrative we hear in the media every day with respect to political will is mind-numbingly pessimistic.

However pessimistic we may be today, it is clear that most times America does find a way forward, even if it takes far too long and costs much more than it should in terms of human suffering and economic costs. It is true that we often only act when we are under extreme pressure but, leaving authoritarian states aside, are other countries any different in this regard? If you listen to commentary on

CNBC, it is almost as if they expect a new "silver bullet" every day that will solve the European debt crisis and US deficits. They express naïve frustration that problems are not being "solved." They profess to be experts on business but daily demonstrate how little they understand about how the world really works. These issues will take years to work their way out because they took years to create. One has to adopt a longer view. One should not become pessimistic just because problems cannot be solved overnight.

Focusing solely on political will in Washington is myopic. If the unemployment rate goes up, the President is responsible, and if it goes down, he gets the credit. The US economy, with $13 trillion in GDP, is incredibly complex. The variety of businesses, from small to large, is incredibly diverse. The US has never had an industrial policy and never will. That China's political cadres think they can centrally plan the second largest economy in the world is delusional. To think that 535 legislators plus the President can cure everything that ails us is equally naïve. Yes, Washington must do its part on what it can control but it is only part of the solution.

Business, labor, education, and the average citizen bear a burden of responsibility equal to those in government. America today has a winner-take-all approach to business and to political and social discourse. Laissez-faire economics was discredited long ago but one would think that, listening to the comments of far too many business leaders, it still lies at the foundation of our business model. Those who sought compromise like Henry Clay prior to the Civil War have been credited with greatness. Compromise today is regarded by some as near-treason. The only way we can find solutions to the imbalances that face us is to work together. Working together will require compromise. It will require respectful discourse. If these occur, we are confident that the worst of the downward spiral can be prevented once a *shock* occurs. The reason it will be avoided is because we will have already begun to address, in a realistic fashion, our overdependence on consumption and the service sector, the issues in the finance and health care sectors, the balance between business and labor interests, and an education system that continues to leave far too many behind.

Naysayers will be skeptical. We already hear whispers of rose-colored glasses. They doubt Americans can find a way forward. What they are betting on is that Americans will not make the right choices when under pressure. Perhaps that is a good bet—we do not really know—but if you had made the same bet hundreds of times throughout US history, you would be bankrupt by now. We cannot ignore the problems that face us but we do not doubt that humans, including Americans, are resurgent. We will give Americans the benefit of the doubt until they prove us wrong.

---

[91] On a side note, the downward spiral has also assumed that current low economic growth continues, but from a slightly different perspective than those who extrapolate. It assumes that, if another *shock* occurs, we will not be able to return to the world of the past because embedded structural imbalances will be too hard to overcome given our current economic sluggishness. Unlike the CBO perspective which does not address the possibility of a shock (such analyses never do so), it assumes a "new normal" due to the shock. It thus assumes both another shock and collective inability to address imbalances in a way that prevents the downward spiral. It is thus a worst-case scenario, far different from those who are extrapolating from trendlines.

[92] Some are worried about the risk of US overextension militarily and the burden this places on us relative to other countries. Overextension is a major theme in this often-cited book: Paul M. Kennedy, *The Rise and Fall of the Great Powers*, (New York: Random House, 1987). Although US military budgets exceed those in the rest of the world by astounding multiples, most analyses show that US military spending, as a percentage of GDP, should decline over the next decade.

[93] "Tax Burden for Most Americans Is Lower Than in the 1980s," *New York Times*, November 29, 2012.

Appendix I
Personal Financial Statement

PERSONAL FINANCIAL STATEMENT & ANALYSIS FOR:

Assets	Amount ($)	Liabilities & Net Worth	Amount ($)
Cash on Hand and in Banks (Schedule A)		Notes Payable to Banks, Other Institutions (Schedule H)	
US Government Securities (Schedule B)		Notes Payable: Relatives (Schedule H)	
Other Fixed Investments (Schedule B)			
Listed Equity Investments (Schedule C)		Notes Payable: Others	
Unlisted Investments (Schedule D)		Real Estate Mortgages Payable (Schedule G)	
Retirement Accounts (Schedule E)		Land Contracts Payable	
Other Equity Interests (Schedule F)		Life Insurance Loans	
Real Estate Owned (Schedule G)		Loans on Life Insurance and Annuities, Retirement Accounts	
Mortgages and Land Contracts Receivable		Estimated Income Taxes	
Notes Receivables		Credit Cards	
Cash Value Life Insurance			
Other Assets: Car, furniture, etc			
		TOTAL LIABILITIES	
		NET WORTH	
TOTAL ASSETS		**TOTAL LIABILITIES AND NET WORTH**	

Cash Income & Expenditures Statement Projected for Next 12 Months			
Annual Income	Amount ($)	Annual Expenditures	Amount ($)
Salary & Wages		Income Taxes - US	
Interest & Dividends		Income Taxes - State & Local	
Real Estate Income		Living Expenses	
Trust Income		Real Estate Taxes	
Business Income		Other Real Estate Expenses	
Alimony, Child Support, etc		Planned Investments	
Pension		Alimony, Child Support, etc	
Social Security		Mortgage Payments	
IRA Distributions		Other Debt Service	
		Credit Card Payments	
TOTAL ANNUAL INCOME		TOTAL ANNUAL EXPENDITURES	
		TOTAL ANNUAL CASH FLOW	

SCHEDULE A - CASH ON HAND AND IN BANKS & MONEY MARKET FUNDS					
Name of Institution	Name on Account	Balance on Deposit	Type	Pledged?	Comment

SCHEDULE B - FIXED INCOME INVESTMENTS				
Custodian	In the Name of	Market Value	Pledged?	Comment
US Government Securities				
Municpal Bonds				
Corporate Bonds				
High Yield-Bonds				
Mutual Funds & ETFs*				

*Designate type using this coding: USG = US Government, M = Municipal, C = Corporate, HY = High Yield, EM = Emerging Markets, BK = Bank Loan, INT = International

SCHEDULE C - EQUITY INVESTMENTS (LISTED)				
Custodian	In the Name of	Market Value	Pledged?	Comment
Domestic Equity				
International Equity				
Limited Partnerships & REITs (publicly traded)				
Mutual Funds & ETFs*				

Designate type using this coding: ALT = currency, precious metals, commodities, etc, US = Domestic, INT = International, S = Sector

SCHEDULE D - UNLISTED INVESTMENTS: LIMITED PARTNERSHIPS & LLCs (ownership <25%)				
Name of LP or LLC	In the Name of	Market Value	Pledged?	Comment
Real Estate				
Non-Real Estate				

SCHEDULE E - RETIREMENT ACCOUNTS				
Custodian	In the Name of	Market Value	Type	Comment

SCHEDULE F - OTHER EQUITY INTERESTS: S-CORPs, LIMITED PARTNERSHIPS & LLCs (ownership >25%, non-real estate)				
Name of S-Corp, LP, or LLC	In the Name of	Market Value	Annual EBITDA	Comment

SCHEDULE G - REAL ESTATE OWNED (and related debt)					
Property	Title in name of	Date Acquired	Market Value	NOI	Current Mortgage Balance
	Cost + Improvements:				
Comments:					
	Cost + Improvements:				
Comments:					
	Cost + Improvements:				
Comments:					
	Cost + Improvements:				
Comments:					
	Cost + Improvements:				
Comments:					

SCHEDULE H - NOTES PAYABLE (non-real estate)				
Custodian	In the Name of	Current Balance	Collateral	Comment
Notes Payable to Banks & Other Financial Institutions				
Notes Payable - Relatives				
Notes Payable - Others				

Appendix II
Financial Plan Worksheet

Assets & Debt Current	Interim Step 1	Date	Interim Step 2	Date	Assets & Debt Final Target	Date	Comments
FIXED INCOME Cash & Money Market US Government							
Municipal Bonds							
High-Yield Bonds							
Mutual Funds & ETFs							
EQUITY (listed) Domestic Equity							
International Equity							
MLPs & REITs (listed)							
Mutual Funds & ETFs							
UNLISTED (non-controlling)							
RETIREMENT ACCOUNTS							
UNLISTED (controlling)							
REAL ESTATE							
DEBT							

Appendix III
Sectors & Industries

Sector	Industry	Outlook
Basic Materials	Chemical Manufacturing	N
	Chemicals – Plastics & Rubber	N
	Containers & Packaging	N
	Fabricated – Plastic & Rubber	N
	Forestry & Wood Products	+
	Gold & Silver	-
	Iron & Steel	N
	Metal Mining	N
	Miscellaneous Fabricated Products	N
	Non-Metallic Mining	+
	Paper & Paper Products	N
Capital Goods	Aerospace & Defense	-
	Construction & Agricultural	+
	Construction – Supplies & Fixtures	N
	Construction – Raw Materials	+
	Construction Services	N
	Miscellaneous Capital Goods	N
	Mobile Homes & RVs	-
Consumer Cyclical	Apparel/Accessories	N
	Appliance & Tool	+
	Audio & Video Equipment	-
	Auto & Truck Manufacturing	N
	Auto & Truck Parts	N

Sector	Industry	Outlook
Healthcare	Biotechnology & Drugs	N
	Healthcare Facilities	N
	Major Drug Companies	-
	Medical Equipment & Supplies	N
Services	Advertising	-
	Broadcasting & Cable TV	-
	Business Services	-
	Casinos & Gambling	-
	Communications Services	-
	Hotels & Motels	-
	Motion Pictures	-
	Personal Services	-
	Printing & Publishing	-
	Printing Services	-
	Real Estate Operations	-
	Recreational Activities	-
	Rental & Leasing	N
	Restaurants	-
	Retail (Apparel)	N
	Retail (Catalog & Mail Order)	N
	Retail (Department & Discount)	N
	Retail (Drugs)	N
	Retail (Grocery)	N

Sector	Industry	Outlook
	Footwear	N
	Furniture & Fixtures	N
	Jewelry & Silverware	-
	Photography	-
	Recreational Products	N
	Textiles – Non-Apparel	N
	Tires	N
Consumer Non-Cyclical	Beverages (Alcoholic)	+
	Beverages (Non-Alcoholic)	+
	Crops	+
	Fish/Livestock	+
	Food Processing	N
	Office Supplies	-
	Personal/Household Products	+
	Tobacco	-
Energy	Coal	N
	Oil & Gas	+
	Oil Well Services & Equipment	+
Financial	Consumer Financial Services	-
	Insurance (Accident & Health)	N
	Insurance (Life)	-
	Insurance (Miscellaneous)	N
	Insurance (Property & Casualty)	N
	Investment Services	-
	Miscellaneous Financial Services	-
	Money Center Banks	-
	Regional Banks	N
	S&Ls/Savings Banks	-
Technology	Communications Equipment	-
	Computer Hardware	-
	Computer Networks	+
	Computer Peripherals	N
	Computer Services	-
	Computer Storage Devices	N
	Electronic Instrumentation & Controls	+
	Office Equipment	-
	Scientific & Technical Instruments	+
	Semiconductors	+
	Software & Programming	N
Transportation	Air Courier	-
	Airline	N
	Miscellaneous Transportation	N
	Railroads	+
	Trucking	N
	Water Transportation	N
Utilities	Electric Utilities	+
	Natural Gas Utilities	+
	Water Utilities	+

Outlook in the aftermath of a severe market collapse:

N means will likely perform in line with the rest of the market

+ means will likely perform better than the overall market

- means will likely perform worse than the overall market

Appendix IV
Classification of Contributors to GDP

G or S	Value Added by Industry as a Percentage of GDP (in %)	
	Industry	**2011**
	Gross domestic product (GDP)	100.0
	Private industries	86.8
	Agriculture, forestry, fishing, and hunting	1.2
	Farms	
	Forestry, fishing, and related activities	
	Mining	1.9
G	Oil and gas extraction	
G	Mining, except oil and gas	
G	Support activities for mining	
	Utilities	1.7
G	**Construction**	3.4
G	**Manufacturing**	12.2
G	**Durable goods**	6.6
G	Wood products	
G	Nonmetallic mineral products	
G	Primary metals	
G	Fabricated metal products	
G	Machinery	
G	Computer and electronic products	
G	Electrical equipment, appliances, and components	
G	Motor vehicles, bodies and trailers, and parts	
G	Other transportation equipment	
G	Furniture and related products	
G	Miscellaneous manufacturing	
G	**Nondurable goods**	5.6
G	Food and beverage and tobacco products	
G	Textile mills and textile product mills	
G	Apparel and leather and allied products	
G	Paper products	
G	Printing and related support activities	
G	Petroleum and coal products	
G	Chemical products	
G	Plastics and rubber products	
S	**Wholesale trade**	5.6
S	**Retail trade**	6.1
	Transportation and warehousing	2.8
	Air transportation	
	Rail transportation	
	Water transportation	
	Truck transportation	
	Transit and ground passenger transportation	
	Pipeline transportation	
	Other transportation and support activities	
	Warehousing and storage	

S	**Information**	**4.4**
S	Publishing industries (includes software)	
S	Motion picture and sound recording industries	
S	Broadcasting and telecommunications	
S	Information and data processing services	
S	**Finance, insurance, real estate, rental, and leasing**	**19.9**
S	**Finance and insurance**	**8.3**
S	Federal Reserve banks, credit intermediation, and related activities	
S	Securities, commodity contracts, and investments	
S	Insurance carriers and related activities	
S	Funds, trusts, and other financial vehicles	
S	**Real estate and rental and leasing**	**11.6**
S	Real estate	
S	Rental and leasing services and lessors of intangible assets	
S	**Professional and business services**	**12.6**
S	**Professional, scientific, and technical services**	**7.8**
S	Legal services	
S	Computer systems design and related services	
S	Miscellaneous professional, scientific, and technical services	
S	**Management of companies and enterprises**	**1.9**
S	**Administrative and waste management services**	**2.9**
S	Administrative and support services	
S	Waste management and remediation services	
S	**Educational services, health care, and social assistance**	**8.7**
S	**Educational services**	**1.1**
S	**Health care and social assistance**	**7.6**
S	Ambulatory health care services	
S	Hospitals and nursing and residential care facilities	
S	Social assistance	
S	**Arts, entertainment, recreation, accommodation, and food services**	**3.9**
S	**Arts, entertainment, and recreation**	**1.0**
S	Performing arts, spectator sports, museums, and related activities	
S	Amusements, gambling, and recreation industries	
S	**Accommodation and food services**	**2.9**
S	Accommodation	
S	Food services and drinking places	
S	**Other services, except government**	**2.4**
	Government	**13.2**
	Federal	**4.4**
	General government	
	Government enterprises	
	State and local	**8.8**
	General government	
	Government enterprises	

Source: Bureau of Economic Analysis

G= goods, S = services

215

Appendix V
Services Under Threat of a Breakdown in the US Business Model

Code	2007 NAICS US Title	Code	2007 NAICS US Title
441210	Recreational Vehicle Dealers	561410	Document Preparation Services
441221	Motorcycle, ATV, and Personal Watercraft Dealers	561422	Telemarketing Bureaus and Other Contact Centers
441222	Boat Dealers	561431	Private Mail Centers
446120	Cosmetics, Beauty Supplies, and Perfume Stores	561440	Collection Agencies
451110	Sporting Goods Stores	561450	Credit Bureaus
451120	Hobby, Toy, and Game Stores	561491	Repossession Services
453220	Gift, Novelty, and Souvenir Stores	561510	Travel Agencies
453910	Pet and Pet Supplies Stores	561520	Tour Operators
453920	Art Dealers	561611	Investigation Services
511120	Periodical Publishers	561612	Security Guards and Patrol Services
511130	Book Publishers	561730	Landscaping Services
511140	Directory and Mailing List Publishers	561910	Packaging and Labeling Services
511191	Greeting Card Publishers	561920	Convention and Trade Show Organizers
512110	Motion Picture and Video Production	611511	Cosmetology and Barber Schools
512120	Motion Picture and Video Distribution	611610	Fine Arts Schools
512131	Motion Picture Theaters (except Drive-Ins)	611620	Sports and Recreation Instruction
512191	Teleproduction and Other Postproduction Services	611630	Language Schools
512210	Record Production	611691	Exam Preparation and Tutoring
512220	Integrated Record Production/Distribution	611710	Educational Support Services
512230	Music Publishers	621610	Home Health Care Services
512240	Sound Recording Studios	624110	Child and Youth Services
522110	Commercial Banking	624310	Vocational Rehabilitation Services
522120	Savings Institutions	624410	Child Day Care Services
522130	Credit Unions	711110	Theater Companies and Dinner Theaters
522210	Credit Card Issuing	711120	Dance Companies
522220	Sales Financing	711130	Musical Groups and Artists
522291	Consumer Lending	711211	Sports Teams and Clubs
522292	Real Estate Credit	711212	Racetracks
522294	Secondary Market Financing	711410	Agents and Managers for Artists, Athletes, Entertainers, and Other Public Figures

Code	Description
522310	Mortgage and Nonmortgage Loan Brokers
523110	Investment Banking and Securities Dealing
523120	Securities Brokerage
523130	Commodity Contracts Dealing
523140	Commodity Contracts Brokerage
523920	Portfolio Management
523930	Investment Advice
525910	Open-End Investment Funds
532210	Consumer Electronics and Appliances Rental
532220	Formal Wear and Costume Rental
532230	Video Tape and Disc Rental
532291	Home Health Equipment Rental
532292	Recreational Goods Rental
541110	Offices of Lawyers
541211	Offices of Certified Public Accountants
541213	Tax Preparation Services
541214	Payroll Services
541320	Landscape Architectural Services
541611	Administrative Management and General Management Consulting Services
541612	Human Resources Consulting Services
541613	Marketing Consulting Services
541810	Advertising Agencies
541820	Public Relations Agencies
541830	Media Buying Agencies
541840	Media Representatives
541850	Display Advertising
541860	Direct Mail Advertising
561311	Employment Placement Agencies
561312	Executive Search Services
561320	Temporary Help Services
561330	Professional Employer Organizations
711510	Independent Artists, Writers, and Performers
713110	Amusement and Theme Parks
713120	Amusement Arcades
713210	Casinos (except Casino Hotels)
713290	Other Gambling Industries
713910	Golf Courses and Country Clubs
713920	Skiing Facilities
713930	Marinas
713940	Fitness and Recreational Sports Centers
713950	Bowling Centers
721110	Hotels (except Casino Hotels) and Motels
721120	Casino Hotels
721191	Bed-and-Breakfast Inns
721211	RV (Recreational Vehicle) Parks and Campgrounds
721214	Recreational and Vacation Camps (except Campgrounds)
722110	Full-Service Restaurants
722211	Limited-Service Restaurants
722212	Cafeterias, Grill Buffets, and Buffets
722213	Snack and Nonalcoholic Beverage Bars
722310	Food Service Contractors
722320	Caterers
722330	Mobile Food Services
722410	Drinking Places (Alcoholic Beverages)
812113	Nail Salons
812191	Diet and Weight Reducing Centers
812910	Pet Care (except Veterinary) Services
813311	Human Rights Organizations
813312	Environment, Conservation and Wildlife Organizations
813410	Civic and Social Organizations
813920	Professional Organizations
813940	Political Organizations

www.ingramcontent.com/pod-product-compliance
Lightning Source LLC
Chambersburg PA
CBHW070925210326
41520CB00021B/6808